D0886735

PACIFIC
BLITZKRIEG
WORLD WAR II IN THE CENTRAL PACIFIC

PACIFIC
BLITZKRIEG
WORLD WAR II IN THE CENTRAL PACIFIC

Sharon Tosi Lacey

University of North Texas Press
Denton, Texas

10 9 8 7 6 5 4 3 2 1

Permissions:
University of North Texas Press
1155 Union Circle #311336
Denton, TX 76203-5017

The paper used in this book meets the minimum requirements of the American National Standard for Permanence of Paper for Printed Library Materials, z39.48.1984. Binding materials have been chosen for durability.

Library of Congress Cataloging-in-Publication Data

Lacey, Sharon Tosi, 1968– author.
  Pacific blitzkrieg : World War II in the central Pacific / Sharon Tosi Lacey.—First edition.
    pages cm
  Includes bibliographical references and index.
  ISBN 978-1-57441-525-4 (cloth : alk. paper)—ISBN 978-1-57441-541-4 (ebook)
  1. World War, 1939-1945—Campaigns—Pacific Area. 2. United States—Armed Forces—History—World War, 1939-1945. 3. Pacific Area—History, Military—20th century. I. Title.
  D767.9.L225 2013
  940.54'26—dc23
                                    2013022386

The electronic edition of this book was made possible by the support
of the Vick Family Foundation.

To my parents, George and Evelyn Tosi,

for their unconditional love and support

— CONTENTS —

— LIST OF MAPS —

Credit: Dave Merrill, Merrill Graphics

— LIST OF ILLUSTRATIONS —

AFTER CHAPTER 2

1. Major General A. A. Vandegrift and his planners on board the USS *McCawley*.
2. LVT-1 amtracs embark on the initial assault on Guadalcanal.
3. Rear Admiral Richmond Kelly Turner and Major General A. A. Vandergrift.
4. Major General A. A. Vandegrift briefs Major General Alexander Patch.
5. Major General Julian Smith, Brigadier Charles Bourke and Brigadier General Leo Hermle.
6. On Tarawa, 2nd Division marines are pinned down.
7. Day 3 of Tarawa assault.
8. Admiral Chester Nimitz, Major General Julian Smith, and Lieutenant General Robert Richardson.
9. 165th Infantry assault wave attacking Makin.
10. Major General Ralph Smith, 27th Infantry Division Commander.
11. Burial at sea of two of the 644 sailors killed on the USS *Liscome Bay*.
12. Brigadier General Graves Erskine, Major General Harry Schmidt and Major General Holland Smith.
13. Major General Holland Smith and Major General Charles Corlett.
14. Men of 7th Division using flamethrowers to smoke out Japanese.
15. Carlos Island, one of the smaller islands flanking Kwajalein, falls to American invasion forces.

─ ACKNOWLEDGMENTS ─

No book is possible alone. As this book began life as a dissertation, my first thanks have to go to Dr. Williamson Murray, Dr. John Gooch, Dr. Holger Afflerbach, and Dr. Robert Foley who guided me through the research and writing. Without their honest criticism and willingness to share their years of experience, I never would have gotten past the first chapter. Dr. Dennis Showalter and Dr. Nicholas Sarantakes provided excellent suggestions that helped me turn this from a dissertation to a book.

Jenny Finchmann, who saved my countless hours—not to mention money—by copying boxes of papers at the Hoover Institute. The staff of the Military History Institute, the Marine Corps Archives, the Eisenhower Presidential Library, and the National Archives for their professionalism and assistance during my research. Wendy Palitz for assistance with photos and maps.

My editor, Ronald Chrisman, whose belief in this book gave me the confidence to move forward.

Everyone should be as blessed as I have been with my family. My children, Edmund, Anastasia, Adam and Ethan Moore, who are my world and the reason to push myself each and every day. They endured me burying myself in my writing for weeks at a time and willingly pitched in to take care of household chores and cook dinner during those times. My parents, George and Evelyn Tosi, who took for granted that their children could accomplish anything. My older brothers, David, Lawrence, and Eric Tosi, who have always set the bar stratospherically high and challenged me to keep up with them.

Last, but not least, my wonderful husband Jim, who is a partner in every sense of the word. He is my fiercest critic and biggest cheerleader and knows exactly when to give me a metaphorical kick in the pants. You are the love of my life and I would be lost without you!

— INTRODUCTION —

From the distance of seventy years, it is tempting to look back on World War II and proclaim that the Allied victory was inevitable. In the Pacific theater, historians gifted with perfect hindsight point to Japan's lack of natural resources, its inferior industrial capacity and the suicidal Bushido code, as factors that combined to make that nation's defeat a certainty. At the time, however, many doubted whether the U.S. military possessed the ability to match the warrior prowess of the Japanese. In the early days of the war America fielded a land force skeletonized by political whim and budget constraints against Japan's millions of combat veterans. When, after an efficient six months of post-Pearl Harbor campaigning, Japan had conquered most of Southeast Asia, there was good reason to question whether America could summon the resources and, most important, the will required for the long struggle necessary to wrest away Japan's empire. In the end, victory rested on how the non-militaristic youth of America could face up to the Emperor's battle-hardened veterans.[1] Many works on the Pacific War relate how the grand narrative of the "pampered sons of democracy" transformed themselves into soldiers and marines every bit as efficient and when necessary, as brutal as any force of Bushido warriors. But this transformation was no accident. Rather, it was the result of difficult and patient work by commanders and evolving staffs that studied and acted upon the lessons of every engagement. For every brilliant strategic and operational decision of the war, there were thousands of minute actions that made brilliance possible. Despite the thousands of works covering almost every aspect of World War II in the Pacific, no one has yet examined the detailed mechanics behind the transformation of the U.S. Army and U.S. Marine Corps during the course of the war. This work fills much of that gap by examining the often neglected details behind the three-year maturation of the joint army-marine force. For it was this transformation, even more so than America's industrial might, which made the Japanese attack on Pearl Harbor one of history's most colossal strategic errors.

Integrating two land forces as culturally distinct as the U.S. Marines and the U.S. Army into a single joint strike force would have been a difficult undertaking in peacetime. In the midst of a great global war it was a monumental task. Unfortunately, for those charged with the job of hammering the two services together, such integration was not anticipated in pre-war planning and certainly not on the scale required for successful operations during World War II. Moreover, there was nothing in the combined historical experience of the services to serve as a guide. Prior to 1942, the largest wartime integration of marines and army units had been during World War I, when a marine brigade made up approximately half of the army's 2nd Infantry Division. While greater than any previous integration attempt it paled in comparison to what was required for success in the decisive Central Pacific Campaign. Moreover, joining the two services in World War I had been greatly simplified by the fact that both forces overwhelmingly consisted of new recruits, all of whom were employing an army-dictated common doctrinal approach to combat.[2] Such were the similarities between the two services that two marine generals rose to command army divisions and both of their division staffs functioned well despite a mix of marine and army officers.

Furthermore, during World War I both services had basically the same role: as light infantry. After the war, however, the two services evolved in vastly different ways. The marines remained light infantry, a decision reinforced by their participation in the Banana Wars in the Caribbean, and focused on the development of amphibious operations. Such operations emphasized frontal assaults and short, but intense, battles. By contrast, the army recognized that mechanization was changing the character of land warfare and therefore reinvented itself as a heavy infantry force. As a result, during the interwar years the army focused on maneuver, massed firepower and prolonged, deliberate operations.[3]

Moreover, although the Marine Corps retrenched after World War I, it remained substantially larger than at any other time in its history. Increased size, a perceived larger role for itself in any future major conflict and a rapidly developing doctrine (with matching organizational and tactical changes) all combined to create a new and unique marine corps culture, in which marines saw themselves as an elite force. The marines enhanced this aura of eliteness by mandating that all marines be volunteers. Although the exigencies of World War II did eventually force the acceptance of draftees, only 3 percent of marines were draftees in contrast to 93 percent of soldiers.[4]

By the time it became necessary to integrate marine and army formations in World War II, everything that had previously made it possible to easily combine units from both services into a single entity had changed. Unlike during the Great War, the marines were no longer a small cog in much larger army machine. In the Central Pacific Theater the marines made up at least an equivalent percentage of the total land force as the army and in the early stages of many operations they provided the majority of the troops engaged. Moreover, this time around, the marines were fighting a type of war for which they had long planned. As far as Marine Corps leadership was concerned it was now the army's turn to conform to marine methods of warfare. On the other side of the hill, the army entered the Central Pacific with a doctrine tailored to the European theater. Furthermore, army leaders were certain that with just a few adjustments their doctrine would prove effective in retaking Japanese-held islands.

How well these two disparate organizations melded themselves into a single joint strike force, capable of synergistically supporting each other, became the determining factor in the level of success American forces met in their march across the Pacific. This work examines the mechanics of how this joint force came into being. As such it is not an operational history of the conflict. In fact, actual descriptions of operations make up only a fraction of this book and are primarily used to establish context and exemplify the crucial aspects of the success or failure of marine-army integration. For purposes of investigation, five battles in the Central Pacific Campaign are studied: Guadalcanal, the Gilberts, the Marshalls, Saipan, and Okinawa. These selections are based on several criteria, the first being that this campaign—the Central Pacific—was arguably the decisive offensive of the Pacific War. Also, it was during this campaign that army and marine units most often found themselves fighting alongside one other. Although there were other Pacific battles where the army and marines fought side-by-side, it was only during the Central Pacific Campaign that such joint actions were interwoven into every major engagement. In addition, many of the commanders present at the start of the campaign were also major players at its conclusion. It is, therefore, possible to follow both their individual growth as combat leaders, as well as their developing attitudes towards combined army-marine operations over a series of battles, all within a single theater.

By definition, joint operations typically combine ground, air, and naval forces under a single unified command aimed at a specific sequence of objectives. Such joint efforts extend far beyond mere operational planning, to include integrated training and equipment acquisition. During World War II, the American military undertook what amounted to a revolution in joint operations on an almost unimaginable scale. Throughout the war, the effort of joining the various services so as to create a synergistic combat effect required the continuous creation of new doctrine and tactics, as well the invention and assimilation of new equipment.

Although this work pays considerable attention to each part of the joint force, including the navy and air force, it focuses on one aspect: that of the ground forces learning to work together. While it is relatively easy to separate the functions of the navy, air force, and ground forces into discrete roles, it is considerably more difficult to do so for two separate land forces operating in the same area of operations. Because both army and marine units had to be capable of working together to accomplish the same missions, it was essential that their simultaneous employment be as seamless as possible. In fact, the overall success of the Central Pacific Campaign rested on army and marine units being nearly interchangeable in combat. Without intending any slight of air force and naval contributions to victory, which are well documented in other works, this book spotlights the growing pains of two services learning to act as one, while still maintaining their distinct cultural identities. This was arguably the most difficult aspect of creating the joint force. It is also the least understood and previously a neglected topic in the Pacific war.

Whenever one attempts to combine culturally unique organizations, individual personalities within each group will have an outsized effect on results. Nowhere is this more demonstrable then in the Central Pacific Campaign, where a few hyper-partisan generals were responsible for most of the interservice friction. Unfortunately, over the past seven decades the narrative of a campaign almost brought to ruin by squabbling commanders—as embodied by the Smith versus Smith controversy—has become one of the dominant legends of the Pacific War. This work clearly delineates the many adverse consequences caused by such personal bitterness.

Still, it was these same commanders' passionate commitment to mission accomplishment that enabled the two ground services to cooperate in an unprecedented manner. By looking beyond the best known controversy—Smith versus Smith—one sees a much brighter picture of interservice cooperation and gets a sense of the importance of a commander's personality in shaping the attitudes of the troops under his command. This work, therefore, goes beyond any previous narrative history of the Central Pacific Campaign to detail the extraordinary interservice harmony that operated with growing efficiency at the command and staff levels charged with getting things done, even as their senior leaders sometimes fought each other as bitterly as they did the Japanese.

Personalities, as important as they are in this story, were far from the only factor affecting the creation of the army-marine joint force. While the marine amphibious doctrine became the basis for the landings, that was only the jumping-off point for each operation. No matter who was in command, both services still needed to develop doctrinal and tactical procedures for land combat that, despite continuing differences, were similar enough to allow for a cooperative effort within a shared battlespace. Such doctrinal similarities must, however, be great enough to allow both services to employ substantially the same weapon systems as they became available during the war. Moreover, it was crucial that there was enough commonality between the army-way and the marine-way that the other parts of the joint team—naval and air power—could support either service with a single set of procedures. In the European theater, where one might expect similar difficulties combining British and American formations into a unified force, many such problems were avoided by supporting each land army with its own national assets to the greatest degree possible. There was no such easy solution in the Central Pacific, where the need to rapidly implement tactical lessons and materiel advances between two culturally divergent services presented a continuous challenge.

By tracing the five major Central Pacific battles in which both army and marine units participated—Guadalcanal, Gilberts (Tarawa-Makin), Marshalls (Kwajalein-Roi-Namur), Marianas (Saipan) and Okinawa—this work explores, for the first time, the mechanics behind the creation of the joint army-marine force. In each of these battles the army and the marines operated either together on a single island or concurrently on parallel islands. Moreover, throughout these five battles, much of the staff at the corps level and above remained the same, providing a thread that allows one to follow the development of crucial joint staffs throughout the campaign.[5]

Comparing, to the greatest degree possible, similar events, functions and outcomes, in various engagements over a three-year period requires a certain degree of analytical standardization. Only by looking closely at similar elements in the preparation and execution of each battle is it possible to examine how the lessons-learned process (usually through after-action reports) delivered new capabilities, technological advances, and doctrinal changes, to the combat forces. Similar analytical standardization also helps one to see how equipment and methodological changes were absorbed and then employed by both the army and marines. Therefore, over the course of these five battles one can easily trace the adaptability of both services as they transformed not only their fighting methods, but also their own cultures.

It is my hope this book clearly demonstrates that even in war on a truly industrial scale, the influence of personalities still has an immense effect on the outcome of events. By examining the personalities and relationships of the ground commanders as they conducted a series of joint missions, one discovers how their interactions affected battlefield performance. In many of the battles analyzed in this work one sees how crucial a role personal biases and resulting interpersonal conflicts played in hampering organizational adaptability. Despite the dedicated efforts of hundreds of junior officers working to integrate the many ingredients involved in creating an effective joint army-marine force, the joint organization was unable to gel as long as toxic leaders remained within the command milieu. Their removal and replacement by commanders determined to fight with an operationally integrated force solidified America's joint land force just in time to face its greatest challenge on Okinawa.

— CHAPTER 1 —

GUADALCANAL:
The Ad Hoc Operation

N o one predicted that the first ground offensive of either theater of the war would occur on an unknown speck of an island in the Southwest Pacific. After all, announced Allied strategy specified the defeat of Germany was the first priority. In the Pacific, the military expected only limited offensive efforts for at least the first years of the war. However, the threat Japan presented by building an enemy airbase less than 1,000 miles from Australia, especially one that interdicted the supply and communications between Australia and the United States, made an immediate offensive against the Japanese imperative. Fortunately, the unexpected Allied victory at Midway in May of 1942 made the success of such an assault feasible.

The major obstacle was the lack of trained units capable of conducting such an invasion. Amphibious landings had long been the purview of the Marine Corps, but its two trained divisions had been divided and sent to guard such places as Iceland and Samoa. By piecing together scattered regiments, the marines barely managed to gather an assault force, while the army busily created new divisions to augment the initial invasion forces. Against all odds and with a minimum of preparation and training, these ad hoc units managed to strike a decisive blow against the enemy and halt the Japanese advance.

Despite ultimate success, the invasion of Guadalcanal was far from a flawless operation. In fact, at times the Americans were close to being routed; only the marines' tenacious defense of a small sliver of beach stood between the ground forces and defeat. Yet these lines held and through six months of grinding combat, the Americans finally crushed the Japanese defenders.

The Guadalcanal operation was the first truly modern joint operation in American history, bringing all facets of land, air and sea power to bear in one battle. It also marked the first time since World War I that army and marine forces conducted an offensive operation together. Without any institutional knowledge upon which to draw, leaders were forced to adapt existing, and usually deficient, doctrine. As the battle proceeded, commanders invented new tactics and doctrine where none previously existed. Those that worked were adopted and expanded for use in future operations. Those that did not were discarded.

Tactically, none of the American ground troops had ever seen a fight like they encountered on Guadalcanal. Although the marines had engaged in jungle combat in Haiti and Nicaragua, that had done little to prepare them for intense close quarters combat in suffocating heat against a seemingly invisible enemy. When it was over the 1st Marine Division's commander offered this startling piece of advice:

> My message to the troops General [George] Marshall's in training for this type of warfare is to go back to the tactics of the French and Indian days. This is not meant facetiously. Study their tactics and fit in our modern weapons and you have a solution. I refer to the tactics and leadership of the days of Roger's Rangers.[1]

STRATEGIC SETTING

Earlier in March 1942, in order to settle arguments over which commander would control the Pacific theater, the Joint Chiefs divided the Pacific between General Douglas MacArthur in the Southwest Pacific Area (SWPA) and Admiral Chester Nimitz in the Pacific Ocean Area (POA). Nimitz then further divided his command into three subcommands: the Central Pacific Area, in which he retained command, the South Pacific Area under Admiral Robert Ghormley, and the North Pacific Area under Admiral Robert Theobald. This arrangement never satisfied anyone, but it did allow the army a greater role in a region where naval power drove operations, while at the same time the navy was pleased that the arrangement kept its precious aircraft carriers out of army control—something Admiral Ernest King, Chief of Naval Operations, greatly feared, given his belief that no ground force commander could ever employ them correctly.[2] At the time, the compromise arrangement appeared sufficient, as no one in Washington envisioned anything more than holding actions in the Pacific until well after operations in Europe were well under way.

However, Japan's sweep through the Pacific in the months after Pearl Harbor, which gobbled up Guam, Wake Island, the Philippines, the Dutch East Indies, Hong Kong, Malaya, Singapore, and Burma, forced the Allies to refocus their attention on the area if for no other reason than to hold back the Japanese tide. While the American naval victory at Midway halted the enemy's advance in the Central Pacific, Japanese forces were still an ominous threat to Australia and New Zealand, along with the concomitant American lines of communication. At the tip of the Japanese advance were two tiny islands in the Solomon chain: Tulagi, a small British harbor, and Guadalcanal, where the Japanese were constructing an airfield.[3] A Japanese presence there would allow them to disrupt the supply routes between the United States and Australia.

The Japanese took these two islands without opposition and initially focused on establishing coastwatcher stations to monitor Allied activity, followed by airstrip construction. Upon completion the airstrips would provide Japan a base from which its forces could easily strike northern Australia, New Guinea, and New Zealand, and interfere with the sea-lanes to America. U.S. forces now had to address this threat to their strongest ally in the region and the unexpected American victory at Midway opened a window of opportunity not only to halt the Japanese juggernaut but also to strike back.

Soon after Midway, MacArthur began advocating an immediate offensive to capitalize on the Japanese defeat: specifically a full-scale assault against the islands of New Britain and New Ireland to neutralize the developing Japanese air bases at Rabaul and the Bismarck Archipelago.[4] Naturally, he saw himself as the logical commander and was confident that with a marine division and two carriers to augment his three army divisions, he could quickly accomplish the mission.[5]

The navy leaders had similar thoughts about an offensive, and King had earlier sent a memo to the president which succinctly summed up the U.S. strategic goals in the Pacific as, "Hold Hawaii; support Australasia; drive northwestward from New Hebrides."[6] The navy envisioned a slightly different campaign than MacArthur and called for the U.S. to first gain a foothold in the Solomons in order to protect its carriers from Japanese aircraft based on the island chain and then to attack Rabaul, which housed the Japanese Seventeenth Army and Southeastern Fleet commands. Naturally, such an operation, based as it was on amphibious landings, should be under the navy's command. However, by chance, the original line dividing the SWPA and the POA divided the Solomon Islands, thus placing Guadalcanal in MacArthur's region. Seeing his chance to command the operation, MacArthur quickly recanted his earlier recommendation and insisted that he had always meant that U.S. forces must neutralize the Solomons first. As notes on the memo observe, "Three weeks ago [MacArthur] wanted to go to Rabaul. Now he gazes at Tulagi [another island in the Solomons]."[7]

Because Guadalcanal fell under his area of responsibility, MacArthur was insistent that he should command the coming invasion. A flurry of memoranda between General George Marshall, Army Chief of Staff, and King argued the specifics of the operations, with Marshall arguing that MacArthur should be in command and King equally adamant that as an amphibious operation it should be a navy show.[8] On 25 June, to Marshall's surprise and annoyance, King submitted a draft plan for the Guadalcanal invasion to the Joint Chiefs for approval. Marshall quickly realized that the issue lay not in the operational details, but rather was a matter of operational command. As a result, he began advocating MacArthur's position.[9]

At this time, MacArthur discovered that King was flagrantly disregarding the chain of command by communicating directly with Admiral Herbert Leary, MacArthur's naval commander.[10] MacArthur was already mindful of how tenuous his claim to command was and he became convinced that the navy intended to assume control of all operations in the Pacific theater, using marines as the assault force and relegating the army to occupation duties. He feared that if the navy succeeded in this effort, the role of the army in the Pacific would consist "largely of placing its forces at the disposal and under the command of navy or marine officers." He further claimed that it was all part of a master plan, which he had learned about "accidentally" when he was Chief of Staff of the Army, in which the navy would gain complete control over national defense and reduce the army to a training and supply organization.[11]

Rather than fight over the details, Marshall appealed to King in terms of what would be best for the success of the operation. On 26 June, Marshall agreed with King that while the arbitrary line separating the commands was irrelevant in determining the commander, the fact remained that

> General MacArthur and his staff and commanders, which include Admiral Leary, have been in the area for months. They have developed sources of information on the islands, they have been reconnoitering the objectives constantly and have been studying and making plans for such an operation . . . To my mind, it would be most unfortunate to bring in another commander at this time to carry out this operation.[12]

King replied by pointing out that the army had command of the operations in Europe and rightly so since those would be ground operations. In the Pacific however, not only were the initial phases inherently amphibious and naval in character, but he was willing to turn over command to MacArthur once the battle became a ground operation. "The primary consideration is the immediate initiation of these operations. I think it is important that this be done, even if no support of army forces in the Southwest Pacific Area is made available."[13]

This implied threat surprised and angered Marshall, who waited several days before replying, "The implication in your last memorandum that this will be done even if no support of army forces in the Southwest Pacific is made available, disturbs me greatly. Regardless of the final decision as to command, every available support must be given to this operation, or any operation against the enemy."[14] In order to forestall any further cooperation issues, Marshall issued a memorandum on conduct to his higher commanders that read, in part, "Vigorous actions must be taken to suppress service jealousies and suspicions . . . It is the clear duty of commissioned officers of the army to do everything in their power to promote harmonious relations and teamwork, avoiding ill-advised comments or attitudes."[15]

On 2 July, King and Marshall had lunch together and Marshall presented the solution that the two would eventually adopt. They broke the operation into three tasks and placed Nimitz in charge of Task One, seizure of southern Solomons and the Santa Cruz Island on 1 August; MacArthur would command Tasks Two (Lae, Salamaua, northern Solomons and New

Guinea) and Three (Rabaul, New Britain-New Ireland) at a date to be determined later.[16] King also agreed to the creation of an army command in the South Pacific Area. As a way to remove the final possible impediment to agreement, the two altered the original line dividing SWPA and POA at 160° east longitude to 159°, thus putting the southern Solomons, particularly Guadalcanal, under Nimitz's command.[17] The planning and execution of Guadalcanal would now fall firmly into Ghormley's and, by extension, Nimitz's territory.[18]

The date for invasion was initially set for 1 August. However, after much pleading, Nimitz granted a one-week extension. Ghormley would have little more than a month to complete the planning and execution of the operation dubbed WATCHTOWER. D-Day would fall on 7 August, exactly eight months after Pearl Harbor.

OPERATIONAL PLANNING

One can characterize the planning of WATCHTOWER as hasty. With so little time, men, and materiel available, some wags dubbed it Operation SHOESTRING. At the helm was Admiral Robert Ghormley, who was considered by many senior naval leaders one of the brightest "young" admirals and a potential candidate for Chief of Naval Operations.[19] In the years immediately preceding the war, he had served as the Director of the War Plans Division and Assistant Chief of Naval Operations before going to Britain as a naval observer. However, while his superiors widely respected Ghormley for his planning and interpersonal skills, they worried that he had not commanded anything larger than a single ship and had spent most of his career as a staff officer.[20] By any measure it was a risky proposition to turn the command of the first American offensive over to someone untried even in a significant peacetime command, let alone the pressures of wartime. It is possible that Nimitz had some doubts about Ghormley's abilities from the beginning, especially as he did not object when the latter announced his intention to exercise command from New Caledonia, over a thousand miles away from the landing site.[21] This would be proven in October 1942, when still in the midst of combat operations in Guadalcanal, Nimitz relieved Gormley for lackluster performance and a pessimistic attitude. He was replaced by Admiral William "Bull" Halsey.[22]

Ghormley kept strict control of all the forces under him, essentially making his headquarters not only the center of joint operations and planning, but also of naval administration. He established air, amphibious, and service subcommands, but would not establish one for ground operations, preferring instead to keep personal control of the army and marine elements in his jurisdiction, an odd choice given that he would not be the operational commander.[23] Even more disturbing was his disinterest in input from the other services. While his staff was ostensibly a joint one, of the 103 officers assigned to it only three were army officers.[24]

Arguments between the army and navy soon erupted, centered on two main areas: logistics and army air assets. The navy favored a combined logistical agency and command of army aviation. Naturally the army disagreed, reluctant to relinquish any more control of its assets to the navy than was necessary.[25] General Brehon Somervell, the Chief of Army Service of Supply, wrote of the logistical issue:

> When you consider our greater strength in the Pacific, in Hawaii, in Australia, in Alaska . . . and our incomparably larger supply set-up, it is inevitable that the operations so undertaken would necessarily become joint in character with all the friction, inefficiencies and divided responsibilities that flow therefrom. We have so dominant an interest; we have so clear a responsibility in the supply of our large forces; we must definitely control the means.[26]

Although the logistical issues remained unsolved, the army circumvented the air issue by assigning General Millard Harmon as the commander of army forces under Ghormley (this was a command arrangement King agreed to in the compromise with Marshall). Of course, this was a command in only the most nominal sense. Harmon was to take over administration, supply, and training of army ground and air forces in the South Pacific and assist Ghormley in preparing plans for their use. However, he had no operational control of the forces and the vagueness of his instructions left them open to interpretation. Due to his aviation experience he functioned as Ghormley's advisor on issues related to army air forces, thus allowing the army to keep a modicum of control of its air assets.[27]

To accomplish this coordination task Harmon set up his headquarters in New Caledonia near Ghormley. Despite the rocky beginning, the two services settled into a harmonious relationship. Harmon wrote to General Henry "Hap" Arnold, Chief of Staff of the Army Air Corps, "There has been no suggestion of any lack of harmony . . . all commands, forces and units in this area are working full out and in full accord to the common end; and this relationship will be preserved."[28] This is echoed in the notes taken by two staff officers in April 1942, "Harmon [is a] splendid cooperator."[29] Vandegrift, commander of the 1st Marine Division, referred to Harmon as a "very capable professional officer"[30] and Vandegrift's chief of staff, Colonel Gerald Thomas, called him "one of our real supporters, one of our real backers."[31] In writing about Harmon's relationship with his staff, Nimitz resorted to a bad pun, "I am sure you will work *harmon*iously together."[32]

However, Ghormley's staff accomplished the invasion planning with little input from the army or the staff of the 1st Marine Division.[33] In fact, the Task Force Commander (Admiral Frank Jack Fletcher) did not even arrive in New Zealand until 15 July, a scant three weeks before the operation. Even worse, Vandegrift had no opportunity to meet with the commanders of the supporting naval force until a few days before the landings. In his final report, Vandegrift wrote:

> There was not sufficient time for the necessary related planning by the commanders and staff of the forces involved . . . As a result the landing force plan of operations was formulated without detailed knowledge of plans of higher and supporting commanders. This was most undesirable from the point of view of all concerned. But it was unavoidable, for the embarkation of a landing force involves the making of decisions irrevocable in character and, to be completed at all, this particular embarkation had, of necessity, to be begun forthwith. The direct consequence of this unilateral form of planning was the absence of a complete meeting of the minds of the commanders concerned.[34]

Harmon concurred stating, "his [Ghormley's] staff organization was . . . never appropriately equipped with ground force or air officers to fully accomplish all of the planning and other staff activities of such a superior headquarters."[35]

The fact that Ghormley only exercised strategic command of the force further complicated the matter, because operational command fell instead to Fletcher and his amphibious force commander, Admiral

Richmond Kelly Turner. In Nimitz's words, Ghormley would have overall command but "no tactical interference" in Fletcher's operation.[36] In his war diary, Ghormley sums up Nimitz's directives:

> The Commander-in-Chief, Pacific Fleet would order Task Force Commanders to report to the Commander South Pacific Force for duty. The Commander South Pacific Force would direct the Task Force Commander to carry out his mission (as given by the Commander-in-Chief Pacific Fleet). The Commander South Pacific Force would not interfere in the Task Force Commander's mission unless circumstances, presumably not known to the Commander-in-Chief Pacific Fleet, indicated that specific measures were required to be performed by the Task Force Commander. The Commander South Pacific Force would then direct the Task Force Commanders to take such measures.[37]

On paper at least, Fletcher, who had won the Medal of Honor at Vera Cruz in 1914, appeared an ideal combat commander. He had spent the months after Pearl Harbor commanding the carrier task force that had supported the reinforcement of various strategically vital South Pacific islands and raided Japanese positions throughout the Central Pacific, New Guinea, and the Solomons. He was also the senior officer present during the battles of Coral Sea and Midway. Nevertheless, those above him were not completely convinced of his competence and King had given him the command only at Nimitz's urging.[38] By the time Fletcher arrived at New Caledonia to assist in planning he had finished eight months at sea without respite and as Vandegrift describes their first meeting,

> He was a distinguished looking man but seemed nervous and tired, probably the result of the recent battles of Coral Sea and Midway. To my surprise he appeared to lack knowledge of or interest in the forthcoming operation. He quickly let us know that he did not think it would succeed. To his arbitrary objections, we replied as best we could, but obviously failed to make much impression.[39]

This matches the observations of others, such as Admiral William Pye, the president of the Naval War College, who sent a message to King noting Fletcher's "general lack of information about the plans."[40] Thomas also observed that Ghormley did not even bother to attend the planning conference.[41]

To add another layer to an already complex command and planning jumble, Fletcher was not immediately available when planning began and Turner, known as "Terrible Turner" for his fearsome temper, took over his portion of the planning.[42] He had been King's Director of War Plans and had helped formulate the general Pacific strategy. He was also a highly divisive character.[43] Although one of the most capable men in the navy, many considered Turner

> A tireless worker, nearly incapable of delegating work. . . . Others described him frequently as irascible, if not actually mean and determined, a hard man to deal with if you opposed his ideas. Like many men of stellar intellect, he displayed little patience for beings of lesser endowments . . . King could hardly have failed to see a great deal of himself in Turner.[44]

Although Turner ably represented King's interests in planning meetings, he managed to alienate so many of his peers that Marshall demanded that King remove him in the name of interservice harmony. However much King may have liked Turner personally, he also had to consider the feelings of his army counterpart, Dwight Eisenhower, and he therefore fired Turner. To soften the blow, King offered Turner the opportunity to command the landing force for Guadalcanal. Despite his temper, Turner had a reputation as an aggressive fighter, which was just as well for his immediate two commanders, Fletcher and Ghormley, proved to be too cautious during the battle.

Vandegrift did his best to get along with Turner. He recalled, "I had known Turner when he was a navy planner in Washington . . . [his] didactic manner proved irritating to some people . . . [at the planning conference] I got along quite well with him since he had not as yet written his plan and perforce relied on mine."[45] On the other hand, in a 1947 interview, Vandegrift's operations officer "gave the distinct impression that he considered Turner to be an opinionated man who considered himself to be qualified to give tactical advice to the commander of ground troops . . . [and] twice to his certain knowledge Turner endangered the Guadalcanal operation." Later in the interview, he qualified his remarks saying, "Turner was obstinate up to a point, but was willing to listen to reason when convinced that someone else knew better than he."[46] In another interview twenty years later, he later called Turner, "a tough hombre, a brilliant fellow, brilliant brain, but ruthless."[47]

However, in practice the command relationship was deeply fractured. Since Fletcher limited himself to controlling the air forces, this left Turner in charge of everything else. The initial plan called for Turner to retain command of the 1st Marine Division, a decision that became an ongoing source of friction between Vandegrift and Turner. The issue of command was not merely a power struggle, but rather a symptom of a deeper rift between the two services about the nature of the operation.

> Turner and many other Naval authorities looked upon the landing force as just a detachment from the force afloat and still connected to the navy's amphibious force by firm command lines . . . Vandegrift wanted a clear-cut command privilege [to make decisions on shore], free from responsibility shared with the commander afloat . . . [he believed that] once firmly established ashore, the landing force commander should command his own land operation.[48]

This battle over command was not a new issue, but one that most had skirted since the amphibious landing at Gallipoli. In 1934 the Marine Corps school published the *Tentative Landings Operations Manual*, which the army and navy eventually adopted with little more than a name change.[49] This manual, along with *Joint Action of the Army and Navy*, became the basic guides for all planning and training for amphibious operations in World War II. As noted after the war, "though experience in the early 1940s constantly refined the techniques of amphibious assault, the basic 1934 doctrine withstood its prolonged trial by fire without significant change."[50]

While the doctrine was basically sound, the glaring deficiency lay in the lack of attention the manuals paid to command relationships. *Joint Action* merely designated that unity of command should go to the service with "paramount interest in the operation."[51] The service landing manuals were not much better, stating, "The attack force commander will usually be the senior naval commander of the units of the fleet comprising the attack force . . . Provision must be made in advance for continuity of command within the landing area during the course of the operation."[52] As such, the landing and support organizations had parallel command functions but the naval commander held veto power as the attack force commander.[53]

Turner took this to mean that his command of the ground forces continued even after the landing. He even planned to land with the marines, going so far as to draw equipment, claiming, "I am not going to interfere with your defense of the island. I'm going ashore to build the naval base."[54] Although Turner eventually relented and stayed on board ship, he remained a source of friction for Vandegrift, always "dipping into affairs relating to Guadalcanal."[55] It was not until Halsey replaced Ghormley that services settled the command issue once and for all. Halsey declared, "Commander amphibious force will command at sea, but the exclusive command ashore is that of commander landing force and commander amphibious force has no authority ashore." Vandegrift made sure that that this agreement was not only put into writing, but also that King initialed it.[56]

Next to the command issue, the major source of friction between the navy and the landing force was logistics. This issue arose when the marines arrived in New Zealand, only to discover that the civilian dockworkers were on strike and the marines had to unload their own ships in the rain. Then they discovered that their food supplies had not been combat packaged and the cardboard boxes disintegrated on the docks, leaving the troops with piles of unidentifiable cans.[57] Further complicating matters, within days, and long before they sorted out the mess at the docks, reloading began. The 1st Marine Regiment commander, Colonel Clifton Cates, remembered that "the nine or ten days we were there—and I might say they are the most hectic I have ever seen—we spent trying to prepare to get combat loaded and get spare parts for weapons, etc."[58] As the operations order called for the marines to take only those items necessary to live and fight, Vandegrift noted that, "even after eliminating seabags, bedrolls, tentage, most post exchange supplies and a good deal of heavy equipment and motor transport, I still had to cut bulk supply—rations, fuel, lubricants—to 60 days and, most tragic, ammunition from 15 to 10 days of fire for all weapons."[59] Even this amount proved too much to unload across an invasion beachhead in the time allocated.

When Fletcher finally arrived, he called for a conference aboard his flagship to discuss the upcoming operation. Thomas attended the meeting along with various members of the 1st Division staff, but

> Ghormley was not there. He did not go to the conference . . . I did
> not go into the conference room. No one went in except Vandegrift,
> and Turner was the only one who went in from the amphibious force.

Peck and Callaghan also were there. It was a most unsatisfactory conference. . . . He [Fletcher] asked Turner and Vandegrift, "How long is it
going to take for you to make this landing and get your supplies ashore?"
They said, "Probably five days." He said, "Well I am not going to stay there
that long. I'll give you two days. Then I'm going to pull the carriers out."
Well, they argued with him a little bit but it didn't do any good . . . The
conference ended, they'd done all they could.[60]

The final plan called for the main body, consisting of over 11,000
marines of 1st and a reinforced 5th Marines, with supporting units to
land on Guadalcanal on 7 August 1942. On the same day, the Northern
Group, under General William Rupertus, would land three battalions
(approximately 3,900 marines) on Florida Island, Tulagi, and Gavutu-
Tanambogo, small islands just 23 miles north of Guadalcanal. The 2nd
Marines (minus 2nd Battalion) formed the floating reserve, with intentions to land on the nearby island of Ndeni.[61]

PRE-COMBAT TRAINING

Unlike subsequent operations, the units participating in the Guadalcanal operations had no prior combat lessons on which to draw. Of course,
there had been peacetime exercises, whose purpose was to perfect their
amphibious landing skills, long a core component of the Corps' mission.
Since 1935 the marines had conducted Fleet Landing Exercises (FLEX),
sometimes in concert with small army detachments, in order to rehearse
the newly developed landing doctrine. Preceded by months of preliminary training, these exercises lasted for several weeks. They allowed the
Marine Corps to rehearse and refine war plans while experimenting with
amphibious doctrine, techniques, and equipment.[62] Not until 1941 did
the army commit the entire 1st and 9th Infantry Divisions to amphibious
training with the 1st Marine Division and the 3rd and 7th Infantry Divisions for training with the 2nd Marine Division. However, only one of
these army divisions—the 7th ID—ever operated in the Pacific; the other
three all served in Europe.

Trained officers and noncommissioned officers (NCOs) from prewar
marine units formed the cadre for each new marine unit upon activation,
ensuring that each new formation began life with a certain percentage of

experienced personnel. As the army began to form its divisions, it would follow this same method.

While the goal was to have units train together for 6–12 months before combat operations, this was not feasible for the Guadalcanal operation. Not only were units constantly dividing to form the nucleus of new divisions, but the Guadalcanal operation was planned and executed in just weeks. Some of the divisions, such as the 1st Marine Division, were able to accomplish some tailored training and exercises, but others, such as the 2nd Marine Division, found themselves scattered across the globe on other missions until called to Guadalcanal.

Although the 1st Marine Division was the only unit to participate in the planning and initial invasion of Guadalcanal, it is worthwhile examining the pre-combat training of all of the divisions that ultimately fought on the island. Doing so gives one a true feel for the chaos of those first months of war, as a number of divisions were literally smashed together out of random units and then expected to fight as a coherent team. It also highlights the fragmented and haphazard nature of the training before this operation. Finally, it provides a first glimpse of many of the units and commanders who played major roles in later operations. Without a fundamental understanding of where these units and leaders began, it would be impossible to follow their maturity as the war progressed.

1ST MARINE DIVISION "THE OLD BREED"

Of all the services, the marines are the most conscious of their history and fiercely defensive of their traditions. As the story goes, on 10 November 1775, as the second man to sign up for the newly formed Marine Corps walked out of the front door of Tuns Tavern, the first recruit confronted him with, "Welcome aboard. Of course, you should have seen how tough it was in the Old Corps."[63] Even among marines, the 1st Marine Division is recognized as the heirs of the "Old Corps," with all the attendant bragging rights.

The creation of the Fleet Marine Force in 1933 split the Marine Corps into two brigades: the 1st Brigade based in Quantico, Virginia, and the 2nd Brigade in San Diego, California, On 1 February 1941, the brigades became the core of the 1st and 2nd Marine Divisions.[64] Adopting a regimental structure, the 5th Marine Regiment became the

1st Marine Division's first subordinate formation, but the 7th Marine Regiment and, finally, the 1st Marine Regiment soon followed. The new division then received assignment to the Atlantic Fleet.[65] After Pearl Harbor, the Corps brought the division up to war strength and prepared for training at the new marine barracks at New River (later Camp Lejeune), North Carolina.

The command of the 1st Marine Division fell to General Alexander Vandegrift, a man "of the Stonewall Jackson breed; a quiet, unassuming man who had learned the fighting trade in the hard marine school, who had a paternal regard for his troops, but never forgot what they were there for."[66] Vandegrift had been an early proponent of Marine Corps aviation. As a brand-new second lieutenant at the School of Application (a forerunner of Officer Candidates School) in 1909, he wrote a paper entitled "Aviation, the Cavalry of the Future." Not only did he receive an "unsatisfactory" on the paper, but his first evaluation report questioned his fitness as an officer.[67] However he persevered and eventually fought in Nicaragua, Vera Cruz, and Haiti and served as an embassy guard at Peking. He had been brought up in the Marine Corps under the mentorship of the legendary General John Lejuene, whose Marine Corps Schools in Quantico fostered an expertise in strategy, planning, and tactics, specifically amphibious warfare.[68] He had spent the late 1930s at Headquarters Marine Corps working directly for the Commandant of the Marines Corps. This experience gave him a first-hand view of the development of strategy and the importance of interservice cooperation at the highest levels.

For the present, however, his focus was on training his new division for combat. The two active units at his disposal, the 5th and the 7th Marines, participated in "intensive training of a practical nature [which] included field exercises, combat firing and service practices for all arms. In addition [the units] engaged in a ten day landing exercise at Solomons Island, Maryland."[69]

Thomas remembered that the training "stressed battalion training and combat exercises, firing, weapons and maneuvers over the countryside and whatnot . . . We had several command post exercises that gave training to the division and the units and the staff . . . we had one really fine field exercise . . . the artillery couldn't do much firing. They were handicapped."[70]

In March 1942, the 1st Marines joined the unit, but the 7th Marines and other supporting elements detached and deployed to conduct defensive operations in Samoa as the 3rd Brigade. They would not rejoin the division until September 1942. While the unit spent the majority its time on Samoa building the island defenses, the regimental commander, Colonel James Webb, tried to balance the duties with training for the upcoming fight. His orderly recalled,

> It seems like the 7th Marines trained constantly while in Samoa, but I received no training that would prepare me to become a rifleman in an infantry battalion soon after arriving at Guadalcanal . . . reflecting on their combat performance in retrospect . . . I am inclined to believe the four months preparation was inadequate . . . it is difficult to train for the physical hardship we experienced along with the fierce combat on Guadalcanal.[71]

The division staff echoed this opinion. Despite the months of training, they felt that "although full advantage was taken of every opportunity and facility, it was considered that the division had not yet attained a satisfactory state of readiness for combat when first intelligence [for movement to the Pacific by the rest of the division] was received in mid-April."[72]

This new plan did not cause undue alarm among the division staff. After all, it merely called for the 1st Division to set up a training base in New Zealand and conduct amphibious training there until 1 January 1943.[73] The unit loaded up and training continued on shipboard en route to New Zealand. One young officer remembered,

> [We] were constantly going over the weapons and map reading . . . and problems, hypothetical problems, with them. So the corporals and the NCOs would then go back and work with their men so they understood it. And we had the men so completely trained like with a BAR. We'd blindfold them and they'd have to disassemble it and put it back together blindfolded, merely so they knew that every touch or in darkness that they could handle it. And machine guns the same way.[74]

The division had been in New Zealand less than two weeks and had not even unloaded its equipment from the ships, when Nimitz informed Vandegrift of plans to invade the Solomon Islands in little more than a month. Vandegrift and his staff rushed to prepare, but because of this shortened timeline, he afterwards felt that there had not been sufficient time to train for and rehearse the operation. While he was eager to put his division through a practice training exercise, the area chosen (Koro Island) proved to be surrounded by coral and completely unsuitable for actual landings. Vandegrift later concluded, "From the point of view of the landing force the Koro rehearsal provided nothing beyond a valuable period of debarkation training and, in the view of the rapid increase of enemy activity, the wisdom of devoting priceless time to such limited advantage appeared dubious . . . With more time available, a more suitable rehearsal area could have been selected."[75]

Since the 1st Division had participated in the FLEX exercises, it is tempting to assume that it was fully trained in amphibious operations and would only need refresher courses. However, because of the cadre system, which drained off many experienced marines to build other units, the division was not at an advanced level of training. Moreover, it had wasted valuable training time during the unloading and immediate reloading of ships assigned to move the unit's supplies and equipment.[76] Cates, commander of 1st Marines, recalled, "There was no training whatsoever of my regiment in New Zealand, because just prior to landing we received orders to be prepared to unload and to combat load for a future operation . . . And we had no training whatsoever."[77]

Nimitz ordered Vandegrift and Turner to conduct a six-day amphibious landing rehearsal in the Fiji Islands beginning 23 July that would have the marines land during "an actual gun and aerial bombardment practice conducted by the aircraft, cruisers and destroyers slated to support the initial landings of the offensive." [78] The start date later moved to 28 July, but the extra time made little difference. The rehearsal, dubbed Operation DOVETAIL, was, in Vandegrift's words, "a complete bust" and his marines would "have been totally slaughtered if the island was in Japanese hands."[79] Not only did operations begin several hours late, but the coral reef surrounding the site severely damaged many of the landing craft when they tried to land at low tide. As a result, the navy pulled back its landing ships after only 42 percent of the landing forces had disembarked. Those who made it off the ships had to wade fifty yards to the wrong beaches, while the naval gunfire and close air support was erratic and inaccurate.[80]

The debacle did not improve during the remainder of the rehearsal as the navy refused to move close to the beach for fear of damaging the boats needed for the real landing. The marines left on board the navy ships contented themselves with practicing getting in and out of the landing boats from the destroyers.[81] Vandegrift consoled his staff with the axiom that "a poor rehearsal traditionally means a good show" and focused on the experience his marines gained from climbing in and out of landing craft for the first time.[82] In just a few days' time, the 1st Marine Division would have a chance to put this experience to the test when it landed on Guadalcanal.

American Division "Born in Battle"

The unit tapped to augment the 1st Marine Division was the newly formed Americal Division. Cobbled together with National Guard units orphaned in the triangularization of army divisions just prior to the war, the Americal Division had the distinction of being the first unit to completely form up and mobilize on foreign soil.

The division originated as Task Force 6814 (codenamed *Poppy*), a conglomeration of stray units hastily assembled in the days after Pearl Harbor and sent to the Pacific from the Brooklyn Port of Embarkation on 23 January 1942 with the mission of providing security for the vulnerable island of New Caledonia. At this point, "the force was not in any sense a division. Its parts had never operated together. Its equipment was scanty; its staff were [sic] strangers."[83] Gathered together from across the United States, the task force had two infantry regiments: the 132nd from Illinois and the 182nd from Massachusetts, along with various surplus support units culled from far-flung divisions in Alabama, Arkansas, Georgia, Kentucky, Michigan, Mississippi, Missouri, New York, South Carolina, Tennessee, Texas and Virginia.[84]

It took over a month for the convoy to reach Australia with a brief stop in Panama, where the unit finally acquired a temporary commander, Colonel Edmund Sebree, a 1918 West Point graduate. Sebree, who became one of a handful of generals to command in both the Pacific and European theaters, quickly assembled a staff and began preparing for future operations, although none of them knew exactly where they were going or what their mission would be.[85] The division did, however, take advantage of the time at sea to conduct training,

which mainly consisted of lectures and conferences on diverse top-
ics such as jungle tactics, tropical diseases, the Japanese army and
gunnery.[86]

After a short stay in Australia, the unit moved on to its final destination of New Caledonia, arriving on 12 March 1942. New Caledonia was a
French colony that had sided with General Charles de Gaulle as opposed
to the Vichy regime. It was under the sovereignty of the Free French government in London, although the Australians were responsible for its
defense.[87] Not only was the island relatively well-developed, but it boasted
rich mineral deposits, especially chrome, nickel, iron, cobalt, manga-
nese, and mercury, all of which could be of great use to the Japanese war
machine. In addition, its location 850 miles northeast of Australia made it
both an important strategic outpost for the Allies and an irresistible target
for the Japanese, who were eager to expand their foothold in the area.
Shortly before Pearl Harbor, de Gaulle realized just how vulnerable the
island was and, with the Australians unable to spare any troops for its
defense, offered it to the United States as an advanced naval and air base
to counterattack any possible Japanese thrust.[88]

Once the division had established itself on the island, General Alexander Patch, also a West Point graduate and then commanding general
of the Infantry Replacement Training Center at Camp Croft, South
Carolina, flew in to take command of this makeshift unit. One of the
recurring bouts of pneumonia that had plagued him since World War I
had delayed Patch from joining the division earlier. His quiet demeanor
masked a man with a fiery temper and an inner strength. Patch looked the
part of a commander: tall and slim in riding breeches and cavalry boots,
a silk scarf around his neck and a black pistol always on hip; however,
he was anything but showy. He eschewed all forms of publicity, preferring instead to spend his time among his soldiers, often strolling up to the
front lines to survey the battle.[89] On Guadalcanal, during night air raids,
even though he was wracked with dysentery, Patch and his aide would
stand outside the bunkers, as if his presence alone could keep his soldiers
safe.[90] Actions such as this inspired strong loyalty from the men under
his leadership. He took each casualty personally, often brooding about
any senseless loss of life. One of his staff officers said of him, "Patch was
compassionate, more than any other commander, in his love and care
of the soldiers . . . Lovable, kind, A modest man. I loved that man."[91]

Patch never let his men see any sign of his weakness and led them through all manner of training and marches despite his severely weakened lungs, which were not helped by his incessant smoking of hand-rolled cigarettes. He would take command of the newly formed XIV Corps after the departure of the 1st Marine Division from Guadalcanal and finish defeating the Japanese forces still on the island. After Guadalcanal, another attack of pneumonia almost killed him, but he recovered and went on to command the Seventh Army in Europe. He was set to lead the Fourth Army into Japan when the war ended and with it his will to fight. Pneumonia, coupled with the emotionally devastating loss of his only son in France, finally killed the seemingly unstoppable general in November 1945.[92]

The arrival of the 164th Infantry Regiment from North Dakota completed the triangularization of the task force. On 27 May 1942, at the direction of the Army Adjutant General, the Americal Division was born.[93] Because of excess artillery and engineer units, its resemblance to a standard army division's table of organization began and ended with its three infantry regiments. For this reason, the new division became one of only two divisions not given a numerical designation.[94] It was an independent command that reported directly to the War Department and Patch was free to take his "military stew of men and equipment" and whip it into shape as he saw fit.[95] As a devout infantryman, there was no doubt that Patch would ensure that his men were proficient in all aspects of ground warfare.

In his former command Patch had trained many of the National Guard soldiers now under him. He was aware of the special issues facing National Guard units: namely that these men had often grown up together and worked side-by-side in their civilian jobs. For this reason it was sometimes difficult for leaders to detach themselves emotionally from their subordinates and push their soldiers to the limits required in combat. While the existing laws made it relatively easy to remove a National Guard soldier from his position, less than 0.75 percent had lost them in the months leading up to the war.[96] Pre-deployment physical examinations managed to remove some of the oldest officers, but their replacements often came from within the unit, a practice that only reinforced the insular nature of these organizations. This local hold on leadership positions did not end until replacements began to fill out the ranks.[97]

Patch and his staff approached the issue with full understanding that "[officers and non-commissioned officers need to] emphasize rigid discipline and control by officers and NCOs in all training and impress them with their responsibilities on the battlefield. Weed out the 'leaders' who are over-solicitous of the welfare and comfort of their men for they destroy the natural ruggedness of a soldier by too much sympathy"[98] To this end, Patch quickly replaced two of the regimental commanders with regular army officers, while he relieved other officers over time for incompetence.[99] Still more removed themselves for "medical reasons." One battalion had 11 of 35 officers, including the commander and executive officer, seeking medical exemptions on the eve of deployment to Guadalcanal.[100] Although junior officers and soldiers expressed their own doubts about the competence of their officers, they were not sure that regular army officers would be much better.

> Our unit, from the North Dakota National Guard had its own problems. Many were political appointments and incompetent. Many were damned cowards! I wrote a book stating my disappointment of West Point, the Old Man's school. We had sergeants in our outfit that were far better qualified to lead men. Our unit was poorly trained as none of our officers (and many did their best) had been properly trained.[101]

To fill in the gaps in the officer corps, the division staff conducted an Officer Candidate School to commission selected soldiers who had proven to be outstanding leaders. In all, nearly 385 soldiers became officers and returned to lead the units from which they came.[102]

Regiment-level training on New Caledonia proved to be nearly impossible. Not only was the division spread throughout dozens of tiny outposts across 180 miles of the island, but the air forces had commandeered much of the division to help build a new airfield. The poor existing road network and severe gasoline rationing compounded this problem. Of course, operating on a shoestring was nothing new to the Guard units, whose large-scale training had largely consisted of two-week summer camps and whose general condition of training and equipment was uneven, to say the least, with quality depending on the command in each individual state. Although the U.S. Division of Militia Affairs worked hard to send updated training procedures to Guard units in every state, the soldiers of the 164th later testified that the training they experienced at weekly drills was "poor" or "uninspired" and the company officers or sergeants too dependent on rote methods and would often simply read the manuals out loud as training. A common complaint was that officers and sergeants seldom did much more than count cadence or watch the drills.

National Guard soldiers laid the blame for this more on lack of proper funds and reliance on old equipment then on poor leadership. Because of budget constraints there was never adequate equipment, such as heavy machine guns or mortars, for real tactical exercises. The system, which had units train once a year in tactics above company level, proved equally unproductive and it was unheard of to keep troops out overnight or in heavy inclement weather in these "glorified scout outings."[103]

Nevertheless, Patch's staff did their best to prepare their soldiers. Australian soldiers trained several men from each regiment in commando tactics, which they in turn taught to their units. Many of the American soldiers were farm boys who had grown up hunting and proved excellent shots, no matter what weapon they used. While artillery units practiced rapid and accurate firing in direct and general support units, small units (battalion and below) trained in defensive maneuvers and jungle tactics and often conducted extended operations across the island as their primary defense mission permitted.[104]

Battalion commanders were often given free reign over their training, something that was not always beneficial.

> An additional shock came when we found he [our now relieved battalion commander] had withheld our 60mm and 81mm-mortar training ammunition from us these past months. He had it all stashed inside a fenced enclosure behind his tent. Word had leaked down that our gasoline ration was in reality four gallons a day for each vehicle. Our battalion commander had withheld half of this in his enclosure. We would lose scores of barrels of gasoline that he had piled up . . . Also lost to us was our machine-gun and rifle-practice ammunition. The only conclusion we could reach was that our commander had withheld the supplies for demonstrations to please the big brass when they came around, demonstrations that would never take place. I never forgave him, for we went to Guadalcanal with little or no experience in firing those important weapons.[105]

By October 1942, the marines' situation on Guadalcanal had become dire and they needed reinforcements as quickly as possible. Despite the deficiencies in training and in contradiction to stated army policy that every division would train together for at least one year before deploying, the Americal Division was the only large U.S. ground force in the region. Less than six months after formation, the division set sail to partake in the first ground offensive of the war, where they would put their inadequate training to the test.

25th Infantry Division "Tropic Lightning"

No other unit was thrown into combat so soon after formation as the 25th Infantry Division.[106] A mere 68 days after activation, the Japanese attack on Pearl Harbor made the 25th Division the first American ground force in combat. On 1 October 1941, as part of a general reorganization of the army, the War Department split the Hawaiian Division, which had guarded the islands since 1921, to create two triangular divisions. This order sent the 19th and 21st Infantry Regiments to the new 24th Infantry Division and the 27th and 35th Infantry Regiments to the 25th Division.[107] In order to round out these regular army units, the War Department then activated the 299th and 298th Infantry Regiments from the Hawaii National Guard.[108] Both divisions remained under the control of the Hawaiian Department, which functioned as a corps headquarters.

In the months immediately after Pearl Harbor, the division's sector included the southern portions of the island, all the naval installations on Oahu and the city of Honolulu while "detachments from the division were on active patrol throughout the vital installations . . . beach positions were constantly improved, guards were stationed at the water and power plants, radios stations, harbor facilities and other strategic sites."[109] Moreover, the division "constructed pillboxes, erected obstacles, final protective lines, barbed wire fences and many other defensive projects too numerous to mention."[110] By this time the 161st Regiment of the Washington National Guard had joined the division. The regiment had been en route to reinforce the Philippines when the fall of Wake and Guam stranded it in Hawaii, where it joined the Hawaiian Department.[111]

In May 1942 General J. Lawton Collins became the commander of the 25th Division. Collins was the former chief of staff of the Hawaiian Department and as such acted as coordinator for the ground defenses of the islands. During his command he earned the nickname "Lightning Joe" for his aggressive style of leadership. He would later lead the VII Corps in the D-Day landings and go on to spearhead the breakthrough at St. Lo, drive through the Siegfried Line and capture Aachen and Cologne before linking up with the Russian army at the Elbe River.[112] General Omar Bradley, the Twelfth Army Group Commander, said of Collins, "Had we created another ETO army, despite his youth and lack of seniority [he was just 45 years old at the start of the war], Collins certainly would have been named the commander."[113] Ironically, Collins was Deputy Chief of Staff of the Army during the unification battle that pitted him against many of the marines he had served with on Guadalcanal, particularly Vandegrift. He would later succeed Bradley as Chief of Staff and still later oversee the formation of the North Atlantic Treaty Organization (NATO).

After the Battle of Midway, Collins realized that not only had the threat to Hawaii lessened but the Joint Chiefs would not allow two regular army divisions to remain in Hawaii much longer. Based on training levels, he determined that the 25th Division would be chosen to deploy first and needed to be ready to go directly into battle.[114]

However, before Collins could fully focus on training, he had to deal with an issue that had haunted the division since formation. A large proportion of the Hawaii National Guard consisted of soldiers of Japanese descent (Nisei). Despite the fact that there were no documented cases of sabotage, the navy was reluctant to have either the 298th or 299th guard any naval installations. Moreover, there was a fear that the non-Caucasian soldiers might be mistaken for Japanese in the heat of battle.[115] In order to appease these worries, the two regiments were withdrawn to Schofield Barracks and placed in reserve. Later these units formed the 100th Infantry Battalion and served with distinction in Europe. Instead, the 161st, which was already attached to the 25th, rounded out the division.[116]

Arguably, Collins was the perfect commander to conduct training for a division headed to combat. Before the war, he had served as the chief of staff of VII Corps[117], which was then dedicated to large-scale training for the General Headquarters (GHQ) of the Army Ground Forces (AGF). Over the course of 1941, VII Corps not only conducted mobilization training testing (MTT) for several National Guard divisions, but executed three months of division-level maneuvers in Tennessee, Arkansas, and Louisiana.[118] These exercises not only tested doctrine and tactics, but also helped identify the most promising leaders for the upcoming war.[119] Because of his participation in the planning and execution of these maneuvers, Collins was well aware of the training challenges his division faced. As he recalled, "There was nothing wrong with the men in the National Guard, it was simply that they hadn't had any real training. Most of them came from cities and there wasn't any place to train [or] to get together prior to the war."[120]

Collins now emphasized realistic training. He knew that it would be difficult to break the men of the defensive mindset engendered by their mission on Hawaii but that

> the success of the division would depend largely on the quality of our noncommissioned officers and company and battalion commanders and that every opportunity should be taken to develop their self-reliance and initiative; that we should hold to firm discipline, based on common sense and confidence between officers and men; and that our main effort in training would be to develop our infantry battalions as the key fighting units, to be closely supported by artillery and air . . . we would spend much of our time on battalion field exercises . . . and on two combat firing ranges . . . we would concentrate our efforts in preparing the division for offensive combat in mobile warfare, in contrast to the relatively stable defensive role on Oahu.[121]

Stanley Larsen, an officer in the 35th Infantry Regiment, recorded the contrast in training after Collins took command. "All our training before WWII and during the first 6 months after the war started was dedicated to defensive action . . . being a very aggressive leader, he [Collins] instituted all kinds of training for offensive actions . . . to present the military's capabilities he prepared a coordinated demonstration of army, air corps and navy might [for Hawaiian officials]"[122]

Other officers recalled the intensity of the training as regiments rotated between defensive positions and field exercises.

> We had numerous exercises to train both officers and men. One was a 35 mile forced march (no stops other than a ten minute break every hour) . . . The plan called for all companies . . . to man machine guns and 37mm guns at preselected beach positions . . . Soon we were relieved of our defensive positions and moved to Schofield Barracks

to train for combat somewhere in the Pacific . . . [which] included amphibious training, that of offloading ship by climbing down cargo nets, entering small boats and the assaulting the beach.[123]

The biggest emphasis was on weapons training due to Collins's belief that every soldier and officer should have a working knowledge of the various weapons used by the division. Many of the 161st officers and NCOs went through the Division Weapons School, nicknamed "Collins' School of Tactical Knowledge," and in turn trained their soldiers. In November 1942, after long hours of marches, lectures, and smaller exercises, the unit was ready to conduct full-scale amphibious maneuvers.[124]

Collins was also one of only two future corps commanders who had attended the Field Artillery school as his second officer advanced course, which affected the manner in which he viewed artillery and close air support. First, he saw the value of forward artillery observers in directing accurate fire as well as the need for artillery to fire massed barrages directly in front of the supported infantry. Furthermore, he viewed artillery fire as a way to knock out enemy emplacements and create maneuver space for ground forces. Not only did he have his regiments train with his supporting howitzer battalions, but he also used artillery to mark targets for aircraft in close air support. He validated his theories with a series of live fire exercises on Hawaii, at times bringing the close air support within 200 yards of his troops—far closer than the 600 yards that was the doctrinal norm.[125]

Later, the commander of the 27th Infantry Regiment recalled just how those months of intensive training paid dividends on the battlefield.

> Despite the time and effort of [defense] projects the importance of individual and combat training was not overlooked and it was recognized that a man skilled in the operation of his principal weapon so that he had personal confidence in his ability to pick off the enemy was a basic essential. Following that the necessity for his knowing the part that he played in the team work of the squad and even the four essentials of a combat squad on a mission. The essentials of doing something constructive, something positive, something involving action and not inaction . . . have since paid dividends and should become SOP [standard operating procedure] for future training and execution at all times. Schools, squad tests, service practice and field exercises . . . gradually developed the fighting qualities recently demonstrated. It was not, however, until the regiment moved

to Schofield Barracks . . . that intensive training in amphibious operations and jungle fighting could be systematically followed . . . The transport trip, due to overcrowding provided little opportunity for training other than last minute instruction in the use of the jungle kit and enemy tactics. I told you then that a good appearing, good marching, good shooting outfit that played the game together was a winning team and your success proved it.[126]

An official report of the operations echoes this sentiment. It claimed that the teamwork developed within the division during training on Oahu was one of its greatest sources of strength that subsequently paid immeasurable dividends. Infantry, artillery, engineers, signalmen, and supply services all learned to work together in combat and as a result "the division functioned as a smooth-oiled, well working machine."[127]

The War Department took notice of the 25th Division's readiness level and selected it to relieve the 1st Marine Division on Guadalcanal. On 19 October, after six months of intensive combat training, the unit received official notification of its impending deployment, although it was not told its final destination. On the eve of the division's departure, Nimitz sent a dispatch to Collins that declared the unit ready for combat. As a result of making good use of its time on Oahu, the 25th Division was now, he believed, "outstandingly fit and ready for offensive combat." Regardless of whether it fought in the SOPAC or SOWESPAC area, "we have high expectations of successful actions by you against the enemy."[128]

2nd Marine Division "Follow Me"

The "Hollywood Marines" of 2nd Marine Division might not have been able to claim the title of "The Old Breed," but they did have a similarly distinguished lineage. Each of the infantry regiments had a proud history of combat service: the 2nd Marines at Vera Cruz and Haiti; the 6th Marines in World War I, the Dominican Republic, Cuba and China; and the 8th in Mexico and Haiti.[129] The division activated on the same day as the 1st Division and the dominating motif of its early years was "detachment." Its detachments gave the 2nd Division many firsts in the war: first sent overseas, first to land on a Japanese-held island and first to exchange fire with the enemy.

The first overseas was the 6th Marines, detached along with elements of the artillery, medical, service, and engineering battalions to form the 1st Provisional Marine Brigade. This ad hoc unit sailed to Ice-land to join British troops to counter a possible German invasion of the island. While there, the unit not only constructed all the buildings for the defense force, but also managed to hold a few field and staff exercises before army units arrived as reinforcements. Together, marine and army units also conducted several large-scale joint command post exercises and firing drills until weather and long dark winter nights made outdoor training infeasible.[130]

In April 1942, the brigade (now reverted back to the 6th Marines) returned to California and rejoined the 2nd Division in the defense of California. It brought with it valuable experience in setting up island defenses.[131] However, the regiment soon lost much of this institutional knowledge as almost half of the experienced officers and NCOs trans-ferred either due to promotion, normal rotation, or to serve as the nucleus for newly formed units.[132]

In October, the regiment sailed for New Zealand. There, it began training to replace the 1st Division on Guadalcanal. The training focused on jungle operations and was accomplished in a region encompass-ing parts of a large sheep ranch. The nearby foothills of forest-covered mountains provided challenging hiking routes and a near-primeval forest proved ideal for scouting and patrolling. The leadership made an effort to make training as realistic as possible and brought in combat veterans returned from Guadalcanal to lecture on their experiences in fighting the Japanese and jungle hardships.

The next to go was the 8th Marines. In January 1942, the marine corps formed the 2nd Brigade around the regiment and sent it to guard the Samoan island of Pago Pago under the command of Colonel Richard Jeschke, an officer who would later be instrumental in the planning the Sicily and Normandy invasions. While there, the unit spent the next three months expanding Samoan defenses interspersed with extensive jungle warfare training.[133]

However, by the time it regained the 8th Marines, the division had lost the 2nd Marines. In order to fill out the 1st Marine Division for the coming invasion, the Marine Corps decided to attach the 2nd Marines as a replace-ment for the 7th Marines, which was part of the defense of Samoa. The unit arrived on 25 July 1942, just in time to participate in Operation DOVE-TAIL. Despite its designation as the division reserve, elements of the unit landed on nearby Florida Island just prior to the main assault, thus earning the distinction of being the first unit to land on enemy territory. The remainder of the regiment landed on Tulagi and Gavutu-Tanambogo, where they conducted clearing operations. On 29 October the regiment joined the main force on Guadalcanal.[134]

The 8th Marines left Samoa and landed on Guadalcanal in November 1942 just in time to link up with the 2nd Marines and the 164th Infantry for the drive on Kokumbona. In the after-action report, Jeschke reflected on the mixed feelings the unit had about the time spent in Samoa and how it affected unit performance in battle. On the positive side, living and training in a remote location allowed for low personnel turnover and fostered initiative and confidence. In addition, "the thorough indoctrination with jungle terrain, vegetation, climate, noises and the intense darkness of tropical nights" meant that the unit needed little or no acclimatization to conditions on Guadalcanal. On the other hand, nine months in the unhealthy jungle climate took its toll on the health of the regiment's marines. Moreover, the location suffered from a "lack of facilities and opportunities for combined offensive training of infantry with supporting arms [and] inadequate facilities for combat practice firing of all weapons."[135]

The last element of the division finally arrived when the 6th Marines landed in January 1943. The regiment immediately became part of the short-lived Composite Army-Marine (CAM) Division, created from the healthy elements of the 6th Marines and Americal Division.[136] Within a day of landing, the 6th Marines were in combat as they relieved the exhausted units on the front lines. For the first time since its formation in 1941, all three regiments of the 2nd Division were now collocated.

Along with the 6th Marines, the division headquarters also arrived, minus the commander, General John Marston. Because he was senior to Patch, Marston stayed behind in New Zealand and his assistant commander, General Alphonse DeCarre, became the acting commander. "The decision to make Patch the island commander on Vandegrift's departure rested on the general policy that the preponderance of strength, either army or marine, [would] more or less determine the commander."[137] Because this decision was made without consulting the Commandant of the Marine Corps, General Thomas Holcomb, it had the possibility of becoming a point of contention. However, the Commandant decided not to press the issue, although he expressed disappointment years later, "I consider it most unfortunate that the division commander should be denied the opportunity and experience of commanding his division in its first action . . . there is no reason known [to me] why General Marston should not have served under General Patch's command."[138] Whatever the reasons for this decision, the marines were no longer in charge on Guadalcanal and the division would fall under the newly created XIV Corps for the rest of the campaign.

OPERATIONS

In hindsight, it easy to take for granted the American victory at Guadalcanal. However, the outcome was not apparent at the time and there were many moments when the American forces seemed headed towards certain defeat. Many of the commanders, particularly Ghormley and Fletcher, were sure that the operation had little chance of success and even positive events did little to shake them from this conviction. Even Harmon expressed doubt at times, writing to Marshall, "we are not prepared to follow up . . . Can the marines hold it? There is considerable room for doubt."[139] However, at the end, one officer summed up the feeling of all the soldiers who participated: "We all had our problems, but we did have a great bunch of marines and a great bunch of soldiers and I think for the first actions that we called Guadalcanal, the first offensive, really set the pattern for the rest of the war."[140]

ENEMY ACTIONS

Success in combat is often equal parts skill and luck and Guadalcanal required more luck than most. In fact, one historian observed that "with the full cooperation of a few marines, the Japanese defeated themselves in detail."[141] Not only were the ground forces fortunate that the battle occurred only on a tiny portion of the island, but also that the Japanese failed to follow up their naval victory at Savo Island by sending reinforcements for a large-scale ground attack. Instead, they chose to commit their forces piecemeal. Admittedly, after Halsey assigned extra battleships to the area in October and destroyed a considerable number of enemy transport ships in November, the Japanese navy was lucky to get any supplies and reinforcements through at all. Conversely, the marines were lucky the Japanese never attempted to destroy American supplies, which lay vulnerable on the beachhead for more than two weeks.

Finally, Japanese commanders never took advantage of their superior knowledge of the terrain gained after months on the island, especially during the period required for the Americans to acclimatize. Instead they seemed to focus solely on recapturing Henderson Field and took little initiative on their own to alter the directives issued from higher headquarters that had little relationship to the situation on the ground.

Tactics dictated by commanders far from Guadalcanal further exacerbated the difficulties confronting the Japanese on the island. Documents that laid down the tactics also gave instructions from which commanders were not to deviate.

> During the course of battle, no commander will retreat except upon orders of a higher command. No unit will take action on its own initiative. No commander will oppose the plans of his superior, or lower the morale of his unit. Casualties result from misunderstanding one's mission, or failure to give proper orders. Further casualties result because lower commanders often lack self-confidence, or desire for notoriety. If the enemy situation is completely unknown, we will not make a frontal assault.[142] Only to defend is not enough; always to attack is going too far.[143]

One can find a clue to Japanese strategy in the area in a speech by General Kotoku Sato, the army/navy spokesman, to the Japanese Diet.[144] He claimed that Guadalcanal and the subsequent New Guinea battles were strategic victories waged in order to occupy the Americans and allow the main forces to consolidate near supply bases in Malaya and the Philippines. He further declared that the two were too far from the main supply line and that "it would have been ignoble strategy for our forces to have sought decisive battle in a location strategically disadvantageous." Moreover, he asserted that only after accomplishing these objectives was "the withdrawal of our forces in both areas carried out in an orderly manner . . . in a calm manner, while always attacking the enemy and keeping him under control . . . with almost no losses."[145] However, despite Sato's claim, while the Japanese managed to evacuate about 10,000 troops and approximately 1,000 were taken prisoner, the rest of the ground forces, over 25,000, died on the island.

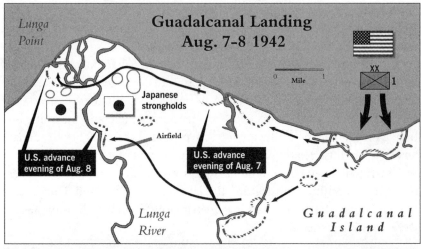

Guadalcanal Landing
Aug. 7-8 1942

Japanese
strongholds

Airfield

U.S. advance
evening of Aug. 8

U.S. advance
evening of Aug. 7

Lunga
Point

Lunga
River

Guadalcanal
Island

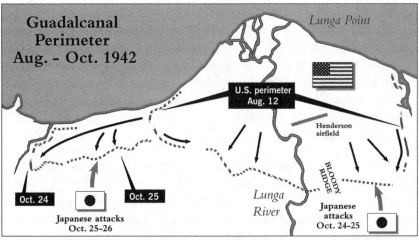

Guadalcanal
Perimeter
Aug. - Oct. 1942

Lunga Point

U.S. perimeter
Aug. 12

Henderson
airfield

BLOODY
RIDGE

Oct. 24

Oct. 25

Lunga
River

Japanese
attacks
Oct. 24-25

Japanese attacks
Oct. 25-26

Japan

Pacific
Ocean

Okinawa

Philippine
Islands

Saipan

Marshall
Islands

Gilbert
Islands

Guadalcanal

Australia

Japanese evacuation
Feb. 8

Florida
Point

Detail
area

Lunga
Point

Pacific
Ocean

2 ⊠ 132

1 ⊠ 161

Feb. 1

Guadalcanal
Island

Final
Phase
Jan. 26 - Feb. 9, 1943

LANDING OPERATIONS[146]

It is hard to evaluate the actual landing versus the operational plan, since the marines landed on Guadalcanal unopposed and it is impossible to determine how the plan would have held up under opposition. By all accounts, the final plan did not materially depart from the original plan of operations.[147] This is remarkable since the landing force staff essentially formulated their plan without detailed knowledge of the plans of higher and supporting commanders. One report noted that, despite several enemy air attacks, the landings on Guadalcanal proceeded "with the smoothness and precision of a well-rehearsed peace-time drill."[148] The preliminary naval bombardment began at 0613, with no response from the Japanese defenders. The first combat group landed at 0910 on Beach RED, just 6,000 yards east of Henderson field, the main objective. The second combat group landed at 1100, followed by the division command post (CP) at 1400. The marines took Henderson Field that day, hampered mainly by the unexpectedly thick jungle. However, the marines did not attain all of their objectives on 7 August. Mount Austen, which overlooked and dominated the landing beach, proved to be much further from the landing beach than the maps indicated. The Americans would not capture the mountain until December.

In contrast, the units that landed on the adjacent islands of Tulagi and Gavutu-Tanambogo experienced fiercer than expected resistance. The Tulagi Group secured the island on 8 August. Gavutu-Tanambogo took a day longer and was finally secured on 9 August.[149] They killed all but three of the approximately 865 Japanese on these islands.

Of course, this smooth initial landing did not mean that the Japanese surrendered the island. Rather this was only the beginning of a six-month struggle. The major blunder during the landing and the action that defined the operation was the logistical issue. During the final meeting before the landing, Fletcher was adamant that he would not keep his carriers in place for more than two days (although he later claimed that he had no memory of the issue coming up during the conference).[150] Although he eventually agreed to three days, during the landing he reneged on his agreement and pulled the carriers out just two days after the landing, with less than half the supplies unloaded. The reasons behind his early departure have been the subject of intense debate over the years. His critics charge him with cowardice and lack of concern for the ground troops; his champions credit him with saving the carriers in the wake of the disastrous American naval defeat at Savo Island on 8–9 August and blame Turner, who refused to release the 2nd Marines to assist in the unloading.[151] Even Vandegrift admitted that he had designated too small a landing party because he had anticipated fierce fighting on the beachhead.[152] Fletcher addressed the issue only once, claiming that he withdrew the carriers early because they were critically short of fuel.[153] Whatever the reasoning, the fact remains that the marines were left with less than 30 days of food supply (including ten days of captured Japanese rations), four units of fire (out of the ten loaded) and a general lack of communications or engineering equipment.[154] It would be weeks before the marines were resupplied and they survived only by immediately cutting the troops to two meals per day. Next to the lack of good maps, this logistical error would do more to threaten the outcome of the operation than the Japanese. As one soldier noted afterwards, "We went in there pretty much blindfolded as well as having one arm tied behind our backs due to a lack of food and equipment."[155]

The immensity of the theater, lack of large ports and the initial lack of advanced bases made resupply slow and cumbersome and supply issues would remain a problem throughout the campaign. When supplies did make it to Guadalcanal, the lack of docks, the small number of service troops, and the absence of a good road network made it difficult to unload and distribute the goods. It was not until December that these issues were finally overcome, too late to do the marines much good as they had already turned the operations over to the army. Vandegrift tersely wrote in his final report that "it must be pointed out that troops cannot be expected to exist indefinitely on short rations and utterly devoid of the necessities of life and some provision for the minimum comfort and standards of decency."[156]

The major lesson that Vandegrift learned from the landing was that an amphibious force should be organized and trained as a permanent unit and not as a provisional grouping of forces brought together for one specific task. He recommended that landing force units should be assigned to specific ships within a transport group and should conduct extended joint training. "Essential teamwork between transport and landing teams can be obtained only by operational practice."[157] To prove his point he noted that a ship in Melbourne, the HMAS *Nanoora*, trained with the division and had repeated a series of elementary landing exercises seven times in the space of ten weeks, each time embarking a different landing team of the division. He noted "strange to her work, she required 21 hours to put ashore the landing team supplies on the first exercise. The time was reduced steadily with each successive attempt until on the final exercise she landed the same quantity of supply in six hours. Improvement in embarkation and boat operations was equally remarkable."[158]

BATTLE SUMMARY[159]

While the 1st Marine Division landed without opposition and managed to capture the airfield and reach the Lunga River within a day, this did not mean that the Japanese were going to give up the island without a fight. Instead, they had moved about three miles east to the Matanikau River, where a destroyer delivered some naval reinforcement troops. At the same time, the Japanese navy surprised and routed the Allied naval force near Savo Island, forcing them to withdraw and leave the ground forces with little air cover.

The first significant contact between the two sides occurred on 12 August, when a patrol led by Lieutenant Colonel Frank Goettge landed west of the Matanikau in order to conduct reconnaissance and contact a group of Japanese supposedly willing to surrender. Instead, an ambush wiped out nearly the entire patrol. In response, on 19 August Vandegrift sent three companies of the 5th Marines to attack these forces in and around Kokumbuna and Matanikau in the "First Battle of Matanikau." This was also the day that the first of the Japanese reinforcements arrived. These troops attacked the marines in the east, near the Tenaru River. A marine counterattack the next day wiped out 789 of the 917 attackers and pushed the survivors back to Taivu Point. Also, during this time the American air forces, called "The Cactus Air Force," arrived and began countering the ongoing Japanese bombing attacks.

A convoy carrying approximately 1,900 Japanese soldiers and marines was headed towards the island, with an anticipated arrival date of 24 August. An attack by Fletcher's carriers and the Cactus fighters sank one of the transports and forced the others to divert. During the rest of the month, the marine battalions from the outlying islands began landing on Guadalcanal as the Americans built up their defenses. In addition, the marines received some supplies from small naval convoys. The Japanese also managed to land almost 5,000 troops at Taivu Point and another 1,000 west of the Lunga. On 12 September, 3,000 Japanese soldiers moved from Taivu Point to fight the Marine Raider Battalion (approximately 800 marines) defending a coral ridge that ran parallel to the Lunga. For two days the Raiders barely held on to "Bloody Ridge" before finally forcing the Japanese west, where they joined with the soldiers at the Lunga.[160] As the Japanese regrouped and waited for further reinforcements, the last battalion from Tulagi, as well as the 7th Marines, arrived. This allowed Vandegrift to establish a full defense around the Lunga perimeter during the short lull in fighting.

Beginning on 23 September the American and Japanese forces skirmished in the area west of Matanikau. Both sides took heavy losses. The marines awaited reinforcement from the Americal Division, while the Japanese managed to land 15,000 more troops for a planned offensive to retake Henderson Field, bringing their total to around 20,000. Although the Americans had roughly the same number—19,500—on ground and more on the way, their hold on the airfield was still tenuous in the face of continuous Japanese attacks.

By the middle of October, disease and sheer exhaustion had ravaged the 1st Marines and Vandegrift begged Halsey for the entire Americal Division and another marine regiment to relieve his worn-out men. No sooner had he asked for this than the Japanese began the attack to retake Henderson Field. It was during this battle that the 164th Infantry arrived, just in time to plug in the holes in the 7th Marine lines along Bloody Ridge. The 164th's entrance into battle was so dramatic that it might have been scripted by Hollywood and it is vital to highlight its seamless insertion into the front lines as a model of adaptive joint cooperation.

As soon as the 164th disembarked from transport ships on 13 October Vandegrift ordered it into battle as the situation on Bloody Ridge became ever more desperate and demanded emergency reinforcement, especially in the 1st Battalion sector commanded by the legendary Lewis "Chesty" Puller.[161] A chaplain was the only one who knew the location of the battalion and offered to guide the 164th into its combat positions. The Americal soldiers worked their way slowly up a jungle-covered hill through the dark and rain to become the first American army units to conduct offensive actions in any theater in World War II. Legend has it that when the chaplain brought the replacements to Puller, he simply said, "Father, we can use 'em."[162] One by one, marines slipped out of their foxholes and made their way towards the army troops to claim their share of the new arrivals. In this completely uneventful fashion, the marines and army inaugurated the joint ground operations that would soon dominate the theater.

In some foxholes the marines simply relieved the soldiers of their weapons and ammunition and continued to do most of the fighting themselves, but in others the marines found the newcomers' fighting prowess notable, particularly considering they were fighting in completely unfamiliar terrain. Together the units beat back the waves of Japanese attacks until the enemy finally fell back without gaining any ground.

In the morning, as the commanders reorganized the front lines, Colonel Bryant Moore, commander of 164thInfantry, sought out Puller and thanked him for allowing his unit to fight alongside the marines. As he noted, "No man in our outfit, including me, had ever seen action and I know our boys couldn't have had a better instructor. I wish you'd break in my other battalions." Puller in turn gave the 164th the highest praise imaginable, "They're almost as good as marines."[163] Vandegrift felt confident enough in their abilities to assign the 164th its own sector.

To exploit their victory, on 1 November Vandegrift sent the 5th Marines, backed up by the newly arrived 2nd Marines, west to Point Cruz (at the mouth of the Matanikau River) to destroy the Japanese headquarters there. However, despite the successes, he halted operations there in order to focus on a threat coming from Japanese troops on Koli Point, an operation that took until 12 November. By this time the 8th Marines, the 147th Infantry, and the 182nd Infantry Regiment arrived, providing a measure of relief to the exhausted veterans.[164] During that time, the Japanese also received a fresh regiment at Point Cruz, although Halsey's carriers managed to destroy a majority of the transports carrying troops and supplies. This proved to be the turning point of the battle, as the Americans managed to hamper every attempt to resupply the Japanese forces. As December wore on, the Americans replaced the worn-out 1st Marine Division with fresh troops from the 25th Infantry Division along with the remaining regiments from the Americal and 2nd Marine Divisions. The newly formed XIV Corps, using the artillery tactics the 25th ID had rehearsed in Hawaii, began pushing the remaining Japanese forces west and finally captured the elusive Mount Austen in mid-December.

In the face of this enormous buildup, on 12 December, the Japanese navy requested, over army opposition, that they abandon Guadalcanal. On 31 December the Japanese prepared to evacuate their soldiers to nearby New Georgia. As the Americans pressed relentlessly west, the Japanese continued resistance, albeit much weaker than before. Beginning 1 February and continuing for a week, the Japanese evacuated their soldiers from Cape Esperance, eventually withdrawing the remaining 11,000 soldiers. On 9 February, Patch announced "the complete and total defeat of Japanese forces on Guadalcanal."

ANALYSIS

Planning

Despite its ultimate success, Guadalcanal's operational planning was an excellent example of how *not* to plan a joint operation. Not only was the planning done in haste, but also in relative isolation. Ghormley's staff did all the planning, with little input from other services. In a report on "The Army in the South Pacific," the army forces commander noted, "the number of army officers on COMSOPAC's [Commander South Pacific] staff was so small and their individual qualifications in some particulars so limited that they were of questionable value. As good or possibly better results would have been obtained had planning activities continued on the basis of close daily association of opposite numbers on the army and navy staffs."[165]

The different service views of the campaign's purpose further hampered army-Marine Corps-navy coordination. Ground commanders saw the campaign as an amphibious operation with the normal division of joint responsibilities. That is, naval forces would secure the seas around the objective for as long as it took ground forces to clear Guadalcanal of enemy. But higher naval commanders viewed the operation as more of a raid than a formal amphibious campaign. Vandegrift's final report noted this disparity and concluded

> had [the]same conception been entertained from the outset by all of the forces involved it would have afforded us an opportunity to modify normal planning by adjusting it to the special circumstances. This in turn would have served to alleviate many of the misunderstandings which later arose with respect to supply and general logistics.[166]

Furthermore, the planners really had no prior operations on which to base their planning, so there were few lessons on which to draw or adapt. Looking at the plan and reports in the days immediately after the landing, the president of the Naval War College, Admiral William Pye, remarked to King that while "the landing was well planned and carried out there seemed to have been little or no long range planning."[167]

Intelligence

A young soldier in the operation later commented, "Had I been asked for my criticisms of the operation at that time I would have stressed the total lack of communications between the higher ups and the troops. We knew nothing. Not where we were, where we were going, where the enemy was or anything about his status. Not once while I was there did I see a map— maybe there were none."[168] This soldier was absolutely correct in one regard: possibly the largest obstacle during the operation was the utter lack of maps, a shortfall that the command was never able to rectify.

An attempt had been made to correct this before the invasion. A mission led by Colonel Merrill Twining, the 1st Marine Division assistant operations officer, flew over the island to take pictures of landing areas and assess their suitability. The operations section also made every effort to exploit all available sources of information, particularly from Australian coastwatchers.[169] Through these means, the 1st Marine Division put together estimates of enemy strength and dispositions as well as an "excellent aerial mosaic and map of Guadalcanal both of which were reproduced in quantity. This cartographic material would have been of invaluable assistance but through a failure of intelligence liaison it failed to reach the division."[170] The maps were created and printed in Australia, then sent in three shipments to New Zealand well in advance of the operation. However, the boxes got mixed in with the piles of supplies awaiting distribution and were not discovered until after the operation.

In the end, the map used for the operation was simply traced from an aerial strip map obtained by Goettge. While it provided a reasonably accurate general outline of the island, the map gave no indication of buildings, foliage, obstacles, or elevations. The Goettge map was supplemented by aerial photos of Tulagi, Gavutu, and Tanambogo done in July and constituted "the sum of the marines' knowledge . . . prior to the landings."[171] As noted in the final report, "Lack of such materials [cartographic maps] severely handicapped all phases of the Guadalcanal operation."[172]

As with the maps, estimates were done using the information given by coastwatchers and former residents, intercepted enemy dispatches, and the scant photographic material. Initial estimates placed 8,400 Japanese on the island. By July the number was reduced to 7,125. Vandegrift planned for 5,000.[173] The actual number was approximately 3,000. Although these numbers did not affect the landing, they are indicative of how inaccurate intelligence was before the operation.

This lack of intelligence was the single greatest failure of the planning phase, but the lack of opposition during the landing reduced its significance compared to the logistical failure. During a conference immediately after Guadalcanal, Vandegrift noted that "we have not put enough time nor effort in the training of intelligence personnel, both in lower units and in the higher echelons . . . What to do with information and how to get it . . . and send it on to where it should go."[174]

The best and most useful intelligence came from the natives who cooperated with the Americans. Their ability to move around the island behind enemy lines allowed them to provide immediate and actionable intelligence to the Americans about Japanese movements. One of these, Sergeant Major Jacob Vouza, single-handedly saved the American forces along the Tenaru River from being ambushed by the Japanese on their 21 August attack. The Japanese captured Vouza scouting their battle lines and tortured him for information about the American positions. When he refused to talk, they tied him to a tree, bayoneted him repeatedly in the arms, legs, chest and throat and left him to die. Despite his wounds, Vouza not only chewed through the ropes, but crawled several miles through the jungle to warn the 1st Marines of the coming Japanese attack, which allowed them time to prepare their defenses. As a result, the marines were able to wipe out nearly all of the 900 Japanese attackers. The Americans learned from this to enlist the assistance of native populations, especially those who had been brutalized by Japanese occupiers, whenever possible.

Training

It is difficult to measure the full effects of training objectively, but some judgments can be made using the percentage of casualties as a measure of individual training, the number of commanders relieved for incompetence and the words of the campaign veterans in evaluating the lessons learned.

Casualties[175]

Looking strictly at the casualties on the Island of Guadalcanal, combat and disease resulted in the death of 1,769 American ground forces and wounding of 5,335 (out of about 60,000) and 25,600 Japanese ground forces (out of 36,200).[176] Fewer than 1,000 Japanese surrendered. These totals do not include the 5,331 American/Allied forces or the approximately 4,743 Japanese lost at sea and in the air. This meant that there were 14.5 Japanese killed for each American death. American casualties amounted to 11 percent of the force. We will compare these percentages with the casualty rates of later battles.

Unexpectedly the major threat on the island was not the Japanese, but the lowly mosquito and the malaria it carried. Overall in the South Pacific, malaria accounted for five times the number of casualties as enemy action and three-fifths of those cases occurred on Guadalcanal.[177] Malaria was so endemic on the island that it caused two-thirds of the men to be incapacitated; by contrast, combat wounds only accounted for one-quarter of incapacitations. According to one soldier, "statistically, I believe the marines had between 90 and 95 percent malaria when we arrived on Guadalcanal in the middle of December . . . I think between 70 and 80 percent of our unit [25th Infantry Division] came down with malaria in the 8 months we were there." The disease so overwhelmed the medical personnel that they deemed those with fevers below 103 degrees healthy enough to fight.[178]

Because the malaria rate was low for the first two months on the island, commanders did not understand the hazard of the disease until rates skyrocketed in October. In fact, one senior officer dismissed the threat saying, "We are here to kill Japs [sic] and to hell with mosquitoes."[179] This attitude trickled down to the lower level leaders and resulted in few prevention measures. The atabrine issued to the men effectively prevented malaria, but rumors about the side effects coupled with the inability or unwillingness of the command to enforce orders to use the drug rendered it ineffective. One soldier recalls the game of hide-and-seek between the men and the medics giving out the pills, "the men walked down the chow line, but before they could eat, they were ordered to 'open wide' while the detested pills were popped into their mouths. An inspector stood further down to check that the pills were actually swallowed. The men were adept at hiding them in their mouths and the grounds around the mess tent wound up peppered generously with those hated pills."[180]

The medical service reacted quickly, establishing a new malarial control unit for each division and investing heavily in both vector control and prophylaxis enforcement.[181] By focusing men and resources, the command managed to reduce the single biggest medical threat on the battlefield in the South and Central Pacific. While malaria continued to be an issue, by the next operation in the Gilberts, it was no longer the threat it had been.

Commanders

In September 1942, Holcomb ordered Vandegrift to send home excess colonels in order to make room for newly promoted officers and so the older officers could be employed in newly created units. This gave Vandegrift the opportunity to send back underperforming officers without formally relieving them for cause. Among those were his chief of staff, Colonel William Capers James, and commanders of the 5th Marines, Colonel LeRoy Hunt, and the 7th Marines, Colonel James Webb, along with four other staff officers.[182] To soothe their egos, Vandegrift officially announced they were leaving because of the new policy and chosen due to the length of time they had served in the unit.[183] One officer, William Whaling, 5th Marines executive officer, became redundant upon his promotion to colonel. With no regiments available, he created a scout-sniper detachment and trained selected officers and NCOs in patrolling and jungle operations. These men then returned to their units to "preach the gospel of long marches, light equipment and scant rations."[184] Thus, although he did not deploy with the division, he contributed to its ultimate success.

Vandegrift received the Congressional Medal of Honor for his leadership on Guadalcanal. However, a more important event for both Vandegrift's and the Marine Corps' future occurred on 22 September. Holcomb arrived for a visit to the battlefield. Already a devoted fan of Vandegrift, Holcomb was impressed by Vandegrift's ability to do so much with so little. Holcomb informed him of his decision to retire in September 1943 and that he planned to recommend to President Roosevelt that Vandegrift be his successor as Commandant.[185] This was an inspired choice as Vandegrift is credited as being the man who saved the Marine Corps from being absorbed into the army during the unification battles of 1947 with his impassioned testimony—the famous "bended knee speech"—before Congress.[186]

Because of rigorous evaluations and replacements by division commanders prior to deployment, only one army regimental commander, Colonel Leroy Nelson of the 132nd Infantry, was relieved for incompetence while on the battlefield, but even that removal was couched in terms that allowed the commander to save face.

However, Guadalcanal planning did show the effect that individual personalities could have on an operation. For example, Ghormley was generally regarded as negative and overly cautious. Commanders on the ground hailed his replacement with Halsey, a man held with the highest regard by Vandegrift and other marines, mainly due to his reputation as a fighter and man of action. The first decision that Halsey made in turning over operational command completely to the landing force commander not only had an impact on the current fight, but in effect determined the command status for all future amphibious operations in the region. His second decision, which was to put additional battleships in the area, had immediate positive impacts on the operations on shore and effectively halted any Japanese reinforcements.

LESSONS LEARNED

Because it was the first of the war, few operations were the subject of such intense scrutiny as the Guadalcanal operation. Mindful of the need to avoid repeating mistakes and needlessly losing lives in the process, Marshall ordered Colonel Russell "Red" Reeder to interview the veterans of the 1st Marine and Americal divisions to gather lessons that the army could utilize in further operations. The Department of the Army then assembled these lessons first into the informal report "Notes on Jungle Warfare" and later into a restricted manual entitled "Fighting on Guadalcanal." This was put together and issued so quickly that the 25th Infantry got it before leaving Hawaii.[187] These interviews provided some of the most unvarnished opinions on the operations and this manual provided the model for a more formal lessons-learned program that grew during the war.

Many of the commanders and NCOs interviewed had specific advice on training. Colonel Merritt "Red Mike" Edson, Medal of Honor winner and commander of the 5th Marines, stated, "If I had to train my regiment all over again I would stress small group training and the training of the individual even more than we did." A junior officer added, "I believe units should have a minimum of 90 days training in jungle warfare . . . I would have some really high class patrol training." Several of his peers echoed this sentiment. Several opined that units should have realistic maneuvers that deprived the men of food, water, and other comforts and use live fire in order to prepare them for the rigors of combat.[188] This was followed up by a tour of army training bases by Chesty Puller and other Guadalcanal veterans, during which they addressed all of the divisions that were destined for the Pacific and shared their knowledge of both the theater and the Japanese.[189]

In his final report, Vandegrift also pointed out that despite his belief that Operation DOVETAIL was a waste of valuable time, "this in no way detracts from the fact that rehearsals are of prime importance but they must be proper rehearsals and made under conditions closely approximating the actual operation and permitting the landing of troops and the enactment of the scheme of maneuver."[190]

One new piece of equipment that proved its usefulness was the newly acquired amphibious tractors in moving equipment to shore, especially in terrain where trucks could not be used. In one instance, the tractor was actually used as a combat vehicle against a cave on Gavutu, although Vandegrift cautioned, "this was an emergency undertaking only as it is not considered . . . a tactical combat vehicle."[191]

The operation also proved the value of using artillery as close support, even in a jungle. As one lieutenant noted, "Close in artillery support is very effective. Even though friendly troops may suffer a few casualties, the effect on the enemy is much greater."[192] Other soldiers echoed this effectiveness: "A report from prisoners indicated that in one unit of approximately one hundred men, all but six were casualties as the result of one artillery concentration . . . he also stated 'except for the artillery we could have continued our defense.'"[193] Furthermore, "the effect of incessant firing of our artillery . . . produced contrasting effects on the nerves of our own troops and those of the enemy. Our infantry often stated that having these rounds continually landing in front of them was one of their best morale builders. In the Jap [*sic*] on the other hand, it produced severe cases of war neurosis . . . he never knew where or when the next round would land."[194]

EFFECT ON FUTURE OPERATIONS

As a marine from the 4th Division summed up, "we learned mostly how to fight from the marines from the first battle in Guadalcanal. Those marines really took a beating . . . they learned, first of all, about how to fight the Japs [*sic*] and their tactics. That's why we learned, like, when they show these movies, these guys coming out and trying to mow us down and all that stuff. We learned all of their tricks on Guadalcanal."[195] Larsen, by then the regimental operations officer of the 25th Infantry, agreed that "the marines and our experiences on Guadalcanal were learning experiences which were to do well for us in all our future combat in WWII." [196]

From an operational perspective, Guadalcanal made it clear that success in the Pacific would rely heavily on interservice cooperation. While this first operation relied heavily on navy-marine planning, the ability of army forces to seamlessly blend in on the ground pointed towards a more active role in future operations. Indeed, as preparations began for the next offensive, the army played an equal role in the planning and execution.[197]

CHAPTER 2

THE GILBERTS:
Parallel Operations
(A Tale of Three Smiths)

As the Americans prepared the Gilbert Islands assault, Guadalcanal's lessons were foremost in the planners' minds. Although American forces were ultimately victorious, many felt that inadequate training and poor intelligence had caused a needless waste of lives. To a large degree planners took the lessons learned on Guadalcanal and successfully applied the solutions to the next phase of offensive operations. At Guadalcanal, however, the landings were uncontested. In the Gilberts, U.S. forces and their amphibious doctrine were to be tested for the first time against a heavily defended beach. U.S. forces eventually prevailed, but only after a bloody three-day contest. In fact, given the size of the forces involved the fighting on Tarawa, the key island in the Gilbert chain was some of the bloodiest and most devastating of the war. It was under this stress that the fissures between the army and marine commanders first emerged. These early cracks eventually became chasms that threatened to engulf and overshadow the joint victories that the services had forged.

STRATEGIC SETTING

When the Allied leaders met in Casablanca in January 1943, the prospects in the Pacific were far different from those just six months earlier. Not only had the Allied successes in the Battles of Coral Sea and Midway halted the seemingly inexorable Japanese march south, but the Guadalcanal and Papua campaigns forced the Japanese to substantially halt offensive operations and move to the strategic defensive. Furthermore, the Allies now possessed sufficient forces to effectively engage the enemy at four widely separated points: the Aleutians, the naval lanes between Hawaii and Midway, the South and Southwest Pacific Areas, and the China-Burma-India (CBI) Theater.[1] As Allied men and materiel continued to pour into the region, the Japanese were forced to stretch their limited means ever further.

At Casablanca, both America and Britain reconfirmed the basic premise of Allied strategy: Germany First. While the United States remained fully committed to this priority, the Joint Chiefs were reluctant to lose the momentum in the Pacific. As Marshall argued, "We must not allow the Japanese any pause. They fight with no idea of surrendering and they will continue to be aggressive until attrition has defeated them. To accomplish this, we must maintain the initiative and force them to meet us."[2] King went on to assure the Allies that operations in the Pacific would in no way divert resources from the European theater.[3] With these assurances, the British reluctantly agreed to increase forces in the area and support King's proposal for a two-pronged attack through the Central and South-Southwest Pacific aimed at seizing and expanding holdings in the Solomons, Rabaul, Western Aleutians, Gilberts, Marshalls, Carolines, and New Guinea as well as increasing efforts in the China-Burma-India theater.[4]

Armed with this agreement, representatives from the three Pacific subcommands (Central, South, and Southwest) met to determine the best plan of attack. As before, MacArthur championed a drive against Rabaul, under his command of course. To support his case he came armed with a complete set of plans for the operation, codenamed ELKTON. Faced with the realities of personnel and equipment shortfalls, however, the planners decided to reduce the objectives for 1943 and focus on expanding the Allied presence in the Solomons, New Guinea, and New Britain. They also decided to avoid further intramural squabbling by postponing final determinations on who would conduct and command these operations.[5]

Despite their best efforts to steer clear of discussing all command issues, there were some that could not be avoided. MacArthur was given command of Tasks Two (Lae, Salamaua, northern Solomons, and New Guinea) and Three (Rabaul, New Britain-New Ireland). Since the new plan was just a variation of this original one, army planners had pushed for MacArthur claiming he was the logical choice. The navy reluctantly agreed, but only after inserting language that kept all ships under navy control when they were not actively assigned to a task force.[6]

Everything began changing when U.S. Joint Chiefs of Staff (JCS) submitted the "Strategic Plan for the Defeat of Japan" at the Trident Conference held in Washington, DC in May 1943. This reformulation of strategic direction was not, however, a plan, as it merely presented a long-range proposal aimed at preparing the Allies for an assault on the Japanese home islands, without announcing a timetable, or presenting any clues as to the command structure or operational details.[7] In order to accomplish the broad goals established by the new strategic plan, the JCS estimated that commanders required 8 amphibious divisions (6 marine, 2 army) and 23 follow-on offensive divisions.[8] Once again, King advocated a push through the Central Pacific Area, with a supporting drive through the South-Southwest Pacific Areas. After much debate, the Allies accepted King's proposals with the caveat that any Pacific operation must take into account the war in Europe and obtain approval by the Combined Chiefs of Staff. The final plan issuing out of the conference called for six specific military objectives within the Pacific theater in 1943–44: ejection of the Japanese from the Aleutians; seizure of the Marshall and Caroline Islands; seizure of the Solomons, Bismarcks, and New Guinea; seizure of Burma; conduct of air operations in and from China; and intensification of operations against Japanese lines of communication.[9]

This plan allowed for some flexibility based on circumstances on the ground and did not set out an order of execution. King did, however set forth two criteria he felt any proposed operation had to meet before it could be approved: would it "further threaten or cut Japanese lines of communication; [and] would it contribute to the attainment of positions of readiness from which a full-scale offensive could be launched against Japan."[10] Despite the high-level agreement at the Trident Conference, the real struggle over operational plans and command issues was just beginning.

In the time leading up to Casablanca and Trident, MacArthur formulated his plans as if the Rabaul-New Guinea-Philippines axis was the main advance, with the Central Pacific drive functioning as a protective flanking action. His argument was that this plan allowed the Allies to have "utterly essential land-based air support all the way."[11] However, joint and navy planners independently came to the conclusion that the quickest way to strike at the Japanese homeland was through the Central

Pacific with MacArthur's offensive as the flanking effort. They also concluded that the arrival of new large carrier forces released them from the need to center their planning on land-based air support.[12] After much deliberation, the Joint Chiefs finally ordered that the main drive proceed up the Central Pacific, but also allowed MacArthur to continue his offensive in what generally became a supporting effort.

Interestingly, the Joint Chiefs had arrived at the Casablanca Conference in January 1943 armed with a paper titled "Seizure and Occupation of the Gilbert Islands," although the final conference communiqué failed to mention the Gilberts.[13] Moreover, Nimitz initially showed little concern for securing the Gilberts, telling King that such an operation would provoke an intense air response at a time when Allied resources were inadequate to respond.[14] This lack of interest was reinforced in the immediate wake of the Trident Conference in May 1943 when army planners initially dismissed the idea that seizing the Marshalls required an approach through the Gilberts. They worried that a Gilberts assault would alert the Japanese to the American strategic design, causing them "to disperse his aircraft widely for a defense in depth" thus making it more difficult for Allied aircraft to target them.[15]

Although the Joint Chiefs themselves apparently had little interest in the Gilberts, the Joint War Plans Committee was looking at them as a way to undertake an offensive in the Central Pacific without diverting too many forces from MacArthur. As the minutes from one of the planning meetings summed up, "the army would not favor operations in the Marshalls at the cost of planned operations in the Southwest Pacific."[16] In reaction to this, the Joint War Plans Committee proposed simultaneous landings in the Gilberts and nearby Nauru.[17] These landings, which would be a stepping stone to the Marshalls and Carolines, could be accomplished with just a marine division and a regimental combat team.[18]

Besides the fact that a Gilberts operation could be conducted on the cheap, there were several other compelling reasons to go through the Gilberts first. The first was that the landings in the Marshalls would be the first attack against a strongly defended coral atoll. By landing in the Gilberts first the services could test amphibious assault doctrine and equipment in a relatively small operation before applying them in a large-scale offensive. The second was that the Gilberts provided protected anchorages for new bases.[19] The final, and most immediately compelling reason was the need for forward airbases from which to launch reconnaissance flights. Carrier-based aircraft were useful for many things, but their short ranges meant that carriers must stay uncomfortably close to the target. Moreover, the longer a carrier stayed in one area, the more vulnerable it became to enemy attack, particularly by submarines. Land-based aircraft not only could be launched from greater distances, but could conduct photographic reconnaissance missions over a greater number of days. This allowed planners to "see" the targets and tides at different times of day. It also painted a far clearer picture of enemy activities in the area.[20] The near-disaster brought about by a lack of maps and good photographs of Guadalcanal had seared into the planners the absolute necessity for gathering as much accurate intelligence of enemy-held islands as was possible, before launching an operation.

The joint staff planners immediately seized upon this plan as the perfect compromise between the army's desire to proceed through the Southwest Pacific and the navy's desire for immediate action in the Central Pacific. They were also drawn to the fact that seizing the Gilberts reduced the number of bypassed islands in Japanese control, thereby limiting Japanese options. Predictably, MacArthur argued that diverting the marine divisions under his command would negatively impact his operations in Rabaul.[21] With this in mind, on 20 July 1943, the Joint Chiefs met to discuss the proposal. After some debate, they approved the plan for simultaneous landings on Tarawa and Nauru and set an invasion date for November, with a follow-on invasion of the Marshalls in February 1944.[22] To appease MacArthur, the JCS agreed to leave the 1st Marine Division under his command and to use an army division as the second unit in the Gilberts. The planners dubbed the new operation GALVANIC.

OPERATIONAL PLANNING

As with any operation, the first step was to choose the participating units and then designate the chain of command. When choosing the units to conduct the attack, joint planners concluded,

> In view of (1) the importance of this operation, (2) the serious implications of a failure in the initial assaults, (3) the fact that it must be a guide to the effectiveness of far reaching amphibious operations in the future as

now planned and (4) the fact that this is the first attempt to seize properly defended and supported atolls, it is considered almost imperative that all troops committed to the assault be battletested shock-troops with amphibious training.[23]

Unfortunately, there were only two divisions available that met these criteria: the 1st Marine Division under MacArthur's command and the 2nd Marine Division under Halsey, although the 7th Infantry Division currently conducting operations in the Aleutians might also be used. Not wanting to open the command debate again and hoping to give the exhausted 1st MARDIV a break, the planners chose the 2nd MARDIV.

The operational plan also called for an army unit. After looking around at the available divisions, Marshall came to the conclusion that the 27th Infantry Division, currently in Oahu, was the only unit that could easily take on the task. In a memo to King, he noted that the 27th was "a well-trained division with excellent leaders. All of the advanced training facilities of Oahu . . . are now available for special intensive training of the 27th in preparation for amphibious operations."[24] Despite preferring the 1st Marine Division as the second unit, the navy agreed to use the 27th.[25]

The operation would fall under the Central Pacific Force (later Fifth Fleet) commanded by Vice Admiral Raymond Spruance, who had replaced an ailing Halsey at Midway and performed brilliantly. Spruance was a taciturn, extremely disciplined officer who never raised his voice or showed any visible sign of stress.[26] He was not one to display emotion or indulge in frivolities, even eschewing comfort in his office where he worked at a stand-up desk (and likewise provided no chairs for visitors). He lived a relatively abstemious life and his one indulgence was long, brisk daily walks, sometimes accompanied by a beloved schnauzer. His Chief of Staff wrote home in frustration, "When he feels the urge for exercise, nothing can stop him . . . with me grabbing at his coattails trying to get him to sign something or give me some decision that will let me proceed until he gets back."[27] He would also swim obsessively, even outpacing Nimitz, who was known for his swimming prowess. While in Hawaii, he noticed that junior officers accompanying him often swam between him and the beach. He discovered that they were running along the bottom of the surf to keep up. After that, in a reflection of his grim humor, Spruance decreed that they must swim on the ocean side of him at all times.[28]

Moreover, he was widely acknowledged as one of the most brilliant strategic and tactical thinkers in the navy. Spruance had been Nimitz's Chief of Staff and they were extremely close friends. As one staff officer remarked, "[Nimitz has] got him to the point where they think and talk just alike."[29] For this reason, Nimitz gave him wide latitude to choose his staff and Spruance had definite ideas as to who he wanted to command under him.

The man Spruance chose to command the assault force, called the V Amphibious Force or V 'Phib, was Admiral Richmond Kelly "Terrible" Turner, the landing force commander from Guadalcanal. Spruance and Turner had been friends for decades, but more than that, Turner was known to be intelligent, analytic and an aggressive fighting man. Always a student of naval warfare, he had also been a strident proponent of naval aviation and amphibious operations during his time as an instructor at the Naval War College.[30] In his usual succinct manner, Spruance summed up his reasons for choosing him as, "Our ideas on professional matters were thoroughly worked out together and we usually thought alike. I was greatly impressed with RKT's brilliant mind, his great capacity for hard work and his fine military and personal character."[31] Nimitz echoed this confidence, calling Turner, "brilliant, caustic, arrogant and tactless—just the man for the job."[32] In fact, the three became so close, that, by their request, they are buried side by side at the Golden Gate National Cemetery, California.

Turner, known for his hard drinking, fiery temper, and sharp tongue, would meet his match in General Holland M. Smith, Commander of the V Amphibious Corps, which was charged with exercising "full and continuing operational command of the amphibious training and operations of all troops in the Central Pacific Area assigned for amphibious attack."[33] Known for his volatility, "Howlin' Mad" Smith was possibly the most polarizing character in the theater. He was widely acknowledged as the father of amphibious warfare and had spent much of his career developing doctrine and training marines. However, his many talents were almost completely overshadowed by his monumental ego and his contempt for almost everyone who was not a marine, including his army and navy compatriots. Then-Captain Charles "Carl" Moore, Spruance's Chief of Staff, who had worked with Holland Smith during prewar exercises in Cuba, thought him "a sorehead, indignant and griping about everything . . . [I had to convince him] that [the navy was] trying to help him, not trying to oppose him."[34] Even the Commandant, Holcomb, found him hard to handle, writing to Vandegrift, "He [Smith] is becoming more impossible all the time. He was most humble and devoted until he got another corps; but now he owns the world and is getting condescending."[35] Interestingly, many marines who worked for him remember him differently, recalling his "warm feeling for everyone around him"; he inspired filial love from his aide and orderly.[36] Until his death, he received scores of letters and cards from marines professing deep affection and thanks for his leadership, all of which he kept.[37]

Given these contradictions in his personality, Spruance knew that he was taking a risk in putting Turner and Smith together as "each was a strong personality, stubborn in support of his own views and [he] foresaw that there would be conflicts of views between the two, but believed, correctly, that he could diplomatically reconcile any differences of opinion between them."[38]

After Tarawa, Holland Smith would be at the center of one of the biggest controversies of the theater (in Saipan, which will be covered in detail in a later chapter), which taints the historical view of army-marine relations even today. While the incident was newsworthy at the time, Smith would really earn his infamy after the war. Not only would he continually revisit the incident on Saipan, but he became one of the most outspoken critics of the decision to invade the Gilberts, even though it had his full support at the time.[39] This earned him the ire of his former comrades and made it virtually impossible for future historians to view his actions with any objectivity. As Julian Smith, 2nd Marine Division commander, diplomatically said of him many years later, "He did doggoned well in the Pacific [but] his combativeness was sometimes a bit misguided."[40] Edmund Love, the 27th Division historian, was just a bit more blunt when he called Holland Smith "the most ignorant and at the same time, deliberate liar who ever wore the stars of a general officer."[41]

Since Holland Smith's writings shaped much of the postwar historical narrative of combative, uncooperative relationship between the army and marines, it is important to compare his later statements with the contemporary record as we go through the various phases of the planning operations in which he participated.[42] Many of Smith's later claims are wholly unsupported by the contemporary evidence, which in turn renders any nuggets of truth existing in his criticisms difficult to divine and mostly impotent. Unfortunately, because many of his opponents, particularly Ralph Smith, 27th Infantry Division Commander, saw nothing to be gained by engaging in postwar sniping, too many of Holland Smith's half-truths and outright lies have gained traction in the historical community. In the same vein, out of respect for his contributions to the development of amphibious operations, many of his marine peers refrained from criticizing him in public. By the same token, those who have taken on his claims, such as Edmund Love and Harry Gailey, have gone too far in the opposite direction and completely demonized Holland Smith. The army historian S. L. A. Marshall, who encountered Holland Smith on Makin, called his actions, "As ridiculous a grandstand play as I have ever seen by a general officer, which is saying a lot . . . he was clearly a bully, something of a sadist and, I guessed, tactically a chowderhead."[43] As history often shows, the truth actually lies somewhere in between these two extremes.

However, all of that was in the future and for now, Smith was simply the man who knew more about amphibious operations than almost anyone else in the Marine Corps. He was also one of only six marines who attended the French Army Staff College and was the first marine member of the Joint Army-Navy Planning Board in 1923. He commanded the 1st Marine Brigade during amphibious exercises in Cuba in 1940 and in the summer of 1941 took over what would eventually become Amphibious Force, Atlantic Fleet. There he oversaw the training of the 1st Marine Division and the 1st and 9th Infantry Divisions in amphibious warfare. In August 1942 he moved to California to take command of Amphibious Force, Pacific Fleet and supervise the training of the 2nd and 3rd Marine Divisions and the 7th Infantry Division. During this time, he oversaw numerous landing exercises and was instrumental in developing landing craft and other equipment for amphibious warfare.

It was during this training that Smith almost lost everything that he had worked for for more than 37 years. In February 1943 he struck a naval seaman with his car and did not stop until the police pulled him over three miles later. They charged him with hit-and-run and drunk driving. When the charges were dropped a few days later, many of his staff was convinced that King, and possibly Roosevelt himself, had intervened on Smith's behalf. As many of his staff quietly requested transfers, Smith was sure that he had blown his chances for a combat command.[44]

Instead, King sent him forward to observe the 7th Infantry Division landing on Attu. He came back full of praise for the planning and execution of the operations but complained that the army was too slow and had taken too much time to clear the island. This would become a common criticism from Holland Smith whenever he had to work with the army.[45]

In theory, Smith would be in charge of training the units selected for GALVANIC, Turner would control the troops at sea, and the landing force commanders would command them after they landed. As with many things, the reality would turn out to be much more complex. Smith was not willing to be cut out of the tactical operations and inserted his headquarters into the operations, adding a layer of bureaucracy that complicated Spruance's attempts to maintain a lean staff. The issue of Smith's actual role shifted with each passing day, as Spruance struggled to balance the need to give commanders on the ground tactical control without eliminating Holland Smith completely. The final decision on Smith's role, which will be discussed in detail later, ended up satisfying no one and needlessly complicated the chain of command.

After choosing his commanders, Spruance left it up to his chief of staff to choose the rest of his staff, with the exception of his flag lieutenant.[46] Spruance's only guidance was to "keep it small . . . staffs should be composed of the smallest number of first class men who can do the jobs . . . [otherwise] a lot of energy is expended in overcoming internal friction."[47] At the end, Spruance's staff was half the size of Halsey's and his men "took grim pride in the fact that any one of them did as much as two or three of Halsey's officers."[48]

There was little time for planning and training: less than four months. Fortunately, the Gilbert Islands, which are actually made up of sixteen small atolls, were not an unknown quantity to the commanders in the Pacific. On 17 August 1942 two companies of the 2nd Marine Raider Battalion had raided Makin and other nearby islands in order to divert Japanese attention from the landings on Guadalcanal and Tulagi. This raid had mixed results. While the marines managed to annihilate the Japanese garrison, they gathered no meaningful intelligence and took no prisoners and no Japanese forces were diverted to the island. Most distressingly, not only were 21 marines killed, but a further nine were left behind in the confusion of returning to the submarines in the heavier-than-expected surf.[49]

In fact, the raid called Japanese attention to their vulnerabilities in the Gilberts, causing them to systematically build up defenses on Makin and nearby Tarawa. Moreover, by September 1942, these new Japanese forces had wiped out the remaining Allied coastwatcher forces throughout the Gilberts, eliminating an important source of intelligence.[50] Despite these setbacks, the invasion force was not going in as blind as the marines on Guadalcanal.

For starters, the planners had detailed maps, which they supplemented with information from members of the British Armed Forces who had worked and lived on the islands. In all, sixteen people who knew the islands were attached to the command staffs for the duration of the operation. Scores of photographs were taken both from the air and from submarine reconnaissance.[51] In fact, the aerial photography was so detailed that analysts were able to estimate the size of the Japanese garrisons from the number of each type of latrine along the shoreline.[52]

On 29 July, the 27th Division received word that its objective would be the island of Nauru, which lay some 390 miles west of the Gilberts, and it became the focus of staff planning.[53] Spruance, Turner, and Holland Smith were united in their dislike of the selected target and argued vigorously against it, although Smith would later claim that he and he alone had objected to the objective.[54] They felt that Nauru was too far from the Gilberts and would force the navy to split its available naval forces over too wide an area, making both landings more vulnerable. Up to this point, the navy had never operated more than 300 miles from an airbase. Tarawa was over 700 miles away from the closest base and navy planners were already a bit nervous about leaving their ships so vulnerable.[55] Furthermore, Nauru had no lagoon for landing boats, contained only a small airstrip and was so heavily defended that taking it would require a full division rather than a regiment. Finally, Nauru would not really help the Allies in the follow-on operation in the Marshall Islands.[56] Instead, they favored the substitution of the lightly defended Gilbert atoll of Makin, which lay only 150 miles from Tarawa.[57]

A letter from Holland Smith, and endorsed by Turner and Spruance, went directly to Nimitz and King (who was visiting Nimitz in Pearl Harbor at the time). Within hours, the JCS approved the change in operation, but the order was not given until 6 October.[58] So the 27th Division, which had been planning the invasion of Nauru for two months, was given a new objective less than six weeks before the attack. However, since the new objective was smaller and less defended, the 27th only needed to commit one of its three regimental combat teams, the 165th.

Overall, no fewer than six separate headquarters had some responsibility for the planning and training for the upcoming operation: Nimitz, Spruance, Turner, Holland Smith, and the two division commanders, Julian Smith and Ralph Smith.[59] However, because Turner's command was only activated on 24 August 1943 and Holland Smith's on 4 September 1943, neither had much time to assemble a staff and prepare individual plans for the November invasion. As a result, the division staffs prepared their tactical plans independently.[60] The 27th ID also received support from the staff of the Commanding General Army Forces, Central Pacific Area, Robert Richardson, who had replaced Harmon. Richardson and his staff were charged with providing administrative, logistical, and training support to all the army ground and air forces under Nimitz. Over the course of the next several engagements, Richardson, who was quite outspoken in his belief that marines were unsuitable for command above the division level, would become one of Holland Smith's greatest nemeses.[61]

To add to the confusion, both the 2nd MARDIV and the 27th ID were under command of Holland Smith for training, but not for the actual operation. For the actual attack, the final plan split the force into two separate attack forces with a floating reserve. The naval assault force (Task Force 54) was under Turner, as was the Northern Attack Force (Task Force 52), which would land on Makin. The Southern Attack Forces (Task Force 53), which would land on Tarawa, was to be commanded by Admiral Harry Hill. These arrangements left open the question of Holland Smith's role once the operational phase commenced.

Holland Smith and Turner argued viciously over the issue of command. As neither man was known for being diplomatic, the quarrel intensified. Neither wanted to escalate the decision to Spruance, who thus far had managed to stay above the fray and expected his chief of staff (Charles Moore) to effect a compromise. Finally, at an impasse, Moore pleaded with Spruance to intervene. Spruance refused, instead assuring Moore that Smith and Turner knew his intentions and would do the right thing. When Moore continued to press for a decision, Spruance dismissed him with orders to "fix it up to suit yourself."[62]

Holland Smith's role teetered back and forth, sometimes changing daily. Ralph Smith's personal diary of the months leading up to the operation reflected this seesaw. On 9 October he indicates, "General Holland M. Smith is completely out of the projected operation. The V Amphibious Corps is not in the chain of command. Ground troops are under Admiral Turner. General H. M Smith's corps may be brought back into the picture." His entry for 13 October reveals, "HMS states that this V Corps is back in the picture and will coordinate with Turner." The next day "HMS placed directly under Turner and will have training functions but no command." Finally on 19 December he writes "HMS situation seems to blow hot and cold. One day he is very decided that he is going to control all of the tactical operations. (showed me letter from 14 Oct[ober] that placed him under Turner) A few days later he was out of the picture again and said that the command set-up would be clarified and that ground troops were to be commanded by ground officers." [63]

The issue of Holland Smith's place in the command structure was ambiguous even in the operations plans. The Central Pacific Force plan states, "The Commanding General Fifth Amphibious Corps will be embarked in the flagship of the Assault Force and will command all landing force troops. Since the employment . . . is subject to capabilities of the surface units to land and support them, directives issued by the Commander, Fifth Amphibious Corps require the approval of the Commander Assault Force before they may be issued."[64] However, a later plan cuts Holland Smith out completely and instructs the landing force commanders (Julian Smith and Ralph Smith) to assume command and report directly to the assault force commanders (Turner and Hill).[65] So confusing was the issue that Task Force 54's final operation plan used the names of each of the commanders rather than their position, as was normal. This seemed to clear up the issue a bit as it stated, "Maj. Gen. Howland [sic] Smith will advise Admiral Turner in regards to the landing forces at each objective [and] to the employment of reserve troops."[66] Curiously, Spruance gave Holland Smith decision authority over releasing the reserve regiment equal with Turner.

This formulation was ambiguous enough for Holland Smith to claim after the war that he was an equal commander to Turner after the troops landed.[67] However, despite Smith's later claims to the contrary, he never had operational or tactical control of any forces after the training phase was completed. Given these command arrangements, it is inexplicable that during the battle he was able to determine when and to whom the floating reserve would be released.

Although both Tarawa and Makin were coral atolls and shared similar topographic features, other than coordinating the times of landing, the plans for each bore little relation to the other. In addition, because the divisions were widely separated, each division wrote its plan in relative isolation from the other.

The Tarawa Atoll consists of 24 small islands forming an open arrowhead pointing southeast. The largest island, Betio, is the farthest west island on the bottom edge. The island itself is shaped like a bird lying on its back, with the head forming the western shore and tapering off to the east. It is little more than two miles long and never more than a half-mile wide. The Japanese occupied Betio in December 1941 and in the ensuing time, especially after the Makin raid, had industriously built up the defenses to the point that the Japanese commander on Tarawa, Rear Admiral Keiji Shibasaki, bragged, "A million men could not take Tarawa in a hundred years." Indeed, by any assessment, Tarawa would be a nightmare to assault. An intricate fortification of coconut logs, crushed coral cement, obstacles, and machine gun emplacements made this the strongest fortress that the Americans would face. Minefields, barbed wire, and concrete and steel obstacles littered the reef. The island was completely flat and direct fire could cover every bit of it. Everything about the island favored the defenders.[68]

Despite confirmed intelligence reports that Tarawa was strongly fortified and held over 4,000 Japanese, 2,500 of them elite Imperial Marines, Holland Smith gave Julian Smith only two regiments, with the third, the 6th Marines, held as a floating reserve. Even worse, the reserve could only be released with the permission of both Turner and Holland Smith. This violated the principle of 3-to-1 advantage when attacking a fortified enemy and hampered Julian Smith's ability to formulate his plan, because he did not know if or when he would get the regiment that Smith had taken to form a reserve. Holland Smith, whose later writings criticized and questioned every aspect of the planning and decision-making for this operation, remained strangely silent on this topic and never offered any insight as to his decision to hold back marines rather than make one of the extra regiments from the 27th ID the reserve. Julian Smith was so incensed at the decrease of his force that he insisted that the final estimate and plan reflect his opposition to this violation of doctrine.[69] He would later remark, "I fought as hard as I could—taking those 6th Marines away from me for the reserve . . . it changed my plan of attack . . . I don't know what was in back of it."[70]

Just as inexplicably, Julian Smith's requests for artillery support on a nearby island and for three days of preliminary naval fire were both denied by his higher headquarters.[71] None of his higher commanders ever provided any explanation as to why they did not give him this requested support. In the end, he would get only two hours of preparatory fires, which proved woefully inadequate. Later, Holland Smith's chief of staff, General Graves Erskine, said, "I think it would have been better to have seized one of the small islands . . . and had the artillery up and started the bombardment on the first day." When asked why Holland Smith was so against doing this, Erskine replied, "I don't know. I'll never know."[72]

In addition to the daunting fortifications the Japanese had emplaced on Tarawa, planners also had to worry about the help nature gave to the defenders, particularly the uncertain tidal conditions. The amphibious craft needed at least four feet of water in order to operate correctly and planners were only too aware that they would not be going in at the optimal tidal cycle. However, delaying the operation for the month or more it would take to get into the proper cycle was not an option. Instead, they relied on the advisors familiar with Tarawa and its tides who swore there would be a minimum of five feet of water on the reef despite the invasion taking place during the neap, or low, tide. Planners remained concerned, especially after a British officer, Major Frank Holland, brought up the issue of dodging, or lower than normal, tides that were possible during this timeframe.[73] Mindful of this possibility and worried that the amphibious tractors might become stranded before reaching the beach, the 2nd MARDIV conducted training on what to do in the event that the landing force had to leave the tractors short of the beach.

The final plan called for three battalions (rather than two regiments) abreast to land on the northern (lagoon) side of the island. The regimental reserve had one battalion and the division reserve had two. Julian Smith would commit these reserves after assessing the status of the initial landing. Before landing there would be two hours of naval fire, which would lift at 0545 to allow for a half hour of air strikes. The landings would begin at 0630.

As the marines stormed ashore on Tarawa, a hundred miles away, the army faced its own problems in seizing Makin Atoll. Makin is a collection of islands forming a rough triangle surrounded by a coral reef. The main island, Butaritari, which runs along the southern end of the triangle, is approximately 15 miles long, but less than 500 yards wide with no natural elevation. Its long southern and small western shores face the open sea, while the northern portion is sheltered by a lagoon. Air reconnaissance revealed two outstanding features. The first was a pair of anti-tank traps that straddled the island approximately two miles apart with a cleared and heavily fortified area in between. Within this area was a series of three wharves that jutted into the lagoon, with a fourth, damaged wharf, lying right outside of the cleared strip.[74]

While the plan was more complex than most landings, it was fairly straightforward.[75] After two hours of preparatory fire, two battalions would land abreast on the western beach. A third battalion would be held in reserve. If not needed to help the western landing force, this battalion would land at the far end of the defended area two hours after the initial assault. The battalions would then push to meet in the middle and sweep through the rest of the island. The idea was to flank and envelop the enemy forces in a pincher and thus avoid facing the Japanese defenses head-on.

Holland Smith had issues with the army plan and instead advocated smashing straight across the defended area from the lagoon and then pushing forward into the teeth of the Japanese defenses—basically the same tactics that he would advocate in every landing in which he had a part. After some wrangling, Ralph Smith got his way and the operation went forward using his plan[76] Holland Smith later derided the 27th operations plan as needlessly complicated, although, at the time, he took complete credit, claiming that his staff oversaw every plan.

PRE-COMBAT TRAINING

As in Guadalcanal, each of the divisions trained independently: the 27th Division in Hawaii and the 2nd Marine Division in New Zealand. However, since the landings would be essentially independent of each other, this was not as major an issue as it was in the training and preparations for Guadalcanal. Holland Smith's staff, located at Pearl Harbor, was able to oversee some of the planning and training of the 27th, but the 2nd

MARDIV trained on its own in New Zealand, although Julian Smith traveled to Hawaii several times to consult with Holland Smith. The pre-combat training resembled that for Guadalcanal with one difference, especially in the 2nd Marine Division: there were now combat veterans available to provide insight into fighting the Japanese. Despite the experiences of Guadalcanal and what the planners expected to face at Tarawa and Makin, neither the army nor the marine divisions conducted any sustained amphibious training. In the 2nd MARDIV, for instance, only one combat team had participated in any ship-to-shore training in the past year.[77]

27TH INFANTRY DIVISION "O'RYAN'S ROUGHNECKS"

The 27th Infantry Division out of New York was one of the three National Guard units whose members all came from the same state.[78] First formed in 1912, the unit, then the 6th Infantry Division, was first mobilized in 1916 to help General John Pershing along the Mexican border. It remained there until it was recalled for training and mobilization in Europe in 1917. During World War I the division participated in the Meuse-Argonne, Ypres-Lys, and Somme offensives, where the division broke the Hindenburg line. The soldiers were so proud of their WWI service that even the unit patch, a depiction of the constellation Orion, was an homage to its WWI division commander, General John O'Ryan.

Between wars, the unit remained relatively stable with four regiments organized into two brigades: the 53rd Brigade consisting of the 105th and 106th Regiments and the 54th Brigade consisting of the 108th and 165th Regiments.[79] The first three mainly drew soldiers from upstate, but the 165th, the heir of the famed "Fighting 69th" recruited from New York City.[80]

After it was mobilized in September 1940, the division moved to Fort McClellan, Alabama, and began training in earnest, culminating in the famous 1941 General Headquarters (GHQ) maneuvers in Louisiana and Arkansas. These exercises, headed by General Lesley McNair, utilized approximately half of the available army manpower and functioned as a giant laboratory for testing combined arms doctrine. The maneuvers were so rigorous that one 27th soldier later remarked in combat, "If it wasn't for the shootin' I'd say the Louisiana-Arkansas Maneuvers were as tough as this."[81] The Louisiana maneuvers revealed the inadequacy of small-unit training as a glaring and widespread deficiency.[82] Unfortunately the Japanese attack on Pearl Harbor, less than a week after McNair delivered the final report, left little time for remedial training prior to units being dispatched into the theaters. As the country rushed to activate and train 38 new divisions in 1942 alone, already formed units, such as the 27th Division, were mostly left to fend for themselves when it came to remedying training deficiencies.[83]

Another troublesome problem highlighted during the Louisiana maneuvers was the generally inferior leadership among the National Guard organizations, as evidenced by the poor discipline and morale within many of these units, especially after President Roosevelt signed an 18-month mobilization extension in September 1941. The extent of the National Guard's morale problem was put on public display by a reporter from *Life* magazine whose interviews with a number of 27th Division enlisted men indicated that half the soldiers planned to desert when their initial one-year mobilization was up in October. They cited dissatisfaction with their officers as one of the main reasons they planned to vote with their feet and go home.[84] A *Time* magazine article about the maneuvers not only highlighted McNair's frustration with discipline due to shoddy leadership, but also blamed this deficiency on the dilution of army leaders by citizen soldiers.[85] An investigation by *The New York Times* found that, among other issues, flagrant fraternization and lack of respect for their officers had a deep and negative effect on the morale of National Guard soldiers.[86]

Others had recognized this leadership problem long before the war. In 1940 Marshall wrote to then-Lieutenant Colonel Omar Bradley: "A serious weakness of the National Guard is the lack of trained staffs from battalion up, meaning staffs that know how to function expeditiously and to the advantage of the troops."[87] Bradley himself would note in his autobiography that "the National Guard could [not] be relied upon for anything more than local riot control . . . [and is] virtually worthless in a major national crisis."[88]

Having worked as a trainer with the National Guard, Marshall was uniquely qualified to pass judgment on the qualities of its leaders and training and he worked to remove ineffective officers as quickly as possible.[89] Of course, Marshall also recognized the particular difficulties of balancing a full-time career with part-time Guard duties by warning, "In considering the capabilities of a National Guard officer to command a National Guard unit, we should not compare him with the best available regular army officer."[90] Problems with National Guard units were evident in the American Division during the train-up for Guadalcanal and there was no reason to assume that the 27th ID was any different.

The root cause of these leadership issues was the static nature of National Guard units. As with many other Guard units, the soldiers and officers of the 27th ID had spent many years together. This had both positive and negative benefits. On the plus side, the unit members knew and trusted one another. Even with deficits in training due to budget and time constraints, this cohesion could be a valuable asset in battle. Unfortunately, the negatives could easily overpower this cohesion. National Guard units tended to be made up of local boys who closely associated with each other outside of the weekly unit drills. The armory was often the center of social events for the families. It was therefore challenging for leaders to enforce strict, impartial discipline on men with whom they lived and worked outside of the unit. Because rank tended to be awarded on a political and personal basis, as opposed to merit, it was easy for poor leaders with political influence to gain promotions and difficult to remove them. When openings did become available, promotions came from within the division, compounding the insular nature of these units. One young volunteer remembered that

> these guys had been together for years and they pulled each other along and did things and overlooked a lot of things they shouldn't have overlooked. There was a lot of nepotism and that's one of the things that disgusted me . . . a lot of the guys that were in the service with me didn't have a high school education and they were promoted very much more rapidly than we were in our outfit, because of the people that had been there for years and they were cousins and brothers and uncles and all that sort of thing.[91]

Another young soldier was blunter: "I thought that 1/3 to 1/2 of the officer corps would be better suited to sweeping out the barracks . . . National Guard (political appointees) couldn't find their rear ends with both hands in broad daylight."[92] Yet another young soldier was even more succinct, noting, "National Guard inferior . . . over-age offi-cers unable to endure field conditions."[93]

Not all of the blame could be placed on the Guard officers them-selves. The army's reluctance to fund Guard units properly meant that only a handful of National Guard officers from each division could attend regular army courses such as Command General Staff School (CGSS).[94] Moreover, unless they were independent businessmen, few members could take time from their civilian careers to attend even the abbreviated version of these courses.[95]

General William Haskell, who commanded the 27th Division for fif-teen years, from 1926 until November 1941, provides a perfect example of the entrenchment of officers in Guard units.[96] While not questioning his competence, Marshall ordered his removal on the eve of war and the division's deployment overseas. In addition to losing its longtime com-mander, the division, which had already been mobilized for a year, also lost about 3,000 men when the War Department authorized the release of men who were "more than twenty-eight years of age . . . whose con-tinued service was causing undue hardship . . . [or] who had more than one year's service." As a result, on 7 December 1941, the unit was down to 920 officers and 13,384 men out of an authorized 1,012 officers, 12 warrant officers, and 21,314 men.[97] Replacements for the officers ini-tially came from within the unit, but eventually, both officers and enlisted would come from draftees and volunteers.

As expected, the bombing of Pearl Harbor changed everything. Despite their manpower shortages, thanks to the GHQ maneuvers the 27th was the best trained National Guard unit in the United States and thus a valuable asset to the War Department.[98] Within hours of the attack all leaves were cancelled and by the morning of 8 December the men of the 27th were on duty guarding critical infrastructure across Alabama. That duty was short-lived and by 11 December, the War Department had recalled the unit to Fort McClellan, Alabama, with orders to prepare for movement to an undisclosed location in 48–72 hours. By 1 January 1942 the units were spread over 1,800 square miles of California and rumors of imminent overseas movement ran rampant.[99] On 27 February, the first elements of the division boarded ships headed for Hawaii, making it the first division to go to the Pacific after Pearl Harbor and the longest war-time overseas-serving National Guard unit of the war.[100]

Although regular army divisions had triangularized in 1941, National Guard units were not ordered to do so until early 1942.[101] So hasty was the mobilization and departure of the 27th ID that it deployed as a square division (the only one to do so). In July 1942, the order to reorganize finally came and the unit lost the 108th Infantry Regiment.

It was not only the physical organization that changed, but also personnel makeup. As replacements from all over the United States arrived to fill in the ranks, the division lost its "local" flavor. By the time the unit departed for Hawaii, it had received enough officers and soldiers to bring it up to its authorized strength. This was a short-lived experience, however, as when the 25th Division departed for Guadalcanal in October 1942 it had 3,500 27th Division soldiers filling its ranks. After replenishment from the replacements flowing into Hawaii the 27th ID was as geographically diverse as any regular army division, although it still retained its National Guard staff and leadership.[102]

While in Hawaii, the division first guarded the outer islands, before moving back to Oahu in October and assuming the 25th Division's mission upon that unit's departure for Guadalcanal. According to accounts, unit training focused on physical and tactical training, which became more intense in September and October, as preparations for further offensive operations in the theater ramped up and the leadership became conscious of the fact that they might have to deploy to combat on short notice.[103]

Just as the large-scale training began in November 1942, the commander, General Ralph Pennell, who had taken over from Haskell, decided that at 59 years old, he was too old to lead his soldiers in battle and asked for relief from his command. Around the same time, the Chief of Staff, Colonel John Haskell (the son of the former commander, a further illustration of the insular nature of National Guard leadership) received orders assigning him to the War Department. Their replacements, General Ralph Smith and Colonel Albert Stebbins, were both regular army officers and were both graduates of Command and General Staff School.

Ralph Smith's quiet demeanor belied the highly adventurous life he led.[104] He learned to fly from Orville Wright himself and received the thirteenth pilot's license ever issued. After a stint in the Colorado National Guard, Second Lieutenant Smith joined General John Pershing's punitive expedition against Pancho Villa on the Mexican Border and then served under Pershing again in World War I, where he received two Silver Stars for bravery and was wounded at the Meuse-Argonne.[105]

Ralph Smith was also an intellectual man. He had taught at the Infantry School and the Staff College and had served on the General Staff between the wars. In addition, he spoke fluent French and was a graduate of the Sorbonne and both the American War College and the French *Ecole de Guerre*.[106] He was regarded as one of the foremost experts on France and the French military, so it is only natural that he was given command of a division in the Pacific where this expertise was useless.

Unlike Holland Smith, Ralph Smith was known for his calm demeanor. His operations officer once said of him, "I have never, never seen him angry. I have seen him disturbed, but I have never heard the level of his voice go up any more than in normal conversation. As a matter of fact, I don't recall the Old Man ever saying even a 'God damn.'"[107]

The unit that Ralph Smith inherited bore little resemblance to the division that had participated in the Louisiana maneuvers. Not only had the division lost some of its most competent leaders when they became redundant after triangularization, but it also took a huge hit when the army took a number of its best noncommissioned officers to form the cadres of the new divisions (the 10th Mountain Division in particular received many of the 27th's NCOs). Finally, still more senior enlisted men were sent to Officer Candidate School.[108]

Dealing with this personnel turbulence as best they could, the division's remaining leaders continued to put their units through their paces in preparation for participation in the upcoming island campaigns. Despite later claims by both Holland Smith and his G-3 that the 27th ID had no amphibious training, for eight months prior to assignment to GALVANIC, the unit conducted basic amphibious training.[109] In order to enhance their capabilities, two officers were sent to the amphibious school in San Diego run by Holland Smith. Upon their return, these officers conducted a one-month training session for all regimental and battalion commanders, executive officers, and other key staff officers and noncommissioned officers. In addition, veterans from the 7th Infantry Division that had landed on Attu provided notes and instructions. Thanks to this and a series of training exercises, by the time the Makin mission was assigned, the unit was well indoctrinated in all aspects of amphibious warfare.[110]

At this point, the focus was on how to make the training as realistic as possible. The men endlessly practiced the art of amphibious warfare and spent many hours using "cargo nets, ropes, boat team drill, debarking, deployment from mock-up boats and passage through wire entanglements and other obstacles" while the battalion staffs focused on planning for everything from boat assignments to shore party organization.[111] The command even brought in veterans of the combat on Guadalcanal to teach the lessons-learned fighting the Japanese.[112] One young artilleryman remembered learning "jungle-fighting, firing all sorts of weapons, bazookas, machine guns, etc. Instructors demonstrated how to survive on edible fruit, plants, etc. and use of bamboo for drinking water."[113]

Due to time and resource constraints training was lacking in two areas. The first was in the operation of the amphibious tractors, called alligators or amtracs, which would carry the soldiers through the water and onto the shore. The 27th ID only had one alligator available for training and did not receive that until 15 October. When the equipment for the landing arrived on 30 October, those alligators were not only of a different type but lacked the necessary armor and machine gun mounts. With time running short, the 165th scrambled to get familiar with the equipment and obtain the necessary accoutrements.[114] The other issue was the inability of the infantry soldiers to communicate with the tank crews that would accompany them. This would not be solved before the operation and would be one of the major lessons that came out of the battle.

The 27th ID conducted a final rehearsal exercise in Hawaii from 31 October through 3 November. A lack of suitable landing beaches forced the staff to conduct the exercise in two phases. In the first phase the landing troops disembarked and simulated the firing of all weapons, including calling in naval and air bombardment. They conducted the second phase, which focused on bombardment, on an uninhabited island. In this phase the soldiers were loaded onto the ships but did not actually land due to the unsuitable landing beach and bad weather that could damage the landing equipment.[115] Again, Holland Smith would later present this as a failing on the part of the 27th ID, when, in fact, the 1st Marine Division had conducted its final rehearsal for Guadalcanal in the exact same way and for the exact same reason.

At the conclusion of this exercise, the main body departed Hawaii for Makin on 10 November to participate in the first assault on defended atolls in the war. At the time, no one had any way of knowing the level of resistance from the enemy.

2nd Marine Division "Follow Me"

At the conclusion of operations on Guadalcanal in February 1943, the 2nd Marine Division limped to New Zealand. It was a broken unit. Death, combat wounds, malaria, dysentery, and other tropical diseases had affected 95 percent of the unit's personnel and New Zealand was not a healthy place in which to recuperate. By the spring of 1943, half of the unit was green replacements, while the other half was still recovering from recurring bouts of malaria. However, there was little time to rest, as a mission loomed quickly and the division was tapped to lead the attack into Tarawa in November. Because the division commander had departed and the assistant division commander was still down with malaria, the training burden fell on the operations officer, Colonel David Shoup, until the new commander and staff arrived in May. His challenge was to get the new marines trained while allowing the veterans to recover their strength, all while helping write the division operations plan for the invasion. He performed these tasks so admirably that when the commander of the 2nd Marines fell ill and could not lead the assault, Julian Smith gave him the command and had him lead the marines onto Tarawa. It was a fortuitous decision, as Shoup performed brilliantly.[116]

The new commander, Julian Smith, has been described as a man whose "entirely unassuming manner and friendly hazel eyes clothed a determined personality that could be forcefully displayed in decisive moments."[117] Others observed that he was the "antithesis of the conception of a high-ranking marine officer . . . [as] a highly-efficient military machine, completely devoid of all human qualities . . . [Smith is] possessed of a genuine feeling of deep concern for his men . . . [and] is never profane or harsh in his speech."[118] One of his battalion commanders, Lieutenant Colonel Raymond Murray called him, "a fine old gentleman, a kindly person . . . you could just love him and we did. You'd fight for him."[119]

Despite his slight, bespectacled appearance, Julian Smith had seen service with marine expeditions in Panama, Cuba, Haiti, Vera Cruz, the Dominican Republic and Nicaragua, where he won the Navy Cross. He once said of himself, "I am not a warlike person . . . Wars just come along and I get involved in them."[120]

It was a bit unlikely, even to Julian Smith himself, that he would get a combat command at all. It was not due to his lack of competence, but rather the fact that he was initially passed over for promotion to brigadier general due to the tropical sprue he had developed while in Nicaragua.[121] Smith had resigned himself to spending the war as a staff officer, when he was handed the reins to the 2nd MARDIV.

Julian Smith found the unit in a state of low morale, brought on, he believed, by a combination of widespread acute malaria and poor leadership. Not only had the division prior to 1942 been scattered around the globe, but each regiment was fed piecemeal into Guadalcanal without the previous division commander being present on the island.[122] As Smith observed, "It had been organized from the regimental combat teams up. And none of those colonels wanted to give up his authority . . . [they were] separate commands just living together as friends."[123] His challenge was to build them back into a cohesive unit.

The 6th Marines were a particular concern of the division commander. When he arrived in New Zealand, Smith found the men in this regiment in a particularly low state of morale and blamed it on the former commander, Colonel Gilder Jackson, who had built a clique of his favorite officers that "had set itself to pick its new regimental commander" and was prejudiced against Smith's pick, Colonel Maurice Holmes.[124] Ironically, Julian Smith later found Holmes lacking and relieved him of command after the operation on Tarawa.[125]

Over the next few months, Smith focused on building unit cohesion and decided that the best way to do this would be through training. For the first couple of months, he focused on weapons training and attempted to use exercises to train his leaders to think and act as a team.[126] Because training areas were few and far between, training was disjointed and he was only able to bring his officers together for a few command post exercises. He also distributed the combat veterans throughout the units. They emphasized the importance of keeping the attack going and ensured that young officers and noncommissioned officers were ready to assume responsibilities one or two levels higher than their rank as their superiors fell.[127]

By September, fewer than 1,800 men were still on the sick rolls and Smith felt that the division had reached, "a high level of training and efficiency . . . [and] is in excellent physical condition. The men and the officers are fed up with inactivity and want to get into action."[128] The division held a final rehearsal exercise off the island of Efate from 7–12 October.

In order to cover up the date of the assault from the enemy, Julian Smith made elaborate arrangements for an amphibious exercise in the division's normal training site in Hawkes Bay, even going so far as to arrange for a dance in Wellington at the conclusion of the training. It was not until they were out to sea that he informed the 2nd Division that not only was there no exercise but that they were actually on their way to invade Tarawa.[129]

OPERATIONS

Despite Holland Smith's later pronouncements, there is no doubt that the Gilberts operation was a necessary one. Although the casualties were high, the short, bloody battle saved lives in the long run. Not only did it set the stage for the successful invasion of the more strategically important Marshalls, but it provided a necessary test of amphibious doctrine and equipment. The operations showed that although previous deficiencies were remedied, more would always crop up. The best that a commander can hope is to never repeat the same mistake twice. As Nimitz observed from a decade of distance, "At the time, we did the best with what we had."[130] One of the transport commanders also mused, "I suppose Tarawa had to happen as it did. There were many new elements in this operation with which we had little or no experience"[131]

Enemy Actions

The Japanese seized the Gilberts as a relatively minor action in their broader Pacific strategy. The Gilberts themselves had little importance for the Japanese, save for their ability to protect the more strategically significant Marshall Islands and provide a place from which to observe American activities in the South Pacific.[132] After the marine raid in 1942, the Japanese realized just how vulnerable these islands were and began to fortify them and moved troops from surrounding island groups to build up the garrisons.

The Japanese commanders were mindful of the following advice offered to garrison troops defending islands throughout the Pacific after the loss of Guadalcanal:

> When it is known that hostile forces will attempt a landing, every unit must concentrate as much of its strength as possible to annihilate the invaders on the beach. Even those who are sick and wounded must, if at all possible, bear arms and participate in the battle with grim determination.
>
> It must be remembered that the hostile troops, upon landing, will not be familiar with the situation and will have no constructed positions.
>
> Furthermore, they will be confused, due to poor liaison and lack of control and will therefore be in a very disadvantageous position. Under such conditions it is possible for even one of our smallest units to destroy a large number of the invaders by fierce and fast attacks.
>
> On the other hand, if the invaders are given time to reorganize and dig in, it will be very difficult to annihilate them later.[133]

The ensuing battles proved just how correct this advice was. However, when the invasions came, these fortifications would not be enough. On Makin, the Japanese were simply overwhelmed by the number of Americans. Furthermore, anticipated Japanese air support never materialized due to the depletion of the carrier planes during battles over Rabaul in early November. On Tarawa, the Japanese had the Americans literally pressed against the sea on the first night and yet were unable to press home their advantage.

There were two reasons for this. The first is that the initial naval bombardments knocked out most of the Japanese communications. No matter how strong the fortifications or how sound the plan, when a commander loses the ability to talk to his troops, he has no way of adapting to the tactical situation. The second is something that was unknown until the 1990s when the translations of the 102-volume Japanese war histories became available: a naval shell caught the Japanese commander and his staff out in the open and killed them around noon on the first day of battle.[134] With no leadership and no communications there was no doubt that the Americans would eventually prevail and the best that the defenders could do was to make the attackers pay for every square inch in blood.

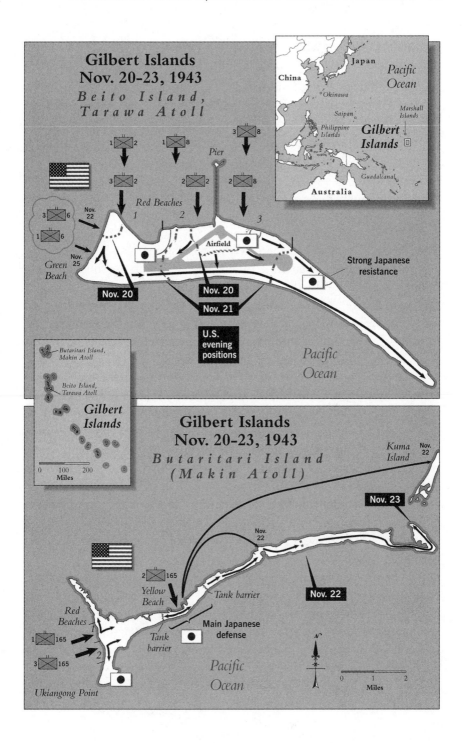

Gilbert Islands
Nov. 20–23, 1943

*Beito Island,
Tarawa Atoll*

Pier

Japan

*Pacific
Ocean*

China

°Okinawa

Saipan °

*Marshall
Islands*

*Philippine
Islands*

**Gilbert
Islands**

Guadalcanal

Australia

Red Beaches
1   2   3

Airfield

Strong Japanese
resistance

Nov. 22

Nov. 25

*Green
Beach*

Nov. 20

Nov. 20

Nov. 21

U.S.
evening
positions

*Pacific
Ocean*

*Butaritari Island,
Makin Atoll*

*Beito Island,
Tarawa Atoll*

*Gilbert
Islands*

0   100   200
Miles

Gilbert Islands
Nov. 20–23, 1943

*Butaritari Island
(Makin Atoll)*

*Kuma
Island*

Nov.
22

Nov. 23

Nov.
22

Nov. 22

*Yellow
Beach*

Tank barrier

*Red
Beaches*

**Main Japanese
defense**

*Tank
barrier*

*Pacific
Ocean*

N

0   1   2
Miles

Ukiangong Point

Landing Operations

An amphibious landing on a small atoll is much different than landing on a larger land mass. Some things on a small island, such as small garrisons, shallow defenses, inability to get reinforcements, and lack of maneuver space, favored the attacker. Other aspects, like the coral reefs, the unpredictable surf, the small area to defend, and the ease of channelizing attackers, favored the defenders. The small area also ensured that the major fighting would occur on the landing beach, just when the attackers were most vulnerable.

Tarawa[135]

The fact that Japanese had spent years fortifying the island, coupled with a certain uneasiness over the erratic tides, led Nimitz to consider postponing the landing. In the end, however, the desire to begin the Central Pacific drive and the knowledge that 2,300 Japanese troops had just landed in the nearby Marshalls, presumably as a layover before being sent to reinforce the Gilberts, outweighed any benefit that might be gained from a few extra weeks of training and planning.[136]

The morning of the invasion, the naval gunfire started on time and relentlessly pounded the small island with large naval ordnance. Naval leaders offered optimistic predictions that the landing would be largely unopposed as nothing could possibly survive the barrage they were pouring onto the island. The commander of the fire support group confidently offered, "Gentlemen, it is not our intention to wreck the island. We do not intend to destroy it. Gentlemen, we will obliterate it."[137] One battalion commander admitted that he worried that there would be no Japanese left for his men to fight and that they would just walk onto the island. The reality would prove a shock and the taking of Tarawa proved to be a bloody struggle.

The naval gunfire, as per the plan, ceased at 0545, so that the air force could take over. However, twenty minutes went by with no sign of the bombers. The Japanese took advantage of the lull to man their guns and resume firing on the transports on the horizon. At 0605, unwilling to risk one of his ships being hit, Hill ordered the naval fire to resume. Minutes later the planes arrived and began blanketing the beach with bombs.[138] As the aircraft finished their runs, the assault craft were already making their runs to the beach. Rough seas, strong winds, and a rapidly receding tide slowed the approach more than expected and the landing time was pushed back from 0830 to 0900.

Unfortunately, no one informed the air fighters, who strafed the beaches at 0825 as originally planned and only returned in limited numbers later. Worried that the smoke would make the landings difficult, Hill ordered the naval fire halted at 0855. When the last small batch of aircraft finished their strafing run a little after 0900, the beach fell silent. The landing tractors still had not reached the beach and the Japanese were beginning to recover, unmolested by the navy or from the air. As the first alligators touched the beach, they were met by withering machine-gun fire. The naval fire had destroyed everything exposed above ground, but pillboxes and reinforced gun emplacements had not been touched. As Julian Smith famously said, "The marines are crossing the beach with bayonets and the only armor they have is their khaki shirts."

Three landings, staggered from west to east, were hampered by both the enemy fire and the amtracs' inability to surmount a five-foot-high seawall made of coconut logs and deposit their cargo of marines beyond the open beach. Japanese machine guns cut down the exposed marines, often before they could even get out of the tractors and onto the sand. What marines did get ashore found it impossible to advance inland due to the defenders' devastating fire. In some areas, the marines held beachheads a scant 50 yards deep.

Even worse, two more waves were coming in to add to the chaos. By now the tide had lowered considerably, making it impossible for the landing boats, which were used due to the shortage of amtracs and also needed a minimum of four feet of water, to get over the coral shoal. Marines exited the craft while they were still at sea and braved a hailstorm of fire as they waded towards shore.

The beach was a confused maelstrom and units were so scattered and intermingled that leaders forgot about commanding their own units and just took command of the marines around them. Eventually, inspired junior officers and noncommissioned officers brought some order to their immediate areas and began to fight back. There was only one assault battalion, Landing Team 2/8, that got through relatively unscathed. Disembarking on the easternmost landing zone, it was separated from the other two beaches by a long pier. As it only suffered 25 casualties during the landing it was the most cohesive unit on Tarawa and was the first major unit to begin the push inland. On the western end, however, the marines' toehold was so tenuous that the commander wired back to Shoup, who was vainly trying to get ashore, "The issue is in doubt."

The beaches became even more crowded as the first tanks landed and began moving through a beach choked with the wounded and dead. With no concept of how to employ the tanks, the marines simply waved them through a hole in the seawall. In a matter of moments all but two were out of action. As if the slaughter on the beach was not enough, some of the landing craft's coxswains, shaken by the accuracy of the Japanese fire, refused to go onto the reef. Instead they ordered the marines off their boats in deep water. Laden with equipment, many of these men promptly drowned. Around noon, Shoup finally landed and began organizing the chaos around him. Renewed naval gunfire support aided his efforts immensely. As if to make up for leaving the beaches unmolested immediately prior to the landing, the navy provided accurate and excellent support throughout the rest of the day.

Communications both across the beach and ship-to-shore remained spotty and Julian Smith was unable to get messages from Shoup. Similarly, he was not getting any information from his assistant division commander, General Leo Hermle, who was pinned down under the pier. As he was effectively blind and had no way of controlling the operation, Julian Smith tried to send a message ordering Hermle to take command of the entire beachhead. It never got through. Moreover, Shoup was unable to communicate with the battalions to his left and had no way of knowing whether they were making progress or had been wiped out.

As the day wore on, Julian Smith first committed the three reserve battalions, although one of the battalions never got the message and spent the night in their boats, waiting for landing orders.[139] At 1330, he asked Holland Smith to release the 6th Marines to him. Two hours after his request, Julian Smith got word that he would get the regiment and could start planning how to use them, a difficult task as he had no clear picture of the situation on the island other than sporadic reports from Shoup and situational reports from air reconnaissance planes.

As night fell on the beach, the marines held less than a quarter of a mile of land. Of the 5,000 men who had landed, more than 1,500 were dead, wounded, or missing. Victory was far from assured and there was a real danger that a concerted Japanese attack could push the Americans off of the island. Worried, Spruance went so far as to beginning to plan for an emergency evacuation of the marines, should the need arise. Due to the lack of communications and leadership, there would be no organized Japanese counterattack that first night.

Makin[140]

Compared to the vicious resistance faced by the landing forces on Tarawa, the army assault on Makin was practically sedate. Like on Tarawa, the majority of the defenses on Makin were situated in a small area, in this case two miles between two piers. Unlike the two hours at Tarawa, Makin received bombardment from both the air and sea for four hours. As the landing craft carrying two assault battalions approached, great plumes of smoke still obscured the island and there was no sign that the defenders had recovered enough to offer effective resistance. When the amphibian tracks began crawling over the jagged coral reef, except for some sporadic rifle fire, the landing was virtually unopposed.

It was fortunate that there was no opposition, because the landing was anything but smooth. The rough tide and jagged reef made it impossible for the amtracs to land simultaneously and, as at Tarawa, the tide was lower than expected, forcing some of the men to dismount and wade in. In fact, initially the terrain presented greater obstacles than the enemy, particularly on Red Beach 1, where due to the jagged coral rocks the shoreline had only 15 yards of usable beach. Once established, one battalion began moving east, hampered mainly by the shell holes that prevented progress of the tanks. The other battalion remained within the beachhead in case it was needed for evacuation and employment on Tarawa.

Once it appeared that the western landing on Makin was secure, a third battalion assaulted the northern landing beach. This landing was much more difficult, as not only was it opposed by enemy snipers and machine guns, but a miscalculation of the tides forced the Americans to leave their landing craft about 250 yards from the shore and wade in through chest-deep water, losing some weapons and equipment in surf. Others, such as the flamethrowers, got wet and were thus unusable.

Fortunately, the enemy chose to move further inland and only three men were lost during this landing. As the battalion commander on Yellow (north) Beach reported, "In my estimation everything went in accordance with plan on Yellow Beach. The complete picture was always clear and pre-arranged tactics were carried out."[141] With both beachheads secure, the Makin assault forces moved inland.

BATTLE SUMMARY

Tarawa[142]

As night fell on the first D-Day, the situation on Tarawa was chaotic. Exhausted marines clung to a narrow strip of beach, while commanders attempted to pull together the scattered pieces of their units and to close the gaps in the battle line. Although the night passed in comparative quiet, as the sun rose the battle erupted anew. New troops, including the battalion which had not received the order to land the day before, began landing. The dodging tides still kept the water level abnormally low and as they clambered out of the boats these marines were cut down with the same overwhelming fire that had decimated the marines' ranks the day before.

Shoup knew that he had to do something to stop the slaughter of his men. Aircraft, naval guns, and artillery pounded the island relentlessly, but seemed to have little effect on the reinforced positions. The marines would have to take these positions one-by-one, often doing so without the heavy weapons or flamethrowers, many of which had been lost or damaged in the surf.

By midday, a makeshift battalion on the western edge of the island had launched an attack backed by naval gunfire and had managed to clear the western beachhead (Green Beach). As this battalion moved off the beach towards the airfield, Julian Smith finally had a large and comparatively safe place to land the 6th Marines. He ordered two battalions of the 6th Marines onto Tarawa and sent one to an adjacent island in order to prevent the Japanese from escaping there.

The beaches themselves were a chaotic mix of corpses, wounded men, and hastily unloaded supplies. By the afternoon however, the tide had turned. The Japanese defenders seemed unnerved that no matter how many Americans they killed, more appeared, guns blazing. With no reinforcement in sight and losing hope, some Japanese committed suicide rather than fight the marines. Slowly the marines moved across the island, destroying gun emplacements and wiping out all enemy positions before them. As evening fell on the second day, Shoup was able to send word to Smith, "Casualties many; Percentage of dead not known; Combat efficiency: we are winning." That evening, an exhausted Shoup turned over command to Smith's Chief of Staff Colonel Merritt "Red Mike" Edson, who had commanded the 5th Marines on Guadalcanal. As one correspondent wired back to his newspaper, "It looks as though the marines are winning on this blood-soaked, bomb-hammered, stinking little abattoir of an island."

With first light of the third day, the marines moved east. Through a combination of accurate fire support and superhuman feats of courage, they broke the back of the Japanese defenses. That evening, Smith landed and assumed command of the 7,000 marines on the island. They still faced 1,000 Japanese defenders.

Six hundred of these defenders would die that night as they mounted repeated counterattacks. By 1300 on 23 November, the rest of the Japanese lay dead, most fighting viciously until the very end. Edson remarked, "This was not only worse than Guadalcanal, it was the damnedest fight I've seen in 30 years of this business."

Makin

As the two battalions moved slowly towards one another, the army faced increasing enemy resistance, especially from snipers in trees. Accompanied by tanks, the two battalions made slow progress, wiping out enemy pockets along the way.[143] The pace slowed further when, just before 1500 on that first day, the 165th Regiment commander, Colonel Gardiner Conroy, was killed by a bullet between the eyes.

For the next two days the Americans slowly cleared out the pillboxes, dugouts, and machine-gun emplacements that appeared impenetrable to indirect fire. By the night of 22 November it appeared that the Japanese defenders had been killed, after 60-plus were killed while making uncoordinated attacks on the American perimeter. By 1030 on 23 November, Ralph Smith cabled to Turner, "Makin taken," signaling the end of combat operations. The combat troops began reembarking for the trip for back to Oahu, while final mopping-up operations continued by the garrison forces for two more weeks. In the end, no Japanese escaped the island.

ANALYSIS

Planning

Planning for the invasion was hampered by two constraints. The first was the short amount of time, especially given the late change of objective for the 27th ID. This would be a challenge for any staff, but the time issue was compounded by the fact that the V 'Phib and V Corps were both in the midst of their own initial organization. Due to this, the divisions largely did their own planning, with less input from higher headquarters, than they would have in later operations. On top of this was the ambiguous role played by Holland Smith, which caused confusion in transmitting orders. Because there was basically no chain of command, the division planners had to maintain close and continuous contact with both V 'Phib and V Corps staff in order to enable the flow of information.[144]

It is worth noting that the final plans for each division perfectly reflected their respective service's approach to combat. Marines are used as shock troops, trained to seize beaches and drive through the enemy. They are prepared to sustain heavy losses in short, brutal battles. The army, on the other hand, is taught to focus on longer-term ground combat and to utilize all aspects of the combined arms. While army doctrine and culture made the main enemy force the ultimate objective, that same doctrine emphasized the avoidance of direct frontal attacks if there were any other effective option available.

Ralph Smith advocated a plan of attack that initially avoided enemy strongholds, but still engaged them in direct and close combat. In order to minimize casualties while moving across the island, he also advocated a more cautious approach than the one Holland Smith advocated. This was an approach that made sense in terms of the army doctrine in which Ralph Smith was trained. In this he found an ally in MacArthur who, still resentful of being deprived of the 2nd MARDIV, wrote after the battle to Secretary of War Henry Stimson, "These frontal attacks by the navy, as at Tarawa, are a tragic and unnecessary massacre of American lives."[145]

This indirect approach infuriated Holland Smith who believed, as many marine commanders did, that the best way to win a fight was to smash through the beach and destroy the enemy strongholds as quickly as possible. His theory was that a unit might take more casualties in early stages of the fight, but by avoiding a protracted campaign, where the enemy might regroup and counterattack, losses would be less in the long run. A prolonged campaign also meant the naval support ships had to remain in one area for long periods, adding to the risk of losing these precious assets. Unfortunately, Holland Smith never saw this difference in outlooks as one of doctrine. Instead, what the army considered a prudent approach to combat he viewed as cowardice and indecision.

Interestingly, Julian Smith's initial plan called for just the kind of flanking assault Ralph Smith advocated. When Holland Smith deprived him of one of the regiments he planned to use in the first assault wave, he had to pare down his plan by giving up the flanking landings. Speaking of the plan later he said,

> Looking back on it, I think that the only thing that I did wrong was that I sent an attack in through the entrance between Red Beach 1 and 2. I would split that attack if I had to do it again. That's the only change I would make on the plans at Tarawa. But my plan was to secure a beachhead on a three battalion front and then on the west end of the island, secure that and then attack from the flank . . . Roll them up and that's exactly what we did although it was a little slower than we'd expected . . . I think if I had landed with 2nd and 8th in parallel [his original plan before losing the 6th Marines] I believe would have taken the west coast sooner than and with less casualties[146]

Intelligence

Despite having much better maps and intelligence than they did for Guadalcanal, the landing operations were nearly undone by the tidal issues. Spruance said afterwards,

> It convinced me that we had to have somebody actually walk over the beach approaches and walk up to the beaches before we scheduled landings on them. Air reconnaissance is wonderful, but it wasn't good enough at Makin to provide adequate information in regard to the beaches or the beach approaches. The Red beaches were just plain *stinko profundo*.[147]

The division G-2 concurred and also cautioned that all operations in the Central Pacific would suffer from the same issue due to the lack of current hydrographic data and tidal charts and the inability to do a thorough ground reconnaissance. Although the tidal charts used in this operation were generally correct, the neap tide rendered them useless. Additionally, the attackers were fortunate to have people who had lived on the island available to provide advice and information. The G-2 highly recommended that all future operations utilize such human intelligence if possible.[148] Although it was unlikely that additional photo reconnaissance would have revealed many of the well-camouflaged Japanese defenses on Tarawa, the Americans would make good use of the airstrips on Tarawa and Makin to conduct photo reconnaissance in support of future operations.

In his criticism of the 27th ID, Holland Smith claimed that Ralph Smith knew from the beginning that there were fewer than 300 Japanese soldiers on Makin and was much too cautious during the operation. In Holland Smith's eyes, the operation should have only taken one day.[149] However, this is in direct contradiction of Holland Smith's own G-2's estimate, which put the number of Japanese soldiers at between 500 and 800.[150] Additionally, at no point during the conduct of the operations was Makin considered feebly defended or a minor operation, as Holland Smith later claimed. While it may have seemed easy in comparison to the slaughter on Tarawa, it was still a struggle against a fierce and determined enemy.

Training

As with Guadalcanal before it, one of the biggest complaints was the lack of adequate training time. In particular, this affected the ability of tanks and infantry to learn to operate together and to overcome the defects in the communications systems. An army battalion commander observed:

> Tanks: there are many things that have to be ironed out before they participate with the infantry in a like assault again. I do believe we could have secured the west barrier two hours earlier and made better progress on the east front on the first day of the tank operations were carried out as well as it was the second day. They should be given more training on that type terrain . . . Individual tank commanders refused to carry out my orders even after I had made myself known to them. This happened with other infantry leaders also but I believe it can be corrected by two organizations training together as much as possible.[151]

One battalion commander even held back one of the tanks to use its radio because that was the only way he could communicate with the other tanks.[152] It is interesting to note that not one soldier was killed or wounded inside their tank. Rather, the only losses among the tankers occurred when the men had to climb out of the tank to pass a message to the infantry.[153]

The lack of training time was further complicated by the formation of new and untested staffs and command groups. The after-action review addressed this issue and recommended, "It cannot be too strongly urged that responsible commanders and their staffs be appointed as far in advance of the operations as possible, in order that they might have time in advance to familiarize themselves with the problem at hand, to get acquainted with their forces and each other and to be prepared to offer advice to the superior commanders."[154]

Finally, GALVANIC proved how important amphibious training was for success. As Julian Smith told one of his combat journalists, "One lesson which Tarawa certainly taught was the need for the use of highly-trained, highly specialized forces in all amphibious operations. It is probably not too much to say that troops which had not had long experiences in such operations and were not led by officers who had made such operations a life study . . . could never have taken Tarawa from its determined garrison."[155]

Casualties[156]

Marine casualties on Tarawa came to 1,147 killed and a further 2,072 wounded against 4,690 Japanese killed for a kill ratio of 4:1 and a casualty ratio of 1:5 and an American casualty percentage of 26 percent. These numbers are shockingly high, especially when compared to the numbers in Guadalcanal, but are not necessarily an indictment of marine tactics. This was the first time that Americans were testing their landing doctrine and they were doing it was against the most heavily fortified island in the region. It is therefore difficult to make a comparison to the landing on Guadalcanal, which was unopposed.

The marines deliberately allowed journalists to capture every aspect of the Tarawa operation on film in hopes of reminding an American public focused on Europe of the cost and difficulty of the Pacific War. However, they were unprepared for just how deeply the pictures of dead marines floating in the water would stir up public emotions. For the first time, Americans confronted the reality of war and not just a set of published statistics at large. Although the total number of casualties was smaller than at Guadalcanal, the fact that they occurred in such a short period of time magnified the shock. Demands for an explanation from the families of fallen marines forced some senators to call for congressional hearings. Vandegrift, who was about to take over as Commandant of the Marine Corps, was able to diffuse this by writing to the senators and reminding them, "A landing attack is recognized by all military experts as the most difficult and costly of all forms of attack. Losses at Tarawa were heavy and losses will be heavy in future attacks of this nature . . . All evidence on hand leads to the conviction that the attack on Tarawa was well planned and skillfully executed."[157] As more information came out from the journalists who had accompanied the marines, Americans slowly began to understand just how well the marines had performed on Tarawa.

The army captured Makin at the cost of 66 killed in action or died of wounds and 130 wounded or injured out of approximately 6,470 personnel. The enemy suffered 550 casualties, including 105 prisoners of war (of which only one was not a Korean laborer). This put combat casualties at a ratio of 2.7 Japanese casualties for every American casualty and 6.7 Japanese killed for every American death.

Unfortunately, naval casualties, among the vessels supporting the Makin landings, were much higher than those on the island. A turret fire on the battleship *Mississippi* during the preliminary bombardment killed 43 and wounded 19; more tragic was the sinking of the escort carrier *Liscome Bay* by a Japanese submarine on the morning of 24 November, which killed 644 men and wounded scores of others. The ship exploded and sank rapidly as a result of a design fault that left onboard ammunition stores vulnerable to torpedoes.[158]

However, it is also true that the longer a ground operation takes, the more vulnerable the navy is as the enemy moves more ships and submarines into the area. As a result, Holland Smith and others on his staff directly blamed the loss of this ship on the slow progress of the 27th ID, claiming that if the operation had concluded early, the carrier would have been away from the area.[159] As he would so many times, Holland Smith would come to a correct conclusion (that *Liscome Bay* would not have been sunk if it had not been offshore of Makin) but would use specious reasoning to get there (that the army should have known the danger to the ship and speeded up its operation). In fact, not only did the 27th ID follow the exact timeframe laid out in their operations plan, but Holland Smith (along with the army and navy official histories) failed to note that the destroyer guarding the *Liscome Bay* had left its picket to investigate a flare dropped several miles away. This left the *Liscome Bay* unprotected and allowed the submarine to slip in unnoticed.[160]

Fortunately, the biggest cause of casualties on Guadalcanal, malaria, was not present in the Gilberts. However, lack of clean drinking water on both islands exposed the men to a number of other tropical diseases present on the island, most of them waterborne. The short duration of the operations ensured that disease did not become a serious issue for the landing forces, although the sheer number of casualties on Tarawa nearly overwhelmed the medical support teams. The greater danger of disease was to the garrison troops that occupied the islands as the coral composition of the islands made burial of the dead difficult and bodies often lay unburied in the tropical heat for many days.[161]

Commanders

Tarawa was the type of battle that brought out the best and the worst in men. Although medals are not always an accurate measure of effort, the marines on Tarawa earned 4 Medals of Honor and 46 Navy Crosses during their 76 hours of unadulterated hell. Interestingly, all four of the Medal of Honor winners were veterans of Guadalcanal; only one survived the fighting on Tarawa. That was Shoup, who was promoted to brigadier general on the spot and made the chief of staff for the 2nd MARDIV.[162] Sixteen years later, he became the Commandant of the Marine Corps. Many other junior officers and noncommissioned officers took control of their sectors as their leaders fell amid the chaos and pressed forward despite mounting casualties.

However, not all marines performed to standard. Furious at Hermle for not leaving the pier (and having no way of knowing that he had never received his message), Julian Smith ordered him back to the ships. Not wanting to stir up controversy, Hermle, who had won the Distinguished Service Cross at the Meuse-Argonne in World War I, would merely say about the event, "We had quite a discussion. What happened from there on is a matter of history."[163] Julian Smith never said a bad word about Hermle, nor did he allow him to go back to the island. Instead, he had him take a battalion to Apemama and relieve the company that had secured it on 21 November. His job was to supervise building the defenses, which sent a clear message that his services were no longer needed as the assistant division commander. Soon after the battle Julian Smith replaced him with Shoup. Hermle would redeem himself later as the assistant division commander of the 5th Marine Division at Iwo Jima, where he was the first general officer ashore under withering fire, not unlike Tarawa, and was awarded the Navy Cross.

Additionally, Julian Smith relieved three other colonels: the commander of the division special troops, who had been left behind as the rear detachment commander; the commander of the 6th Marines, who, as mentioned earlier, was someone Julian Smith had handpicked for the position; and the commander of the 2nd Marines, who had fallen ill and was replaced by Shoup at the last moment. In every one of their fitness evaluations he commented that they did not have the temperament to lead men in combat, which is possibly the worst thing to say about a marine and guaranteed to destroy a career. There was nothing personal in these evaluations. In fact Julian Smith liked all four of these men, but he would not risk putting marines under their command if he had the slightest doubt about their ability to lead in combat. All three were shuffled off to staff positions where they could contribute to the war without putting marines in danger.[164] A few months afterwards he wrote to Vandegrift, "The changes in officer personnel have been beneficial. I think the division is much better off now than at any time since I joined it. It was rather hard to give the three colonels unsatisfactory fitness reports, as all of them and their families have been old friends, but I certainly could not trust them in action."[165]

No officers from the 27th ID were relieved, although with only one regiment in the fight, this is not surprising. However, Ralph Smith's critics, especially Holland Smith, claimed that all of his regimental commanders should have been relieved. Whether or not that is true, it is a ridiculous accusation coming from a leader who had himself never been tested in battle. However, there are some doubts as to whether Ralph Smith would relieve a commander even if there was sufficient cause, for as S. L. A. Marshall said of Ralph Smith, "His extreme consideration for all other mortals would keep him from being rated among the great captains."[166]

Holland Smith would later charge that the 27th ID soldiers were too timid and lacked leadership. One of the charges he made was that Colonel Conroy's body lay in full view of the unit for two days after he was killed.[167] This claim is patently and unequivocally false. The official command journal, whose entries were entered, dated, time stamped, and numbered on the spot, indicates that his body was recovered and buried within 24 hours.[168] This was reinforced by sworn statements from both the 1/165th battalion commander and the division chaplain who performed the burial service.[169]

Holland Smith also charged that the soldiers were firing wildly and indiscriminately at nothing. There is a nugget of truth in that accusation as there was quite a bit of wild firing from these troops who were in battle for the first time. The 2nd MARDIV, with its combat veterans who emphasized fire discipline, did not have as many problems with this.[170] Of course, this is not necessarily an apt comparison because the marines were in continuous combat for the entire operation.

An army battalion commander admitted, "I believe much of the indiscriminate firing both during the day and night was caused by an overemphasis placed on the fact that Japs [sic] fight from trees. No doubt there were some but I think that part of the enemy tactics could be de-emphasized without losing the caution of being on the alert."[171] This statement is supported by a company commander who said that Guadalcanal veterans advised soldiers to spray the trees with gunfire whenever they entered or left an area, in case there were snipers in the tree. After all, as they were told, bullets are cheaper than men.[172]

Ralph Smith did not try to gloss over this issue and told the lessons collection team, "Promiscuous firing by trigger happy individuals is a serious danger to our own troops. It is a great temptation for men in battle for the first time to fire and ask questions later. Prior training and strict discipline for offenders can eliminate this to a large extent."[173] He later said, "Of course it's true. This was the first action of the 27th Division and all troops were keyed up. They don't know what's going on and they piss their pants. That's the kind of thing which always happens."[174]

Despite Holland Smith's accusations, this issue was not unique to the 27th as "the problem of controlling the individual firing of infantrymen is a difficult one . . . [and] usually occurs among troops unused to combat."[175] In fact this exact same topic would be addressed in other issues of "Combat Lessons," implying that it was a common problem with new soldiers. As the lessons learned team noted, "combat-experienced personnel, with proper direction, will develop intelligent initiative in individually opening fire."[176]

Ralph Smith also admitted that it took a little while for soldiers to get their "fighting spirit," but that once they did, they performed admirably. One of the 165th battalion commanders said, "I think its training was good and I think the units were very good. I do think there was one thing that hurt us. We spent a long time on the beach [in Hawaii] in defensive positions . . . I think that took the edge off."[177]

LESSONS LEARNED

As with Guadalcanal before it, the army G-3 staff swooped in to gather information from the returning soldiers and marines. The best of these were put into "Combat Lesson," a publication that gathered the best lessons from all the theaters and put them out to the military every few months. Additionally, both divisions, V Corps and V 'Phib, each compiled after-action reviews of the operations and sent them to Nimitz's staff. Soldiers and marines were quite voluble about their experiences. The Marine Corps history of the battle marks the importance of GALVANIC to the body of knowledge about amphibious operation, noting, "From analytical reports of the commanders and from their critical evaluations of what went wrong, of what needed improvement and of what techniques and equipment proved out in combat, came a tremendous outpouring of lessons learned."[178]

In addition, the Makin operation marked the first time that a historian accompanied an army unit in an operation. It was here that S. L. A. Marshall instituted his now-commonplace technique of conducting group interviews with combatants immediately after a battle. This ability to capture soldiers' memories while fresh and, when possible, on the ground upon which they fought, revolutionized not only the way that the army collected history, but also the way that it captured lessons learned for immediate implementation.

Some of the most important suggestions were on the tactical level. Leaders complained that the men carried too much equipment for a short duration and that they should not be carrying packs as they assaulted a beach.[179] Not only did packs weigh down the men, causing several to drown after exiting landing craft in deep water, but they also hampered their ability to move quickly across the beaches, which is when they were most vulnerable.

Next, the men gave universal praise for the use of flamethrowers as an effective weapon against enemy pillboxes. Unfortunately, in this operation, not only were there not enough to have one in every platoon, but many were damaged by water during the landings. Units requested an increase from 24 to at least 192 per division (at least 1 per rifle platoon) and that equipment be waterproofed.[180]

Another weapon that was a huge success was the new anti-tank rocket launchers or bazookas. The men of the 165th found them extremely effective against the light tanks and coral bunkers on Makin.[181] They probably would have helped on Tarawa as well but the marines did not receive them until a week before the operation. With no time for training on this new weapon, the marines left without them.[182]

The men judged the medium tanks extremely successful in the operations and recommended that these replace all light tanks. As stated before, not only was additional combined training needed but the tanks needed a radio system that allowed them to talk to the infantry commanders.[183] One suggestion was a telephone mounted on the outside of the vehicle as a fix while the services studied the issue further.

Finally, amtracs were judged a necessity for island landings. There were no mechanical failures of any of them and no losses except for those hit by enemy fire. That said, the men requested that the amtracs be improved with landing ramps, self-sealing fuel tanks and armored plating as "small arms fire penetrated unarmored parts of the amphibian tractor, punctured pontoons, punctured radiators, wounded and killed personnel."[184]

There were a few concrete policy changes that Nimitz put forth quickly before the next operation. The first was that not less than one division would be used against any enemy garrison the size of Tarawa.[185] The second is that preparatory fire would last several days if at all practicable.[186] Finally, he determined that training rehearsals must be conducted under circumstances and against beaches that closely resembled the actual objective. Commanders were also told not to worry as much about damage to equipment since the realistic rehearsals and training would save lives and speed up operations in the long run.[187]

EFFECT ON FUTURE OPERATIONS

The biggest positive from the capture of the Gilberts is that for the first time, commanders would not have to rely solely on carrier-based aircraft, but could now use land-based aircraft, which could carry larger payloads and provide better intelligence. Within a month, the airfields on both islands were operational and launching sorties against the next target, the Marshall Islands.

From an operational point of view, these operations proved the essential soundness of American amphibious doctrine and revealed weaknesses in the employment of naval gunfire, both in planning and in employment. Additionally, the operations revealed the strengths and weaknesses of the equipment. Finally, the Americans gathered invaluable information on the composition and strength of Japanese bunkers and fortifications, as well as the best way to neutralize them. The Americans would make the adjustments and test their solutions just two months later as they conducted assaults on Kwajalein and Roi-Namur in the Marshall Islands.

Major General A. A. Vandegrift and his planners on board the USS *McCawley* enroute to Guadalcanal. Second from the right is Colonel Frank Goettge who would lead an ill-fated patrol on the island. *Credit: U.S. Marine Corps*

LVT-1 amtracs embark on the initial assault on Guadalcanal. *Credit: National Archives*

Rear Admiral Richmond Kelly Turner and Major General A. A. Vandergrift on flag bridge of USS *McCawley* near Guadalcanal. *Credit: National Archives*

Major General A. A. Vandegrift briefs Major General Alexander Patch before handing over command of the American forces on Guadalcanal. *Credit: U.S. Marine Corps*

Major General Julian Smith, Brigadier General Charles Bourke and Brigadier General Leo Hermle oversee 2nd Marine Division training in New Zealand in preparation for operations on Tarawa. *Credit: U.S. Marine Corps*

On Tarawa, 2nd Division marines are pinned down behind the Japanese-constructed seawall. *Credit: U.S. Marine Corps*

Day 3 of Tarawa assault, M3 Stuart tows a 37mm antitank gun, escorted by Marine riflemen. *Credit: U.S. Marine Corps*

Admiral Chester Nimitz, Major General Julian Smith, and Lieutenant General Robert Richardson inspect battered Japanese defense on Tarawa. Colonel Merritt Edson looks over Nimitz's shoulder. *Credit: U.S. Marine Corps*

165th Infantry assault wave attacking Makin, finds it slow going in the coral bottom waters. Japanese machine gun fire from the right flank makes it more difficult. *Credit: National Archives*

Major General Ralph Smith, whose relief during the Saipan operation threatened to destroy army-marine relations. *Credit: National Archives*

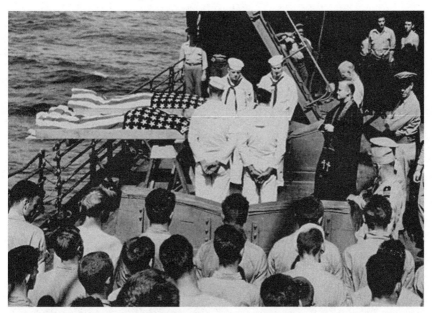

Burial at sea of two of the 644 sailors killed on the USS *Liscome Bay* when it was sunk by a torpedo off the coast of Makin. *Credit: National Archives*

Brigadier General Graves Erskine, Major General Harry Schmidt and Major General Holland Smith study a map of the Marshall Islands. *Credit: U.S. Marine Corps*

Major General Holland Smith and Major General Charles Corlett on the bridge of USS *Rocky Mount* shortly after the first wave of troops reach Kwajalein Island. *Credit: U.S. Marine Corps*

Men of 7th Division using flamethrowers to smoke out Japanese from a block house on Kwajalein while others wait with rifles ready. *Credit: National Archives*

Carlos Island, one of the smaller islands flanking Kwajalein, falls to American invasion forces driving ashore in landing craft. *Credit: National Archives*

Major General Harry Schmidt briefs Admiral Nimitz's staff at the conclusion of operations on Roi-Namur. *Credit: U.S. Marine Corps*

American troops rush ashore from a landing boat during amphibious training on Guadalcanal in preparation for the invasion of the Marianas. *Credit: National Archives*

L-R Admiral Harry Hill, Major General Harry Schmidt, Admiral Raymond Spruance, Lieutenant General Holland Smith, Vice Admiral Richmond Kelly Turner, Major General Thomas Watson and Major General Clifton Cates during the Marianas operations. *Credit: U.S. Marine Corps*

Army reinforcements disembarking from LSTs form a graceful curve as they proceed across coral reef to the beach to Saipan. *Credit: National Archives*

Victorious Marines on Higgins LCVPs head to Saipan's shore two weeks into the invasion. *Credit: National Archives*

First wave of marines to hit the beach in Saipan take cover behind a sand dunes while waiting for the following three waves. *Credit: National Archives*

Using every available means of transporting supplies to the front lines on Saipan, these marines loaded this ox cart but had to use a lot of persuasion and a little teamwork to get the ox underway. *Credit: National Archives*

Admiral Spruance and Lieutenant General Holland Smith confer on Saipan. *Credit: National Archives*

Admiral Raymond Spruance, Vice Admiral Richmond Kelly Turner, Admiral Chester Nimitz and Major General Sanderford Jarman off the coast of Saipan. *Credit: National Archives*

Major General Clifton Cates and *Time* & *Life* Correspondent Robert Sherrod. His articles on the 27th Infantry Division would touch off a firestorm between the army and marines.
Credit: U.S. Marine Corps

Lieutenant General Simon Bolivar Buckner and his planning staff for the Okinawa invasion, including Major General Oliver P. Smith and Colonel James Roosevelt.
Credit: U.S. Army

Major General Thomas Watson oversees weapons training of the 2nd Marine Division prior to the invasion of Okinawa. *Credit: U.S. Marine Corps*

The day before landing on Okinawa, Brigadier General Merwin Silverthorn briefs Major General Roy Geiger and his staff. *Credit: U.S. Marine Corps*

Off the coast of Okinawa, landing craft of all kinds blacken the sea to the horizon, where stand battlewagons, cruisers, and destroyers. *Credit: National Archives*

A demolition crew from the 6th Marine Division watch dynamite charges explode and destroy a Japanese cave on Okinawa. *Credit: National Archives*

Early days of Okinawa invasion. *Credit: National Archives*

Major General Lemuel Shepherd consults a map on Okinawa with the city of Naha in the background. *Credit: National Archives*

Major General Lemuel Shepherd and Lieutenant General Simon Bolivar Buckner overlook the city of Naha, Okinawa. *Credit: U.S. Marine Corps*

Japanese night raiders are greeted with a lacework of anti-aircraft fire by the marine defenders of Yontan airfield, Okinawa. *Credit: National Archives*

Major General Pedro del Valle and Brigader General Louis Jones on Okinawa.
Credit: U.S. Marine Corps

— CHAPTER 3 —

THE MARSHALLS:
The Perfect Operation

With victories on Guadalcanal and the Gilberts, the Americans not only succeeded in wresting valuable territory from the Japanese, they also verified the basic soundness of U. S. amphibious doctrine and equipment. However, both operations also revealed a distressing number of weaknesses. With just six weeks between the Gilberts and upcoming operations in the Marshalls, there was scant time for planners to incorporate the lessons learned into training and to fix a myriad of remaining equipment issues. Still, the invasion of the Marshalls clearly demonstrated just how quickly the Americans were capable of adapting and avoiding making the same mistake twice.

The operations in the Marshalls unfolded much like those in the Gilberts: two divisions, one army and one marine, conducting independent planning and training followed by parallel operations. However, in the Marshalls leaders applied many of the specific tactical and operational lessons learned in combat just weeks before. On the one side, operators had to quickly modify and upgrade equipment. On the other, planners needed to adjust the naval and artillery fire support to ensure maximum effectiveness, as well as modify landing plans to take full advantage of the increased fire support. The net result was an operation so perfectly executed that one observer remarked that "no previous battle has ever enjoyed such complete cooperation, coordination and teamwork . . . no paper maneuver could have envisioned a more powerful, smashing, successful blow to an enemy stronghold."[1] When it was over, the United States had shattered the outer ring of Japan's strategic defense and possessed the bases needed to conduct air and naval operations deep into Japanese held territory.

STRATEGIC SETTING

At the Casablanca Conference, the Allied leaders agreed to focus future Central Pacific operations first on the Marshall Islands and then on to the Marianas and Carolines.[2] Consisting of 32 island and 867 reefs, the Marshalls cover more than 400,000 miles of the Pacific and lie just 565 miles from Tarawa. Taking the Marshalls would not only protect the Allied lines of communication and extend their control of the sea a further two thousand miles, but would also force the Japanese to divide their already stretched naval forces throughout the theater. Moreover, the Marshalls offered excellent anchorage for ships and ample space for runways.[3]

Unlike Guadalcanal and the Gilberts, which the Japanese seized during their prewar expansion, the Marshalls belonged to the Japanese by mandate.[4] Once a German possession, the Japanese seized the islands in 1914 and after the war the League of Nations formally gave them possession of the area with one stipulation: the Japanese could not establish fortifications or military or naval bases there. However, in 1935, Japan withdrew from the League of Nations, which was, in any event, powerless to enforce the stipulation. Therefore, Japan had almost nine years to build up the defenses on the islands and used that time building airfields, naval bases, and garrisons across the atolls.

The original American plan called for the simultaneous seizure of the Kwajalein, Maloelap, and Wotje atolls. These three atolls contained 65 percent of the Japanese airfields in the islands.[5] The first was in the geographic center of the island group and the latter two were on the eastern edge. Follow-on operations planned on Mille and Jaluit would neutralize remaining Japanese airbases in the area.

Joint planners dubbed the operation FLINTLOCK and set the invasion date for 1 January 1944, just five weeks after the anticipated completion of GALVANIC. However, by the end of October, Nimitz asked King to push the start date to 31 January, citing the need for further training, the unknown outcome of the upcoming battle in the Gilberts and the need for further photo reconnaissance. Weighing the risk of giving the

Japanese an extra month to prepare to meet an assault against the need for adequate American training, the Joint Chiefs agreed to push the operation back, while recognizing that an unexpected setback in the Gilberts might cause a further delay.[6]

As the planners moved forward, Nimitz, Spruance, Turner, and Holland Smith studied the lessons coming from the Gilberts—in particular the danger of splitting the landing forces and, in turn, the naval forces, too far apart. Rather than aiming for five different atolls spread over hundreds of miles, Nimitz and his subordinate commanders decided to focus on a smaller, more focused, landing operation. As Nimitz observed, "The experience gained in the occupation of the Gilbert Islands [and] . . . the assault troops and shipping available will permit the inclusion of only two major objectives in the initial invasion."[7]

Turner and Smith advocated taking Wotje and Maloelap before moving either back to Hawaii or on to Kwajalein. Nimitz, on the other hand, favored skipping those two and just taking Kwajalein, while neutralizing surrounding islands with air and naval power. This mirrored the MacArthur strategy of leapfrogging outer islands and striking into the heart of an enemy stronghold.[8]

Spruance, Turner, and Smith were united in their opposition to this plan.[9] In his later recollections, Holland Smith remembers the planning differently, claiming that *he* thought that the original plan was too ambitious and that *he* was the first to advocate for striking a single atoll.[10] However, Spruance and Turner both recalled Smith supporting them against Nimitz's plan.[11] In any event, Nimitz prevailed and, as Turner later admitted, "As it turned out, that was the best plan."[12]

The final objectives, which were not agreed upon until mid-December, called for an attack on the islands of Kwajalein and Roi-Namur, which lay in opposite corners of the Kwajalein atoll with a subsequent landing on Eniwetok (dubbed Operation CATCHPOLE). Several days after fixing the objectives, Spruance requested one further change. A reconnaissance flight over the Majuro atoll had revealed that the airfields there were lightly, if at all, defended and the atoll would provide needed fleet anchorage for the navy. Nimitz agreed to send an expeditionary force to occupy the island (dubbed Operation SUNDANCE).[13] With the broad outlines of the operation set, planners now turned their focus onto the particulars.

OPERATIONAL PLANNING

Now there was an objective, but no units available to conduct the operation. In August, the newly formed and activated 4th Marine Division started undergoing amphibious training in California in anticipation of conducting the landings on Roi-Namur, the lesser defended of the two islands. This left the planners looking around for a division available for the more challenging operations on Kwajalein.

As it happened, events unfolding in the Aleutians would solve the dilemma. On 15 August, the 7th Infantry Division, which had already conducted amphibious combat operations on Attu, landed on Kiska to find that the Japanese had abandoned the island. Suddenly free, battle-tested, and already trained in amphibious operations, the 7th ID was the logical choice to conduct the landings on Kwajalein and two of its regiments headed to Hawaii to prepare. Additionally, Nimitz tapped the 106th Infantry Regiment, part of the 27th ID, and the 22nd Marine Regiment to conduct the follow-on operation on Eniwetok.

Seizing the Kwajalein atoll was more complicated than simply landing on the two main islands, Kwajalein and Roi-Namur. The atoll had dozens of smaller islands populated with Japanese garrisons and defensive positions. These islands not only presented a potential threat to the landing forces, but they also guarded the deep water passes into the lagoon area. Since the lagoon had a deep anchorage, the navy planned to move some of the transport and fire support ships into there, to safeguard them from submarine attacks. Moreover, clearing adjacent islands gave the divisions a place to land supporting artillery and communications units as needed. For these reasons, the divisions had to plan to take several additional islands as part of the preparatory phase of the operations.

As in past operations, the issue of command and control once again reared its divisive head. The final plan called for two attack forces, plus the follow-on attack on Eniwetok. Turner decided to assume command of the Southern Attack Force (Kwajalein), since it was the more important of the two main objectives. This allowed him to coordinate directly with the 7th Division commander, General Charles "Cowboy Pete" Corlett, should the landing force find itself in a situation like that at Tarawa. He made Admiral Richard Conolly the commander of the Northern Attack Force (Roi-Namur) and Admiral Harry Hill the commander of the Majuro and

Eniwetok attack forces. Each of these commanders would have authority over their landing force, although Turner still exercised overall command of the entire operation.[14]

Turner had had a similar command structure in the Gilberts, although in that operation he controlled the attack at Makin, which did not require his full attention after the landings and allowed him to shift focus to Tarawa and back up Hill there as needed. Here he was taking command of the main attack against the more heavily defended island. Corlett protested that having Turner dual-hatted as both the Expeditionary Force commander and Southern Attack Force Commander violated the principles of "clear-cut command channels and unity of command." His main worry was that Turner, as the overall commander and his own higher headquarters, would have to divide his attention between the two landing forces and would not be able to give his *undivided attention* to the objective of the 7th Division." Corlett was concerned that events in the Northern Attack Force sector might force Turner to shift this attention and deprive the 7th ID of its Attack Force commander.[15]

Moreover, since the plan called for all three commanders (Turner, Smith, and Corlett) and their staffs to be on the same flagship, the possibility existed that Turner, as the Expeditionary Force commander, might have to physically move away from the operation if there was an emergency at Roi-Namur, taking the 7th ID staff with him. Corlett first suggested that Turner appoint another naval commander for the Southern Attack Force. When that failed, he expressed concern that there would not be enough room on the ship for all three staffs. Corlett felt that if Smith was to have no direct command of the landing forces, then he and his staff should move to another ship.[16] Part of this probably stemmed from the fact that he and Holland Smith knew and disliked one another, ever since the Aleutians, where Smith had been an observer of Corlett's division on Kiska. Corlett was known to be "abrasive, high-strung, short-tempered, and unpolished" and not afraid to speak his mind, often unprompted.[17] In other words, he was very much like Holland Smith.

However, it appears that Nimitz and Spruance did not have the same worry and the plan stood as written. More problematically, the command schematic did not address the role of Holland Smith once combat operations began. As with the Gilberts, there seemed to be no room in the command structure for a corps commander in division and regiment-sized assault landings.

The three services struck a compromise that seemed to satisfy Smith's ego while keeping the command structure as streamlined as possible. As in the Gilbert operations, the attack force commanders (Turner and Conolly) were in charge during the initial amphibious phase, with the landing force commanders taking command as soon as their divisions were established on shore. At this point, Smith would be considered in command; however, as in the Gilberts, his powers were severely limited and he could not make "major changes to the tactical plan or make unscheduled major landings without the approval of Admiral Turner."[18] Even requests for naval gunfire support and air support were made directly from the Landing Force Commanders to the Attack Force Commander.[19]

Corlett later addressed this unusual command arrangement in remarks to the Commandant of the Marine Corps, writing, "It is my opinion that a corps commander did not add anything to the success of this operation . . . Turner realized the unwieldy and awkward [command] situation because he told . . . Smith that 'Corlett and I will deal directly with each other' or words to that effect." He further stated that "the commander of the landing ground troops must deal directly with his naval task force commander. Harry Schmidt did this with Admiral Conolly and I did it with Admiral Turner after [he] eliminated the echelon of delay [Smith's corps headquarters]." [20] Turner himself emphasized Smith's marginal role in a letter to the 4th MARDIV commander, writing, "Saipan [which took place four months after the Marshall landings] was the *only* place where Holland Smith was charged with tactical command."[21] In other words, once again, Smith was the commander on paper, but not in actuality.

However, Smith remembered this differently. He claimed that he instructed Schmidt to take command the moment he set foot on Roi-Namur.[22] This seems a bit ridiculous and redundant since the operations plan clearly laid out that Schmidt was to do that anyway and besides, it was not Smith's prerogative to issue such an order in the first place. Corlett was even blunter. Hearing of Smith's plan to land on Kwajalein with him, Corlett informed his nominal commander that he was not welcome on the island until the battle was finished. He agreed to allow some of Smith's staff to land as observers, but stated, "If I find that they tried to issue any orders, I'll have them arrested."[23] This blunt talk must have had some effect on Smith's psyche as, despite their mutual dislike, Smith did not disparage Corlett personally in his memoirs (in fact, he avoids referring to him by name at all), although he did vocally criticize the operations of the 7th ID on Kwajalein, claiming—as he almost always did with the army—that they were too slow in securing the island. Smith even complained to Vandegrift that the 7th ID's slow progress on Kwajalein has "tried my soul."[24]

As with the Gilberts, each landing was essentially independent and the two divisions formulated their own plans and then submitted them to their higher headquarters planners for approval and integration. Because the final decision on target islands was not made until just six weeks before the operation, the divisions had limited time to formulate detailed plans. Corlett had his staff work up plans for invading any coral island, reasoning that if the broad outlines were in place, the staff could swiftly complete more specific planning once they received the final target.

Kwajalein was a crescent-shaped island two and half miles long and about 800 yards wide. The nearest island, Carlson, was about two miles away and intelligence indicated that it was only lightly defended. Another nearby island, Burton, had relatively extensive defenses and held about 1,000 Japanese troops. The Japanese also occupied a few of the smaller islands nearby.

Corlett, with his experience with planning Attu and Kiska, and mindful of the lessons of Tarawa, was convinced that the key to swift victory was the intelligent use of indirect firepower. First, he instructed his staff planners to regard the island as a "heavily fortified fortress." This meant that long, intensive preparation fires, delivered from as many sources and directions as possible, should precede any attack. Secondly, once ashore, the landing forces were to make full use of the overwhelming naval firepower at their disposal. Finally, he advocated landing the division artillery on nearby islands in advance of the main landing.[25]

This was the same tactic that Julian Smith had advocated, and was denied, at Tarawa. Corlett recalled that when he first suggested landing the artillery on the adjacent island (Carlson), his entire staff, including his artillery commander, expressed doubt as to whether the island was big enough. In response, Corlett had an area the size and shape of Carlson taped off and physically moved all of his artillery battalions into the area. The units fit and the plan was written as Corlett envisioned.[26]

The 7th ID final plan contained five distinct phases. In Phase I, elements of the 17th Infantry Regiment would land on the four small islands (Cecil, Carter, Carlos, and Carlson) nearest Kwajalein and the field artillery would set up on Carlson in order to provide fire support to the main landing force.[27] Phase II would be the main attack onto Kwajalein, which would take place after two hours of devastating preparatory fire. Rather than assault the middle of the island into the teeth of the Japanese main defenses, two regiments would land abreast on the westernmost beach of the island (184th to the north and 32nd to the south) and then advance eastward along the island. Two factors influenced this decision. The first was that the surf was gentler at that end of the island and the coral reef narrower, which would allow the landing boats to come in closer to the beach. The second was that it would be easier to land supporting artillery on the undefended Carlson Island rather than on Burton, which held a garrison of approximately 1,000 Japanese.[28]

Phase III consisted of moving across the island and clearing it of the enemy. Once the Americans had secured Kwajalein, the division reserve would begin Phase IV and occupy the other islands in the division sector (Burton, Burnet, Blakenship, Buster, and Byron). Finally, Phase V called for the capture of the remaining small islands in the sector.[29]

Like the 7th Division, the 4th Marine Division staff began training and planning before they actually received their final objective. Unlike the 7th ID, the 4th MARDIV was located in California, which required the staff to shuttle back and forth to Hawaii in order to consult with V Corps staff.

Roi-Namur was actually two islands, separated by just 400 yards and joined by a causeway over a narrow manmade sandy neck. Roi, the western island, was only 1,200 yards long and 1,250 yards wide. On it was a large airfield that took up practically the entire island. Namur was even smaller, only 900 yards long and 800 yards wide and contained all of the support buildings for the soldiers on the island.[30]

Because of the unusually large and rocky coral reefs and heavy surf, the only possible approach was from the lagoon. The passages into the lagoon were guarded by five small islands (Jacob, Ivan, Abraham, Albert, and Allen) and these would have to be secured before the naval ships could move in. For this reason, much of the 4th MARDIV plan mirrored that of the 7th ID. Phase I would involve the 25th Marines occupying these smaller islands and establishing artillery on Jacob and Ivan.

The next day, Phase II would commence with the 23rd Marines landing on Roi and the 24th Marines landing on Namur and each would sweep across. As with the 7th ID, heavy aerial, naval, and artillery fire would precede and support the landings. The final phase involved securing and repairing the airfield and capturing any remaining islets near the island.[31] If all went as planned not only would the Allies have taken Japanese land for the first time, but they would also have a large, three-runway airfield and deep-water port to support further operations.

PRE-COMBAT TRAINING

As seen in all the previous operations, the two divisions trained independently of each other, with the 7th ID in Alaska and the 4th MARDIV in California. In this case, however, it was the army division that had the combat and amphibious assault experience and the army would take the more heavily defended island.

7th Infantry Division "The Bayonet"

The 7th Infantry Division was initially created in December 1916 and deployed to France just a couple of months later. However, although elements of the division saw combat, it did not conduct any operations as a whole division. Just as the unit prepared to launch an offensive against the Hindenburg Line, the Armistice ended the war and the division found itself on occupation duties for the next year. Soon after returning to the U.S., the unit deactivated.

On 6 July 1940, the unit reactivated in Fort Ord, California, under the command of General Joseph "Vinegar Joe" Stilwell. The division was made up of the 17th, 32nd and 53rd Infantry Regiments, all largely composed of reservists and draftees and all of its initial training was conducted on the Pacific Coast. Stilwell, a notoriously tough but fair trainer, drilled his men long and hard.

Upon returning from annual training in the summer of 1941, the division experienced the first of many upheavals that marked its first years of existence. First, in September, General Charles White succeeded Stilwell, who became the III Corps Commander and later took over the China-Burma-India Theater. While assigned to guard the Pacific coast, the division lost a large portion of its officers and NCOs, who were taken to form the cadre of two new divisions. As the 7th ID was a motorized division, White anticipated service in North Africa and focused maneuvers in the Mojave Desert.[32]

In late 1942, the unit received a new commander, a new regiment, and a new mission when General Albert Brown replaced White, the 159th replaced the 53rd, and Allied victories in North Africa portended the end of combat in that theater. Instead, the unit abruptly shifted focus to amphibious operations and the soldiers were told that they were headed to fight in the Aleutians, on the island of Kiska, which the Japanese had occupied in June 1942, while the American Pacific Fleet focused on the fighting at Midway. After some dithering, the Japanese had finally committed to building an airfield on the island as a launching pad for attacks on the U.S. West Coast.

As planning progressed, the focus shifted from Kiska to Attu, as planners believed that the latter island had only 500 Japanese soldiers (as opposed to Kiska's estimated 9,000) and the capture of Attu would completely cut off Kiska's lines of communication, leaving it to "wither on the vine."[33] Later intelligence showed that the estimates were off by a magnitude of 10, resulting in the need for a full division to take Attu. En route to the Aleutians, the 7th ID learned that they would be that division and the 17th and 32nd Regiments landed on 11 May in the midst of a heavy fog.

An operation that planners estimated would take only three days ended up taking more than two weeks of vicious fighting and resulted in Brown being relieved by Admiral Thomas Kinkaid in the midst of the battle. When Attu was finally secured on 30 May, the division had lost 549 killed and about 3,300 wounded or ill.

In the meantime, the 159th regiment, which the 7th ID had left behind in California, was training for amphibious operations on Kiska under the watchful eye of Holland Smith and Corlett, who would take over the division after the campaign. It was joined by the 184th Regiment, a California National Guard unit, which would eventually replace the 159th when that regiment became the garrison force on Attu. Operations were scheduled to begin on 15 August, using the 184th and many of the veterans from Attu.

Unlike on Attu, however, the only casualties on Kiska were inflicted by friendly fire. Unseen by the Americans, over 5,000 Japanese soldiers packed up and abandoned the island weeks before the American landings. Holland Smith, who was an observer of the operation, is typically scornful, claiming that he alone had determined that the Japanese had abandoned the island but that the army and navy would not listen to him.[34] He also complained in his final report that the 7th ID was too slow and deliberate in its operations—a complaint that he would have against every army unit with which he came into contact.[35]

In late August, the division was alerted to its new mission in the Central Pacific and turned its attention to upcoming operations in the Marshall Islands. On 4 September Corlett officially took command and that same afternoon the division, which had been loaded and afloat for several days, began the convoy to Hawaii, to begin training for the upcoming operation. The smooth sandy beaches of Oahu were a far cry from the solid, rocky, fog-shrouded beaches upon which these soldiers had previously landed. A staff officer observed:

> Every officer and soldier knew that an amphibious landing conducted on the smooth, sunny beaches . . . is indeed an elementary affair. They had learned to gauge wind, surf, fog, rain and waves with boat reactions and team work in their landings on the cold, dark, rocky shores of the Aleutians, the best amphibious training area known. The actual landing on a sunlite [sic] beach of the warm Pacific held no terror for them, even when complicated by coral reefs.[36]

Nevertheless, Corlett did not allow the 7th ID to rest on past laurels. His staff spent hours with veterans of the Tarawa landing in order to extract lessons to use in their training. Afterwards, Corlett gave his staff what he divined as the three guiding principles for the training: every soldier must be able to fight effectively while moving through the water to the beach; everyone down to the squad leaders must know how to coordinate with and use mortars, tanks, engineers, artillery and air support; and leaders must ensure that every soldier understood the plan completely and was a tactician in his own right.[37]

These directives were reflective of Corlett as a leader. Although he could be abrasive and short tempered, he was known as a superb and meticulous trainer who had been conducting amphibious training in Alaska as the commander of Fort Greeley since 1941. His special focus was on combat loading, ship-to-shore communications, and indirect fire support for the landing forces. His time in Alaska routinely forced him to interact with the local naval commanders and he was known as one of the few army officers who had strong positive relations with the navy. For this he earned the endorsement of the notoriously prickly Admiral King.[38]

Corlett had just a few short months to prepare his men for yet another landing in a very different climate from that in which his men had trained. To support his first two training directives, Corlett made sure that every landing exercise was as realistic as possible. Much of the training took place in a bay where it was possible to fire weapons inshore and the men learned to time the fire of their weapons on the landing craft with the waves. They invited aviators to observe operations so that they could better understand what the men on the ground might need. Most importantly, the unit had time to train with the alligators and DUKWs (army amphibious truck), learning not only how to operate, embark, and disembark from them, but also how to best use these vehicles operationally and tactically.[39]

Mindful of the communications and coordination issues between the infantry and tanks on Tarawa, Corlett ensured that the tank battalion participated fully in all training. Frequent meetings between his staff and the tank commanders allowed the division to develop its own doctrine for using the tanks on the battlefield and even allowed them to develop a rudimentary phone system to allow infantrymen to communicate with the tankers, without the tankers having to leave their vehicle.[40]

The final of his three training principles could not be accomplished until the men were loaded on the transport ships and headed to their objective. Each battalion commander was given a sealed package marked "SECRET" and directed not to open the package until at sea. Inside there was a map and a summary of the situation and plan for each officer and non-commissioned officer with instructions to make sure that every man in the unit understood both. As Corlett later summed up, "On the eight day trip to Kwajalein, every soldier learned what he was going up against. The mystery was gone. The men knew what to do and how to do it."[41]

4th Marine Division "Fighting Fourth"

Early in 1943, as the 1st and 2nd Marine Divisions recovered from extended operations in Guadalcanal and the 3rd Marine Division was on its way to operations in the Southwest Pacific, pieces of existing but unassigned regiments were being used to create a new division. Unlike the first three divisions, whose regiments had some history dating back to World War I, the 4th Marine Division was the first division built with completely new regiments. These men created the division history and legends as they went along. In all, the division would spend 21 months overseas and just 63 days in actual combat. However, their landings and combat operations were some of the costliest and most hotly contested battles of the war: Roi-Namur, Saipan, Tinian, and Iwo Jima. When the war was over, the 4th was the first division returned to the United States for deactivation.[42]

The first regiment, the 23rd Marines, was originally part of the 3rd Marine Division, located in Camp Lejeune, North Carolina. In February 1943, it was detached to form the nucleus of the new 4th Division. In May, the regiment was split in two and half was used to form the 25th Marines. The third rifle regiment, the 24th, was organized in Camp Pendleton, California, in March 1943.[43] It would be fall before these disparate parts of the division united on the West Coast. The 23rd and all support elements moved across the United States by train, while the 25th sailed from Norfolk, Virginia, through the Panama Canal and finally arrived in California in September 1943. Finally the 4th MARDIV was complete.

By then, the division had been formally activated and was conducting training in anticipation of overseas movement sometime at the end of the year.[44] The assistant division commander, General James Underhill, remembered that "it was a pretty raw division to start with. There weren't very many combat people . . . very few officers that had combat [experience in WWII] . . . the older officers, might have gone all the way back to World War I. And some local skirmishes in Central America, in Haiti and Santo Domingo . . . but not any real warfare [experience]."[45]

Commanding this new division was General Harry Schmidt, who was fresh from serving as the Assistant to the Commandant of the Marine Corps. He had been a marine for over 30 years and in one of those odd twists, had served his first tour in the Marianas Islands and was fairly familiar with the Central Pacific.

Like the 7th ID, the leaders of 4th MARDIV knew in early fall that their target would be in the Central Pacific, although they did not know that it would be Roi-Namur until early November (and the men would not be told until a few days before the landing).[46] Also, starting in November, the unit had the benefit of the lessons learned from the Tarawa landing and several key division leaders, including the assistant division commander, had been observers at Tarawa.[47] As a result, the 4th MARDIV focused on "utilization of amphibious tractors as assault troop carriers and in the type of tactics required for coping with a strongly entrenched enemy on a small atoll."[48] All the observers noted that in the chaos of the battlefield, all leaders and marines needed to be prepared to "adapt themselves to unexpected and unfamiliar situations [and] be able to take the men and materiel available and do the job at hand."[49]

While the 4th MARDIV conducted the usual combat training, special attention was given to certain specialized training such as demolitions and the operation of equipment such as boat guns and mounted rocket launchers.[50] However, due to limited availability of equipment, especially the tractors that were being fitted with extra armor plating and the fear of damaging these irreplaceable vehicles, the division did not receive the full benefit from its two rehearsals.[51] Indeed, after watching one rehearsal where two landing vehicles collided, one observer later remarked, "All this was very poor for morale just before combat."[52]

Additionally, the unit had no time to conduct rehearsals once deployed to the forward area. Rather, after the division embarked from San Diego on 13 January 1944, save for a single day in Hawaii for the division staff to consult with the V Amphibious Corps, the marines only disembarked when they stormed the beaches of Roi-Namur.

OPERATIONS

It is tempting to use the success of this operation as a mallet to hammer the operations on Tarawa; however that would be unfair and disingenuous. The fact is that without the lessons learned at Tarawa, the operations in the Marshalls might not have been so easy. While Tarawa was the proving ground for new equipment, the Marshalls were the proving ground for developing Tarawa-informed doctrine. In the Marshalls the landing forces were able to finally bring together equipment and doctrine in a way that had not been done previously. While a number of lessons remained to be learned, they would mostly be refinements of what was now established doctrine. As far as the leaders were concerned, there was nothing new to develop or discover and further operations would require little more than tweaking of the proven basic doctrine and equipment.

However, it was here at the Marshalls that the interservice issues came to the forefront as a leadership concern. These disputes had been pushed aside in pursuit of the common goal of creating a workable common doctrine and equipment. Nevertheless, tensions, especially between Holland Smith and various army commanders, continued to smolder just beneath the surface. Both the army and the marines were acutely aware that their roles in the Pacific overlapped and there was a constant tension as to who would have command of the ground forces.

Enemy Operations

The Japanese had long regarded the Marshalls as a natural geographical shield against an Allied push towards the heartland of the Japanese naval defenses in the Carolines and Marianas.[53] In order to protect these vulnerable islands, the Japanese developed Plan Z in May 1943, which put island commanders in charge of their own defenses, but based the fleet at Truk, where it would be available to reinforce any threatened island.

The Japanese had owned the Marshalls since 1914 and had spent a great deal of time fortifying this, along with other islands, as part of their defensive system in contravention of the League of Nations. However, Japanese planners did not grasp the full import of the Marshalls until 1941 and even then only viewed them as another block in their defensive perimeter. Starting in September 1943, large numbers of army personnel were sent to the islands as reinforcements, but they were mainly scattered among the various atolls and not really concentrated in any one area in great numbers.[54]

However, as the Allies made gains, the Japanese pulled into a tighter and tighter perimeter and eventually several chains, including the Gilberts and Marshalls, were written out of Plan Z. This did not mean that they were ignored, but rather that they were now the outside ring of the defense. The Japanese no longer cared as much about retaining the islands, but rather viewed them as a means to merely slow any attacks from the Allies. As such they received more reinforcements and supplies but could not expect naval support if invaded. In short, they were to fight to the death to keep the Allies out of the heart of the Japanese defenses.[55]

The defensive plan for the islands followed the Japanese tactical emphasis on stopping the Americans on the beaches and counterattacking before the troops could consolidate and move forward. This mindset was not only a product of the Japanese recognition of the vulnerability of forces during landing, but also had a measure of practicality. Coral islands are small and there was not much land on which to build defenses in depth. For this reason, as at Tarawa, the defenses were concentrated on the beachheads, with little or nothing behind them. Oddly, unlike in the Gilberts, there were no offshore mines, obstacles, or wires. Even the beach defenses had few obstacles or wire, relying instead on an extensive system of trenches, pillboxes, and bunkers. Of course, some of those differences could be attributed to the fact that the Gilberts were defended by specialty troops of Japanese marines, while regular soldiers of the Japanese army manned the Marshalls.[56]

Furthermore, Japanese air power was nonexistent in the area. Those planes not destroyed on the ground in the weeks leading up to the invasion were evacuated to the nearby island of Truk, where they would be out of range of American firepower.

The Japanese had also learned some lessons from Tarawa. They understood the need to keep the Americans out of the lagoons and to cover the logical landing sites. However, nothing in their Tarawa experience alerted them to or allowed them to prepare for the hailstorm of devastating fire that would rain down upon the islands in the days leading up to the invasion. Moreover, despite the unprecedented firepower unleashed on the island, the commanders around Kwajalein never realized that that island was the main focus of the invasion.[57]

The Japanese also understood that the Marshalls would be a logical step in the American strategy, but the commanders disagreed as to which island would be the target. A Japanese naval officer later confessed,

> There was divided opinion as to whether you would land at Jaluit or Mille. Some thought you would land on Wotje, but there were few who thought you would go right to the heart of the Marshalls and take Kwajalein.[58]

This command confusion was noted by the American intelligence analysts who spotted the rush of Japanese troops from Kwajalein to Mille and Jaluit as well the flurry of activity as defensive installations on these islands were hastily erected there. Therefore, when the final landings came against Kwajalein and Roi-Namur, the Americans managed to achieve both tactical and strategic surprise.[59]

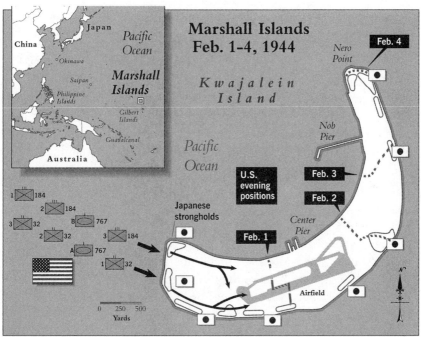

Marshall Islands
Feb. 1-4, 1944

Kwajalein Island

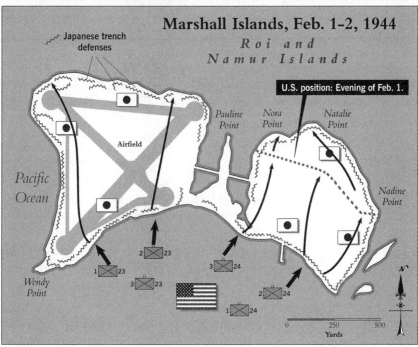

Marshall Islands, Feb. 1-2, 1944

Roi and Namur Islands

Landing Operations

As the assault forces prepared for the landings, three major changes, which had been requested for the Gilbert operations, were granted for this operation. First, the preliminary naval and aerial bombardment would be significantly longer. This was possible because the new island bases in the Gilberts considerably eased logistic strains. Secondly, artillery units were to land on adjacent islands the day before the assault in order to provide cover for the landing troops. Finally, not only would the landing troops have enough amphibious landing tractors to land each wave, but the tractors, dubbed LVT(A)s, were equipped with extra armor and a 37mm gun, a modification that was requested in the wake of the Tarawa landing. These tractors would provide extra firepower and protection for the first landing wave.

Additionally, the Marshall operations saw the introduction of two new pieces of amphibious landing equipment. The first were the new amphibious gunboats, which would precede the first wave. These gunboats (called LCIs) were equipped with three 40mm guns and several rocket launchers and provided close-in firepower focused on destroying any enemy machine gun positions on the beaches. Interestingly, at a conference in Hawaii between the Gilberts and Marshalls operations, Marshall asked about equipping landing boats with machine guns and rockets. Holland Smith dismissed this as "an indication of his unfamiliarity (like most army officers) with amphibious technique."[60]

The other piece of landing equipment to make its debut in the Marshalls was the introduction of the DUKW, the army's version of an amphibious truck. The army, along with General Motors Corporation, had been working on this truck since 1940 and the Marshalls would provide its first test in combat. These trucks could carry up to 25 troops or 5,000 pounds of cargo and the 7th ID had one hundred at their disposal. Since they were the perfect size to land howitzers, the staff gave 60 to the division artillery and kept 40 for division logistics.

Finally, the operation saw the introduction of two specialized units. The landing difficulties at Tarawa, particularly on the undetected submerged coral heads, and the knowledge that most of the remaining island objectives were also coral atolls, spurred the creation of naval underwater demolition teams (UDT). Trainers from the Naval Construction Battalion (Seabees) came to Oahu in November 1943 to train 180 men and officers from the three services in the art of underwater reconnaissance and demolition.[61] The two teams were deployed to Kwajalein and Roi-Namur to support the upcoming landings.

The other unit, the Joint Assault Signal Company (JASCO), grew out of the realization that not only would the landing parties be scattered on various islands throughout the atoll, but that all these units had to be able to coordinate the air, naval, and artillery support that was similarly scattered. The plan was that these teams would be able to pinpoint calls for support as needed during the battle. Each battalion received a JASCO team to direct the naval and air strikes and liaison with the battalion air-ground teams.

Kwajalein[62]

The preliminary air attacks on the atoll had begun on 5 December 1943, during which several Japanese merchant ships were sunk. Periodic attacks on Kwajalein and surrounding islands over the next two months ramped up on 29 January 1944, two days before the planned landing. At this point there were neither enemy planes nor any boats in the area. In short, there was absolutely no way for the Japanese to send reinforcements to the targeted islands. Beginning on 30 January, over 400 air sorties and hours of naval fire bombarded the island relentlessly and this was merely the beginning.

Early in the morning of 31 January, as UDT 1 slipped under water to check for obstacles, rubber boats carried elements of the 7th ID to Cecil and Carter Islands, which were thought to have small garrisons. Once these islands were cleared, the plan was to bring both forces to Chauncey Island, where they would remain as a defensive force. The Carter landing force encountered a small, but determined, Japanese force and suffered one killed and one wounded before securing the island. However, choppy seas had forced the other landing force slightly off course and they mistakenly landed on Chauncey, a mile north of Cecil. After a short battle, the platoon re-embarked for the correct island, while leaving a small force behind to deal with the remaining members of a beached Japanese tugboat.

In midmorning, further American troops landed on Carlson and Carlos, capturing both by mid-afternoon. Not only did this successfully complete Phase I of the landing operations, but the 7th ID now possessed communications and artillery bases from which to support the main landing. The operations on the subsidiary islands were so far ahead of schedule, that the five artillery batteries were able to start full-scale artillery bombardment that evening, as opposed to the planned harassment fire, on the main island. This fire lasted all night long.

At 0530 the next morning, the first wave of the main landing force moved forward under a hail of artillery, naval, and air fire. The regiments landed on the western edge of the island, with the more experienced 32nd Infantry taking the right, or ocean edge and the 184th taking the left, or lagoon edge.

Despite the overwhelming firepower that had pounded them for the past several days, a small force of Japanese defenders manned the few remaining pillboxes and greeted the first wave with machine gun and grenade fire. While the defenders inflicted some casualties, they did not slow the invasion and all four waves landed within fifteen minutes and began moving inland.

The destruction that greeted the landing forces was unlike anything seen in the war up to that point. As an observer remarked in his official report, "The island looked as if it had been picked up to 20,000 feet and then dropped. The devastation on the landing beach was so great that it was almost impossible for tanks to cross the beach. All beach defenses were completely destroyed."[63] The engineers had more work clearing out debris and smoothing roads than they did breeching enemy obstacles. The Americans had landed and now prepared for their push across the island.

Roi-Namur[64]

Just as on Kwajalein, as 31 January dawned, the naval and aerial attacks that had been going on for two days continued to pummel the small islands near Roi-Namur. The landings on these small islands were initially delayed by the rough seas and damaged communications equipment. Confusion at the transfer points from LSTs to the LVTs that held the amtracs compounded these problems for the troops. Because the plan had been revised after the final rehearsal, there had been no chance to coordinate or discuss the final landing plans. Additionally, the lack of radio communications made it easy for rumored changes to the plan to be mistaken as fact. As a result, the transfer area became what was described as "an amphibious traffic jam."

However, despite the delays and confusion, by evening the passages into the lagoon and all the initial objectives had been gained with a minimum of Japanese opposition. Most importantly, the artillery emplaced on Ivan and Jacob was prepared to support the main landing force the next day. As the ships moved into the lagoon, it was found that the Jacob pass was too shallow to permit the destroyers to enter. Fortunately, the Ivan pass was not, and the navy cleared it in preparation for the main landings.

Mindful of the difficulties posed by the weather and communications failures, Conolly decided to invoke his rough weather plan, which eliminated the need for the landing troops to transfer between landing crafts at sea and allowed the landing craft to enter the lagoon before launching the tractors, thus decreasing the distance that the amtracs would have to travel. However, this did not completely eliminate all problems. Issues stemming from the previous day's confusion meant that the landing forces had lost forty-eight amtracs and were short vehicles for the invasion.

The regiments fell behind schedule as the navy and marines scrambled to get the assault boats into formation and come up with an alternative for the missing tractors. The landing time was moved from 1000 to 1100 and coordination made to continue the punishing fires that poured on the small islands. At this point, the Japanese began shelling from Namur, although this was quickly quelled.

Finally, the attack launched and the first waves hit the beaches at about 1155. Unlike at Tarawa, careful coordination allowed the indirect fire from artillery, ships, and bombers to continue until just before the landing forces reached the beaches. As a result, the defenses on the island were thoroughly destroyed and the marines met only slight resistance. The 23rd Marines commander, Colonel Louis Jones, summed it up with a message back to Schmidt: "This is a pip . . . No opposition on the beach . . . Give us the word and we will take the rest of the island."[65]

BATTLE SUMMARY

Kwajalein[66]

As the first day went on, the Americans met more determined resistance from the Japanese defenders, although it was not nearly as heavy as the

32nd had faced on Attu. As expected, the fortifications were much heavier on the ocean side, where the Japanese had been focusing their attention for years. As night fell, along with a period of heavy rain, the Japanese began dropping mortar rounds into the 184th lines. The left flank broke briefly, but the Japanese did not exploit this breech and the Americans were soon able to restore order. The Japanese continued to stage counterattacks all night and it was described in the command journals as "from midnight on, the enemy was very active, screaming and yelling in a fanatical manner, and one counterattack after another was attempted until daybreak."[67]

For the next two days, the Americans doggedly moved east and conducted coordinated attacks between the two regiments. They captured the airfield and moved past tank traps, including one almost 300 yards long. Despite the wreckage, the island was still a fortress honeycombed with underground tunnels and bunkers from which the Japanese began emerging in large numbers. Japanese resistance was steady throughout the two-day advance, consisting mainly of snipers, machine guns, and white phosphorous shells. The night brought further counterattacks, although the army easily repulsed them.

On 3 February, the Americans began what they assumed was the final offensive drive through to the end of the island. With only a mile to the northern tip of the island, Corlett was so optimistic that he even told his troops to "finish the job by 1500." However, the regiments were moving into the toughest section of the enemy stronghold and, to their surprise, made little progress that day. The island was not secured until the next afternoon. Organized resistance ended in spectacular fashion. As the Americans moved against the last three defensive positions on the northern tip of the island, the defenders opted for a mass suicide, destroying their remaining positions in a stunning explosion. The island was secure.

Roi-Namur[68]

Flush with the unexpected ease of the landings, the 23rd Marines rushed headlong across the beach, not even waiting for official permission. Although they encountered some resistance, they were soon backed by the medium tanks that were sweeping across the airfield. The regimental commander soon called them all back in order to conduct a more orderly attack across the island.

The combination of devastating indirect fire, coupled with the initial unexpected infantry-armor attack left the Japanese unable to coordinate any defense or counterattack. By 1800 Roi was secured and units posted around the causeway to ensure that no Japanese could escape to or from Namur.

On Namur, the assault was a bit slower. On Roi almost all of the vegetation had been cleared to build the airfield and as a result there was clear visibility across most of the island and few places available for the enemy to conceal himself. By contrast, thick foliage limited visibility on Namur. In addition, the majority of the Japanese defenders were on this side, as opposed to Roi, so the 24th Marines met much fiercer, although not particularly organized, resistance.

Around 1305 hours, marines came upon a large concrete building and placed satchel charges inside to destroy it. As they detonated the charges, the building exploded in a series of blasts that engulfed the entire island in brown smoke and rained debris on everything around it, killing twenty marines and injuring a further hundred. It turned out that the concrete building was full of torpedo warheads and the two other explosions were smaller magazines nearby, although it was unknown if they were set off by the initial explosion set by the marines or if the Japanese had set off the other two in order to kill as many Americans as possible. This incident alone accounted for a substantial portion of the casualties on Namur.

That night, Japanese defenders harassed the marines, but there was no large-scale counterattack. As with all men in combat for the first time, and not unlike the 165th Infantry on Makin, the marines nervously fired at imaginary snipers. This indiscriminate shooting became so bad that Schmidt himself emerged from his command post to calm the men. Additionally, medium tanks from Roi came across the causeway to assist the morning attack.

This proved wise as the Japanese finally mounted a counterattack with first light. Backed by the tanks, the marines were able to break the attack, leaving the way clear to advance northward. The 24th Marines then swept across the island, encountering desultory opposition and finally declared it secure at 1418. In just three days, the marines had secured all of their objectives.

ANALYSIS

Planning

Planning at the corps and higher levels for the Marshalls invasion had two important advantages over planning for the Gilberts. The first was time. The Marshalls had been a planned target since May 1943 and high-level planning and surveillance had been going on ever since. This is a marked contrast to the Gilberts, which was planned and executed in a scant four months. However, dithering over the selection of which islands to target removed much of that advantage from the division and lower echelons, who were given less than six weeks to plan tactical operations.

The other advantage was the lessons learned from the Gilberts. Aware that they could not afford another slaughter like the Tarawa landing, planners used the extra planning time to determine how to minimize casualties while quickly subduing the island.

The easiest way to do this was to obliterate the enemy and its defenses before any American even set foot on the beach. Planners understood that accomplishing this would require four steps: eliminating all enemy aircraft within striking distance of the island and their continued neutralization throughout the operation; gaining early use of the Kwajalein lagoon; occupying Majuro atoll; and conducting heavy and protracted bombing of the objective.[69]

As mentioned earlier, the Americans managed to do the first quite early on and Japanese aircraft had a minimal effect on operations. In fact, no Japanese aircraft made it into the area until 12 February, well after the end of the operations.

The second was important not only to protect American vessels from submarines, but also to prevent the enemy from escaping from one island and reforming on another. While trying to determine the best landing area, intelligence officers noticed that the Japanese had begun building more defenses on the lagoon side of the island. In the past, defenses had been concentrated on the ocean side, the most likely American avenue of attack. However, the Japanese had also learned a few lessons from the Gilberts. The Allied landing in the lagoons there had alerted Japanese planners to their importance and vulnerability.

On Kwajalein, the ocean side had a large reef (100+ feet wide) that was completely bare during low tide. On the lagoon side, the reef ran

500–800 feet, making a landing from that direction even less appealing. Fortuitously, the ends of the island not only provided suitable landing beaches, but also avoided landing troops directly into the face of the Japanese defenses. There was an element of irony in the planners choosing the western edge of the island for the landing site, since Ralph Smith's plans to do just that on Makin were derided by Holland Smith as foolishness and borderline cowardice.

On Roi-Namur, on the other hand, the shape and separation of the two islands made it logical for the two regiments to land abreast and sweep north, each independently of the other. Additionally, the reefs on the lagoon side were much smaller and there were no issues with surf inside the sheltered lagoon. For this reason, a lagoon landing was the safest and quickest landing spot.

The third step, the capture of Majuro Atoll, which lay 265 nautical miles southeast of Kwajalein, was critical, as it would protect the Allied lines of communication both within the Central Pacific area and to the South Pacific. It also provided a protected anchorage for an advanced naval force.[70] The plan called for the capture of this lightly defended island concurrently with the other landings. The planners had no clear idea of just how lightly defended the island was and were surprised when reconnaissance troops found just one Japanese soldier on the island and took the atoll without opposition.

Finally, the last step was accomplished handily. The three days of preliminary bombing completely destroyed the island. In fact, when viewing the rubble, the engineer units actually complained that they did not envision "the complete devastation of all enemy installations and materials which required the replacement of all facilities."[71] In other words, there was little left on the island that was usable. Furthermore, observers noted that even in the pillboxes that were not destroyed, the concussion from the bombs killed or injured the personnel inside. The few survivors who surrendered noted that "the continued bombardment . . . was very demoralizing."[72]

Intelligence

One of the reasons for taking the Gilberts before the Marshalls was to have a place from which to launch land-based photo reconnaissance, which was clearer and more detailed than the carrier-based equivalent.

This proved wise, as there was universal praise for the quality of the photos received by the attacking units. As Conolly stated in his final report, "Intelligence information, largely from interpretation of photographs taken from aircraft, proved accurate and adequate and was invaluable."[73]

However, the divisions did have some issues with the distribution of these photographs. In some cases, there were not enough sets to give to each of the landing teams. In others, the photos were not given to the landing force until a couple of days before the operation, leaving them scant time to compare the photos to their landing plans.[74] Schmidt spoke for all of the land-based forces when he said, "Ships were under the impression that the photographs were for them only and were hesitant to turn them over to the units which had real use for them."[75]

Another issue dealt with what the photographs did and did not show. While they were excellent at revealing enemy fortifications and defenses, they could not show hydrographic or tidal information.[76] In other words, the units had no idea how deep the water was or how treacherous the reefs were where they were going to land. After the debacle during the Tarawa landing, ground commanders were understandably skittish about trusting the tidal tables distributed by the navy.

This had been the purview of the new UDTs who, in addition to clearing underwater obstacles, were supposed to report on any tidal or topographic features found in the water leading up to the landing zone. In fact they had done just that, making a complete reconnaissance to within 50 yards of the beaches, but these reports were never distributed to the divisions.[77] Fortunately, this had no impact on the Marshalls operations and this error could be easily remedied before the next landing.

A further weakness was the continued lack of detailed maps. Furthermore, those available were not reproduced and distributed until a few days before the landings and many proved to be worthless as they were "incorrectly gridded [and] difficult to read."[78] This problem was compounded by the fact that almost all recognizable landmarks were leveled by three days of punishing fire. Therefore, units had little on which to orient themselves initially: a minor problem on a small atoll, but something that would have been a critical issue on a larger island or during a more protracted operation.

The final criticism was the lack of trained interpreters. While the marines carried a large contingent of Nisei, the army had no equivalent section.[79] For the first time, the landing forces captured a relatively large number of prisoners, all of whom needed to be interrogated. Without the ability to do that on site, it was necessary to transport the prisoners back to the naval vessels, losing valuable time on actionable intelligence. In fact, the forces in the Pacific had gotten so used to not capturing Japanese soldiers that they did not put much value on their intelligence officers once operations began. As one complained, "It is evident that some unit commanders do not appreciate the importance of combat intelligence and the functioning of their respective intelligence officers." Another complained of being employed as the regimental anti-termite officer during the day and only worked on intelligence activities at night.[80]

Training

A common complaint throughout all three operations—WATCHTOWER, GALVANIC, and FLINTLOCK—was that the training and rehearsal times were too short and that there was not enough time for training with joint and combined assets.[81] As Spruance observed, "The peculiarities of amphibious warfare require that detailed operational planning be accomplished well in advance to permit rehearsals stressing coordination."[82]

Although the 7th ID made a huge effort to conduct training with the tank and artillery units, the leadership still judged it inadequate and there remained a number of communications issues. Furthermore, the divisions noted that "It is highly important the army and navy personnel who work together be staged and trained together for an extended period of time prior to an operation . . . the non-availability of navy personnel and the frequent change in plans by CINCPAC [made it impossible]."[83]

This was a particular issue for the 4th MARDIV, which trained remotely from the rest of the invasion force. Yet, even the 7th ID, which was co-located in Hawaii with the V Corps, had little interaction with its higher headquarters during training. As Corlett bluntly stated, "To the best of my knowledge the CG of the V Amphibious Corps [Holland Smith] and his staff officers did not benefit the 7th Infantry Division . . . all of the above were conspicuous in their absence from the 7th Infantry training, except for one exercise afloat."[84]

Another area where the divisions noted training deficiencies was in small unit and night operations.[85] Commanders urged more attention be paid to developing the abilities of small unit leaders in order to operate more efficiently on the ground.[86] Corlett in particular noticed the inefficiency in assaulting only one lightly defended target at a time, noting:

> [In the] Training of small units, more problems should be conducted involving the simultaneous assault on two distinct lightly defended objectives. In the operation just completed, many instances occurred when a platoon might have been reducing two or more lightly held enemy strong points simultaneously, whereas, only part of the platoon was concentrating on a lone enemy position while the remainder of the platoon awaited its reduction before going on to the next.[87]

The marines also pointed out that small unit leaders needed to learn when to direct and when to lead. Both the marines and army also addressed the folly of ceding the night to the enemy, who favored counterattacks and infiltrations under cover of darkness.[88]

Finally, both divisions remarked on the inadequacy of the dress rehearsals due to lack of time, equipment, and personnel. Although the 7th ID had been able to conduct a couple of fairly robust rehearsals on manufactured training sites that closely resembled the actual island, the 4th MARDIV did not have the same luxury. Instead, their combat loading for the rehearsal was also their combat loading for the operation. As Schmidt noted, "The full benefit of two division rehearsals was not attained because of limitations as to landing areas, the necessity for conserving irreplaceable equipment and the impracticability of conducting full scale unloading problems."[89]

Casualties[90]

The total number of army troops on Kwajalein was 21,342 against approximately 5,112 Japanese soldiers. The 7th ID on Kwajalein suffered 177 killed and 1,037 wounded against 4,938 Japanese killed and 174 wounded or taken prisoner. This comes out to a kill ratio of 27.9 and casualty ratio of 4.1.

The 4th MARDIV had 20,104 marines against 3,563 Japanese. The marines on Roi-Namur suffered 195 killed and 545 wounded against 3,472 Japanese killed and 91 wounded/taken prisoner. This works out to a kill ratio of 17.8 and a casualty ratio of 4.7.

It is tempting to compare the casualty numbers in the Marshalls against those in the Gilberts and make assumptions about the abilities and wisdom of the tactics and commanders. However, that would be a false comparison as the marines on Tarawa, in particular, landed against some of the most determined resistance of the war. Instead, it can be argued that casualties were low in the Marshalls *because* of the Gilberts.

To begin with, the sheer amount of firepower poured onto Kwajalein and Roi-Namur dwarfed that on Tarawa. Furthermore, the leaders had learned just what type of munitions and what angles were required to destroy the Japanese fortifications. In fact, Corlett estimated that 50 to 75 percent of the enemy on Roi-Namur had been killed by air bombardment and naval gunfire before the marines even set foot on the island.[91]

Secondly, the men in the Gilberts faced specialized Japanese marines who had been fortifying their positions for years. By contrast, the troops in the Marshalls were a combination of Japanese army and Korean laborers. Although the area was fairly built up, as had been mentioned earlier, the fortifications were not as robust as those on Tarawa. Moreover the Japanese thought that the Americans would attack the outer atolls in the Marshalls first and focused their manpower and equipment accordingly.

However, it would not be amiss to compare the two islands in the Marshalls to each other, especially in light of Holland Smith's later criticisms of the army habit of slower, more deliberate operations in order to minimize casualties. First, the army was taking on the larger, more entrenched enemy than the marines. Second, not only was Kwajalein thickly forested, but it was also more highly fortified than Roi-Namur. Third, Kwajalein was more than twice the size of Roi-Namur. Finally, every commander must have been aware of the criticism leveled at the marines over the number of casualties at Tarawa and wished to avoid the image of American men being heedlessly sent into a death trap. In all, it appears that 7th ID was correct to take its time and minimize the casualties if it did not risk the success of the mission or endanger other forces. Nonetheless, that did not prevent Holland Smith from volubly bemoaning, "I could see no reason why this division, with ample forces ashore, well covered by land-based artillery and receiving tremendous naval and air support, could not take the island quicker."[92] He also wrote to Vandegrift, complaining that "the slow progress [of the army] has tried my soul."[93] It appears that nothing the army did would ever satisfy Holland Smith.

Commanders

The relative ease of operations in the Marshalls meant that no commanders were relieved and there was no need to look for blame. Instead the issues of command centered more on chain of command, as discussed earlier, and the positioning of commanders. Furthermore, the issues between Holland Smith and the army that had begun in the Gilberts continued to simmer. However, Smith found it much more difficult to talk poorly about Corlett, given the success of the operation with so few casualties and Corlett's natural combativeness. According to S. L. A. Marshall, at one of their early meetings Holland Smith criticized Ralph Smith to Corlett, who flatly stated, "Don't you ever talk about me that way." In another instance, during a press conference immediately after Kwajalein, Corlett overheard Smith criticizing the speed of the army operation and he felt compelled to break in and defend his soldiers. Corlett informed the reporters that Smith could not know about either battle since he was shipboard the whole time.[94]

Over time, Corlett continued to criticize Smith's leadership. Not only was he emphatic in his after-action review that the V Corps and its staff had done nothing to help in planning or training, but over the years he went out of his way to emphasize how little Smith had done for the operations. A perfect example was his letter to Lemuel Shepherd, then the Commandant of the Marine Corps:

> The corps commander issued a field order, pretty much a copy of the navy order . . . After that the corps commander or his staff did not contribute anything to the 7th Division plan, which included the amount and type of naval gun fire and air support and the complete logistical plan; prepared entirely by [Corlett] and his staff, which was submitted [to] Turner and his staff and to . . . Smith and his staff at a joined [sic] meeting and it was accepted by both . . . without changing one word of the plans and orders.[95]

Corlett had also been outspoken from the beginning about his unhappiness with being crammed onto the *Rocky Mount* with Smith and Spruance's staff.[96] As stated before, he preferred that Turner not be dual-hatted as the Assault Force Commander and Attack Force Commander, although in this particular operation it had worked out fine. In his opinion

> Where there are two or more main objectives, the over-all Naval Commander and Commanding General Expeditionary Troops should be boated together free to move where their presence is required. The Commander of the Land Force at each principal subordinate objective should be boated with his Naval Task Force Commander, who can devote all of his time and attention to the local objective.[97]

Further, Corlett was adamantly opposed to the need for a corps commander in such an operation, writing, "Where the land area is too small for the operation of two or more divisions, there appears to be no requirement for a corps overhead."[98]

The victory in the Marshalls also proved a professional jumping-off point for the ground commanders. In April 1944, Corlett took command of the XIX Corps and led them through D-Day, thereby earning the distinction of commanding in three separate theaters of the war.[99] At the end of the war, he commanded the XXXVI Corps and was planning the attack on the Japanese mainland. His three regimental commanders remained in the division, leading their regiments through the battles of Leyte and Okinawa.

As for the marines, Schmidt would lead the 4th MARDIV through Saipan and then replace Holland Smith as the V Corps commander. In fact, the entire leadership of 4th MARDIV stayed intact through Saipan, save the assistant division commander, James Underhill, who moved to Fleet Marine Force. He was replaced by the 25th Marine commander, Samuel Cumming.

LESSONS LEARNED

The various echelons of participants compiled no fewer than fourteen different lessons learned reports on the Gilberts. Unlike at Tarawa, a good many of the lessons were positive and mainly a validation of previous tactics and equipment. In fact, the V Corps report actually went as far as to say, "The cooperation and coordination of action in FLINTLOCK was the most satisfactory ever experienced . . . Progressively, naval and land forces are learning the problems of the other and the cooperation and coordination now realized is gratifying."[100] As Richardson wrote in his after-action review, "The successful establishment of bases in the Marshall Islands . . . at a relatively low cost in casualties and in a minimum of time demonstrated the fundamental soundness of the methods and tactics taught in preparation for and used in the whirlwind campaign".[101]

The first positive note sounded was the success of the indirect fire campaign. Not only did these fires allow substantially unopposed landings, they also assisted the landing forces as they moved inland by "destroying resistant targets, cratering and demolishing field fortifications and clearing foliage and undergrowth to open fields of fire and reduce enemy concealment."[102] By destroying the Japanese plan to stop the landing forces at the beaches, the Americans ended any chance the Japanese had to mount an organized defense. By contrast, the Americans had plenty of time to regroup before conducting coordinated attacks inland. In some cases, U.S. forces advanced three hundred yards or more before encountering enemy fire.[103] In fact, so thorough was the damage that survey teams coming in after the operation could not determine which type of munition was responsible for the damage of various targets.[104]

Interestingly, Holland Smith and his staff, who had been so opposed to Julian Smith's plan to land artillery on an island adjacent to Tarawa, now became one of the foremost proponents of this tactic, crediting it as one of the two main factors in capturing an objective with minimum casualties (with the other being the prolonged initial bombardment).[105] In fact, units at all levels recommended that this tactic be used whenever practicable and it would become a standard practice in other islands whenever there was an island near enough to the landing site.

As mentioned earlier, this operation saw the use of two new specialized units: UDTs and JASCO. Due to the lack of underwater obstacles, validation of the usefulness of the UDTs would have to wait until a later operation. However, the JASCOs were in place and received mixed reviews.

On the positive side, the army considered the concept of a JASCO a complete success. Having one team to coordinate all of the fires allowed the naval and artillery bombardments to last longer and come in closer.

The army praised the unit, claiming that "communication during the bombardment and assault phase were more successful than for similar periods of any previous operation, despite the magnitude and complexity of this operation."[106] Unlike at Tarawa where the troops had minimum support as they waded in, this coordination allowed naval gunfire to continue until the first wave was 300 yards from the beach and the artillery until they were only 200 yards away. Furthermore, the JASCOs continued to call in fire on the flanks and further inland throughout the rest of the landings.[107]

As with many other things, the criticism of the JASCO had to do with time. As a hastily assembled ad hoc unit, the JASCO did not arrive until just prior to rehearsals. In some cases, the JASCO units were poorly trained and equipped and required augmentation from the existing unit communications personnel.[108] This did not detract from their potential usefulness and the recommendation was that "each JASCO be given a thorough and rigid course in training prior to any operation with the emphasis placed on procedure drills with actual ships to increase the success of the communications."[109]

The first new piece of equipment introduced by the army, the DUKW, proved to be an unqualified success, as did the newly armored amtracs. The recommendation was that units use the DUKWs to move artillery and supplies, with the amtracs continuing to be used to move troops. The marines lamented their lack of DUKWs and requested them for future operations.[110] The army agreed, stating, "Procurement of these vehicles for use in future operations has been confirmed."[111]

The LCI gunboats also proved to be highly valuable to covering the landing forces. The only changes recommended by the divisions were larger caliber guns and more protection for the machine gunners.[112] The army pointed out that these new gunboats offered "at once an extremely effective striking force and a highly mobile and flexible reserve" and recommended the exploration of new uses for this equipment.[113]

The fixes for two other issues from the Gilberts proved to be less than successful.

The first, the attempt to waterproof the flamethrowers, was a complete failure. At Makin, the army proved the utility of flamethrowers in ferreting defenders out of tunnels, caves, and pillboxes. However, this essential tool was still too prone to water damage.[114] A further experiment in mounting the flamethrowers on tanks also proved to be less than helpful, since it was too hard to maneuver.

The final issue left over from the Gilberts was the lack of tank-infantry communications. The improvised telephone system was unsatisfactory for a variety of reasons, chiefly the fact that about half of them had been smashed in the landing craft or ruined by water during landing.[115] Some of those left working shorted out the tank inter-communication net, leaving the tanks unable to talk to each other. Even more dangerous was the fact that the vehicle and the infantryman had to halt to communicate with one another, holding up the advance and leaving the other troops exposed. For these reasons, the recommendation was to only use the phones in case of emergency.[116] However, this solution satisfied no one as it did not address the root of the problem—the inability to communicate—nor did it correct the issue. This would prove to be the one tactical weakness that was not resolved by the end of the war.

EFFECT ON FUTURE OPERATIONS

As Corlett correctly noted, "Each operation in the Pacific presents a separate and distinct tactical problem, requiring special troops, organizational equipment and training."[117] While generally true, the fact was that there would be no more changes to the basic doctrine and equipment during the rest of the war. While there would be small changes around the edges, the Marshalls had proved once and for all that the Americans had got it right. This was especially remarkable since amphibious tactical doctrine had been set in the 1930s and did not change appreciably throughout the war.

However, the fundamental character of future operations would change. Although there were still some "smaller scale" operations in Pelelieu and Iwo Jima, the operations in the Marianas and on Okinawa would harken back to Guadalcanal. No longer could the invading troops count on capturing an island in a matter of days. Instead, future invasions would be protracted operations. No longer could the divisions train and plan in isolation. As army and marine cooperation was required in combat, it was also necessary in training. Unfortunately, the combination of long distances and short timelines made this impossible and the services never did achieve this cooperative training.

With the mechanics of amphibious operations settled, the cultural differences between the two services began to assume more importance. This issue had been swimming around the edges of all the operations, particularly in the statements of Holland Smith, who had a clear antipathy for the army in general and Ralph Smith in particular. Without the buffer of parallel training, planning and operations, this issue would grow to consume relations between the two services. It would come to a head in the Marianas. This event continues to color historiography of that operation and, to a certain degree, of the entire history of joint ground operations.

— CHAPTER 4 —

SAIPAN:

Smith Versus Smith

After the relative ease of the Marshall operations, army and marine leaders believed they had mastered the technical details of amphibious landing operations. Armed with battle-tested equipment and battle-hardened troops, they collectively believed they were ready to tackle the key strategic element laid out in the 1943 Cairo Conference—the seizure of Guam and the Japanese Marianas—five months ahead of schedule.[1]

Unlike earlier landings involving the storming of atolls by relatively small forces, which ended in a matter of days, the Marianas would require weeks of slow painful ground operations conducted by several full combat divisions. For the first time since Guadalcanal, army and marine forces would fight side by side for an extended period. This close contact during the prolonged battle of Saipan exposed each service to the other's culture to a greater degree than any previous battle. Inevitably problems arose, as at the heart of marine doctrine was quick amphibious strikes followed by withdrawal for recuperation before moving on to the next island assault, while the army centered its doctrine on sustained ground operations over a period of weeks or months.

On Saipan, the inability of American senior leaders to understand and make use of the respective strengths of the various services had fateful and long-lasting consequences. Foremost among them was that prolonged exposure to each other coupled with the lack of technical issues to distract the individual service staffs allowed the ongoing personal feud between Holland Smith and the army to bubble to the surface. His low opinion of the army in general, and the 27th Infantry

Division in particular, meant he was continually on the lookout for an excuse that would allow him to remove what he viewed as weak leadership at the top. Unfortunately for the 27th Division's leaders, they gave him ample cause for action. The end result was the relief of General Ralph Smith, an event that came to overshadow the remarkable joint victory on Saipan. In fact, Ralph Smith's relief has colored all histories of the Pacific theater and threatened interservice cooperation for a generation.

STRATEGIC SETTING

At the Casablanca Conference in January 1943, Admiral King declared that short of invading their homeland, the Marianas were the key to defeating Japan.[2] Because of the lack of adequate anchorages, King's position was not universally supported by navy planners, although Nimitz did agree with him.[3] Claiming that the lack of anchorages was secondary to the importance of using the Marianas to interdict Japanese lines of communication, King stuck with his proposal. In this, he received support from the Air Force Chief, "Hap" Arnold, who coveted the Marianas as a heavy bomber base. Just 1,270 miles from Tokyo, well within the B-29's range, bases in the Marianas would allow Allied airpower to penetrate the Japanese inner defense perimeters.[4]

Backing King and Arnold was a study by the Joint Strategic Survey Committee that reinforced the idea that the Central Pacific was the main effort in the Pacific, with MacArthur's Southwest Pacific as the supporting theater.[5] The final decision was made at the Cairo Conference in December 1943, when Roosevelt and Churchill agreed to add the Marianas as a target, with an invasion target date of 1 November. However, as the victories along the Central Pacific proceeded ahead of schedule, Nimitz began pushing for the acceleration of planning and execution of the Marianas offensive, and that it officially be placed under his command. MacArthur had different ideas. Now that large naval forces were available in the Pacific, he thought the best use of the preponderance of them was to support his advances through the South and Southwest Pacific.

To avoid another interservice struggle, Marshall stepped in and recommended that the Joint Strategic Survey Committee conduct an analysis to determine whether to support operations through MacArthur's area before striking the Marianas or to make the Marianas the main effort.[6] The JSSC recommended the Marianas as the next major offensive target, but failed to address issues over the allocation of resources between the respective Pacific theaters.[7] Neither Nimitz nor MacArthur was satisfied with this outcome and both presented further proposals to the Joint Chiefs of Staff.

Finally, on 12 March 1944 the Joint Chiefs issued their new plan: the main objective would be the Marianas-Carolines-Palau-Mindanao starting with the occupation of the southern Marianas on 15 June. Moreover, the Central Pacific would receive the lion's share of available resources. Dubbed Operation FORAGER, it would be the largest amphibious operation in the Pacific to date, involving three landings, three marine divisions, a marine brigade and two army divisions.

Recognizing that the stress of continuous combat would be too much for any one staff, Nimitz hit upon the idea of alternating commanders. Spruance and Halsey would take command of the fleet in turn, falling in on the same set of ships and allowing their staffs planning and preparation time. When Spruance had command, it would be named the Fifth Fleet; under Halsey it would be the Third Fleet. This flipping of staffs would also have the added benefit of making the Japanese believe that the Americans had an additional fleet in the Pacific.[8]

The Marianas were originally a Spanish possession that the Germans purchased in 1899. The Japanese used the distraction of World War I to seize the islands along with the Marshalls and Palaus. After the war, the League of Nations formally granted the islands to Japan, with the exception of Guam, which became an American territory and housed a small naval garrison consisting of 153 marines and 271 sailors. Hours after the Pearl Harbor attacks, Japanese forces rectified this, launching 30,000 men ashore and quickly overrunning the small garrison.

Unlike the coral islands in the Gilberts and Marshalls, the Marianas, the northernmost islands in Micronesia, are a chain of fifteen volcanic islands. The ten northern islands in the chain possessed little military value, but three of the southern islands—Saipan, Tinian, and Guam— were centrally located in the Pacific theater and placed virtually every remaining Japanese territory—the Philippines, the Ryukyus, and the Home Islands—within range of American bombers.

Saipan, however, presented new tactical and operational problems. Unlike the previous invasion targets, not only was the island covered with limestone cliffs, caves, and thick vegetation, but 70 percent of it was under sugar cultivation. These sugarcane fields impeded movement, provided concealment for defenders, and contained all manner of disease-carrying insects and biting animals. The islands also contained relatively large civilian populations and numerous towns. These 30,000 civilians presented planners with a particularly thorny problem when they considered pre-landing bombardments. Furthermore, the specter of house-to-house fighting in the towns kept many of them awake nights.[9]

The landing beaches of all three islands presented a special challenge. They were ringed with coral reefs and narrow beaches, many of which ended in cliffs. On Saipan, those beaches that did not end in cliffs gave way to marshes or sugarcane fields. Moreover, along the center of the island was a jagged seven-mile-long ridgeline. On the southern end of the ridgeline rose Mount Tapotchau. On the northern end was Mount Marpi. Both mountains dominated the area in between, offering the Japanese a clear view and unfettered fields of fire over the Americans advancing down the valley—soon to earn the nickname "Death Valley."

The best landing beaches ran down the western coast, which also contained the major towns, including the three largest on the island: Charan Kanoa, Garapan, and Tanapang. Additional military targets included three airfields: Aslito Airfield on the southern part of the island; the Charan Kanoa, a strip on the west coast; and a third unnamed strip at the north end of the island. Planners could count on the use of a robust road network in the south, but even this small advantage would end as the invasion force moved north.[10]

OPERATIONAL PLANNING

The operation was larger than any other planned in the Pacific up to that point, involving three separate landings: the Northern Attack force would land first on Saipan and, once they secured the island, move on to Tinian; during this time the Southern Attack Force would land on Guam. Three separate objectives, to be assaulted by two separate landing forces, ensured that the command structure would be somewhat complex. As with all other landings in the Central Pacific drive, Nimitz was the overall commander and it was Spruance's turn to command the fleet. As in past operations, Turner was dual-hatted as both the Expeditionary Task Force commander and the Northern Attack Force commander. Finally under him was Holland Smith. As during past operations, he was the commander of the expeditionary troops and responsible for the amphibious training of the landing forces. Marine General Roy Geiger, commander of the III Amphibious Corps, had the same responsibility for the forces scheduled to attack Guam.

Unlike past operations, however, upon landing on Saipan, tactical command would pass to Smith rather than to the landing force division commander. This meant that Smith, for the first (and last) time, would actually land on the island and direct tactical operations beyond the initial landing. Some of the army's leadership in the Pacific questioned whether he was up to the task—doubts shared by a number of marines—as operations were likely to be a drawn-out affair. This ran counter to the marine doctrine of accepting high initial casualties in exchange for a rapid conclusion to the fight. Saipan was not the kind of fight marines specialized in and there was nothing in Smith's makeup that led army officers to believe that he could adapt to the new realities of the Pacific Campaign.

As if the command relationships were not tough enough, Smith decided to add new complexities to the structure. Once the operations on Saipan were completed, he planned to pass tactical control for the invasion of Tinian over to Harry Schmidt, commander of the 4th Marine Division. But since Smith retained his position as commander of all marines in the Central Pacific he also dictated that once combat operations on Saipan ended, he would move to oversee Schmidt's force and Geiger's corps during their respective landings on Tinian and Guam. However he would not hold a tactical command for those operations, instead reverting to the administrative command he had held in earlier operations.

Nimitz set the date for the landings on Saipan on 13 April—providing Holland Smith and his staff just two months to plan and train for the largest and most complex amphibious operation in marine history. Smith immediately split his staff in half to reflect his dual roles: the Red Staff functioned as the Northern Landing Force staff (Saipan and Tinian) and the Blue Staff served as Headquarters Expeditionary Force staff. Although touted as truly "joint," there were actually few army officers on the staff. Although army officers headed up the intelligence and logistics staffs, there were no army officers in the G-3 (operations) section responsible for actually writing the tactical plan.[11] Thus, from the beginning, the plan was geared towards the marine tactical mindset and objectives were set on the preferred rapid marine timeline with little concern for conditions on the ground. With this in mind, Holland Smith planned to secure the island in three days and then attack Guam.

In fact, Holland Smith hoped to not use the army at all. He later exulted, "For the first time we were to operate in the field as organic units instead of a joint command. We were a marine field army, commanded by a marine general, going into action independently."[12] With this mindset, it must have galled Holland Smith to have to utilize the 27th ID when his beloved marines got bogged down on the island.

When completed, the plan called for the 2nd and 4th Marine Divisions to land adjacent to one another, while the 27th Division remained as a floating reserve, ready to land wherever needed. The 77th Division, still in Hawaii, was available should things go badly, although it would take some weeks for it to arrive. After the conclusion of major combat operations and with the island then secured, the army would provide the garrison for Saipan, while the marines would garrison Tinian.

Because of the combination of reefs and cliffs, there were a limited number of beaches suitable for landings. With few options that could accommodate a two-division front, the staff finally decided on the southwestern beaches. Two regiments of the 2nd MARDIV would land to the north and two regiments of the 4th MARDIV would land south of them. The dividing line between the divisions would be the town of Charan Kanoa, which contained large sugar refineries, whose rail lines connected it to a large number of sugar plantations.[13] After landing, the plan called for the 2nd MARDIV to advance across the island to secure Mount Tapotchau and Magicienne Bay before heading north. The 4th MARDIV would capture Aslito Airfield and Nafutan Point.

Pre-combat Training

In the few short months between the end of the Marshalls operation and the beginning of FORAGER, the marine divisions, in response to lessons-learned in prior operations, underwent a significant reorganization. The intent was to streamline the divisions in order to allow them to focus on offensive tactical operations. Each division was reduced by 2,500 men and those removed then became part of new, separate 535-man amphibious tractor battalions attached to corps headquarters. These tractor battalions were available to support a division's landing and logistical operations, but the division no longer concerned itself with the administrative burden of supporting those units. Moreover, the creation of the corps artillery and provisional engineering group placed the burden of shore party operations on the corps rather than the landing force.[14] In addition, they disbanded the "special troops" units within each division, such as the naval construction battalion, special weapons battalion, and scout company.

There were also numerous equipment changes in response to the after-action reports. The most notable was that medium tanks replaced the light tanks used in earlier operations. Furthermore, the universal praise for flamethrowers in earlier operations resulted in a ten-fold increase of the portable variety from 24 to 243 and the addition of 24 tank-mounted flamethrowers per division. The divisions also lost a number of howitzers, but received a greater number of mortars and automatic rifles, resulting in greater overall firepower capability.[15]

Altogether Smith had two marine divisions (the 2nd and the 4th), an army division (the 27th), and a marine brigade at his disposal. These divisions, with the exception of a few battalions of the 27th Division, had all been battle-tested in island warfare. In fact, the only unit that had not been tested under fire was Smith's corps staff.[16] At the time of the operations, the 2nd and 4th Marine Divisions had undergone reorganization. However, with all of their reinforcements and attachments, each division possessed approximately 22,000 marines assigned, not counting supporting units. Furthermore, the replacements had been trained by veterans who were rotated back through training units. By contrast, the 27th Infantry Division, fully reinforced, had only 16,400 soldiers. Oddly, the V Corps plan did not issue any instructions for training. As a result, each division established its own priorities and conducted its own training.

Astonishingly, neither Holland Smith nor his staff conducted any inspections of the divisions or their training. Considering that these divisions would have to operate on the ground together and that the differences between army and marine tactics had caused friction in the past, this lack of centrally directed and supervised training is surprising. Given Holland Smith's vocal criticisms of the 27th ID leaders and soldiers, one would expect that he would want his staff to oversee their training in Oahu. On the positive side, however, Smith did ensure that the corps staff underwent an intensive training program, which included participation in a simulated landing exercise.[17]

2nd Marine Division "Follow Me"

Of all the units participating in FORAGER, the 2nd MARDIV, after its bruising operations on Guadalcanal and Tarawa, had the most experience. Its marines had taken the worst the enemy could throw at them and emerged victorious, making it the logical choice to lead the landings. While its least experienced regiment, the 4th Marines, had not participated in a large landing as a unit, most of its men were former raiders who had extensive experience in jungle operations.[18]

In April, General Thomas Watson took command of the division. He had served in the War Plans Division and commanded the 3rd Marine Brigade in Samoa. When the brigade deactivated in November 1943, Watson moved to command of Tactical Group One and led the assault on Eniwetok Atoll as part of the Marshall Islands campaign. Watson was nicknamed "Terrible Tommy" for his legendary impatience: a fellow marine general commented, "He would not tolerate for one minute stupidity, laziness, professional incompetence, or failure in leadership . . . His temper in correcting these failings could be fiery and monumental."[19]

Watson's principal training emphasis was ensuring his small unit leaders were adept at handling the unit's new tactical organization. The old 12-man rifle squads were increased by one man and then divided into three four-man rifle teams (plus a squad leader) with increased organic firepower, all of which improved the squad's flexibility on contact with the enemy. However, despite focusing on individual and small unit tactics, the division also made time for combined arms training at all levels up to division, culminating in two-and-a-half weeks of amphibious training exercises that included all division elements.[20]

These exercises were plagued with accidents. During one rehearsal heavy seas caused the cables holding three LCTs to break free and the vehicles fell overboard. Two LCTs were lost, along with twenty-five marines killed or injured. In addition to the human cost, the sunken LCTs went down with the mortars that Watson had designated to protect his flanks as the 2nd MARDIV moved inland. To make up for this loss of firepower, Turner decided to escalate planned rocket barrages on the beach defenses, in the hope that the increased preliminary fires would inflict sufficient damage on the Japanese defenders so that they would not be able to coordinate flank attacks on the advancing marines. Rather than risk losing any more mortars during training, Turner ordered all landing craft carrying mortars to return to Pearl Harbor.

In another incident, a round exploded while being unloaded and set off a string of explosions that enveloped six fully loaded LSTs, resulting in over 500 more casualties. Fortunately, the division was able to replace materiel and personnel losses rapidly and the invasion convoy sailed only one day behind schedule.[21] Considering that there had been just three LSTs available for Tarawa, the fact that the navy could now replace six on short notice was nothing short of astounding. Still, however easily the equipment was changed, the loss of 500 trained combat marines was potentially devastating.[22] Although the divisions received replacements, these marines were not adequately trained on the equipment or familiar with the landing plan. Despite training every available moment during the journey they were still far below the standards set by the rest of the division.[23]

4th Marine Division "Fighting Fourth"

The experiences of the 4th MARDIV on Roi-Namur could not compare to what the 2nd MARDIV had faced, but it did provide a certain level of combat experience. In the absence of a training directive, or even training facilities and aids, the division first focused on restoring disciplinary and physical standards, while constructing improvised training sites.[24] Even after finally receiving a training directive from V Corps on 3 March, the division found itself plagued by inadequate training facilities, poor weather, insufficient transportation, and delayed equipment replacement, all of which cut into available training time and significantly impaired the division's preparations.

As unit training continued at a delayed pace, the division staff focused on operational planning, which was accomplished in close coordination with their supporting units and the 2nd MARDIV. After gaining corps approval of their basic plan, the staff issued new training guidance and schedules refocused on the tasks required to make the plan successful.

Still making do with inadequate equipment and facilities, the division conducted a wide variety of training exercises through battalion and regimental combined arms operations. Its leaders also began tackling the thorny problem of ensuring the troops received sufficient training and rehearsal time for the conduct of landing operations, while also training on the tasks that were crucial for success in prolonged operations once ashore, including long-range operations.[25] Not used to long ground operations, planners did not appreciate the complexity of the task facing the division and their training guidance would in certain critical respects be inadequate. Afterwards the major complaint coming from the division's marines was that too much training time focused on patrolling and not enough on setting up defensive positions.[26] This is surprising given the emphasis Chesty Puller and his team had placed on defensive preparations during their tour of training bases.

Remembering the infantry-tank communications problems suffered on Namur, the unit gave special attention to its training as part of a unified team. Infantry commanders received all available training time to rehearse how they should control tanks in combat, a program made that much harder due to the division's tank battalion not receiving all of its assigned tanks until immediately prior to the unit's departure. Despite the lack of actual tanks for training, the tank battalion managed to run a school for infantry officers that at least provided them with rudimentary knowledge about the capabilities, limitations, and tactical uses of tanks. Unfortunately, all of this excellent training was for naught, as none of the officers assigned to attend the classes ended up in positions where they would ever have to exercise control of the tank units.[27]

One of the most useful training exercises was known as DUCKBILL, during which the division was given a general task organization, plan of attack, and intelligence that would apply to the actual operation and conducted a full study and planning session. Units down to the battalion level produced operations orders and thus provided staffs some needed experience in planning under conditions that were evolving and with limited information. In other words, exactly what they would have to deal with in the chaotic conditions of combat. Since the officers had the general outlines of the operation, many of the issues resolved during the exercise saved time when doing the actual planning phase.[28]

27th Infantry Division "O'Ryan's Roughnecks"

Up until this point in the war, the 27th Division had been broken up and used piecemeal during various operations. Not only did this mean that the division had no experience fighting as a cohesive unit, but it also limited the time available for training. Divided for operations on Makin, Eniwetok, and Majuro, the division did not reunite on Oahu until a scant two months before the scheduled invasion of Saipan.[29] Thus, it was as if three random regiments had been thrown together and the division had no chance to develop the esprit and trust that comes from training and fighting together.

Despite some changes within the staff, the leadership of the 27th ID remained essentially the same as it had since the beginning of the war. This meant that all nine battalion commanders and two of three regimental commanders were still New York National Guard officers.[30] The lack of regular army officers had caused minimal issues during earlier operations, which had involved no more than a regiment at any one time. However, in longer operations, discipline and tactical expertise come to the fore as battlefield necessities. Unfortunately, for reasons previously discussed, National Guard leaders, even those with combat experience, were often reluctant to enforce necessary disciplinary measures on men they frequently knew in the civilian world, nor did they possess the tactical expertise typical of regular army officers.[31] For example, most of the staff principals (notably the division G-2 (intelligence), G-3 (operations) and G-4 (logistics) lacked the formal schooling in their functional areas that regular army officers had received as a matter of course. Moreover, there was little training time available to remedy these deficiencies. A weak division staff put the 27th ID at a disadvantage and placed their commander, Ralph Smith, behind the power curve from the start of operations.[32]

Lessons learned in recent operations did drive the training to focus primarily on small unit tactics, night maneuvers, and combined arms operations. Mindful of the hardships faced by units on Guadalcanal, when the landing forces found themselves essentially abandoned for over 30 days, the leaders placed an emphasis on physical conditioning, identification of edible plants, personal hygiene, and first aid.[33] Smith also considered it especially important for the troops to embark at peak physical conditioning, as there would be limited opportunities for physical

training during the 15–24 days on cramped ships.[34] Previous experience
had shown how much conditioning men could lose in that time and a long
campaign would push the men to the limits of their physical endurance.

In conjunction with the navy, the division did conduct advanced
amphibious training, although the soldiers never embarked in the alligators or landing craft because of the fear of damaging them. This culminated in a large scale, multiday rehearsal with the actual transport ships
that would take them to the objective. The division staff also conducted
two joint staff exercises with their navy counterparts to ensure that all
parties understood the accepted procedures and rehearsed the coordination of interservice staff work. In fact, the army troops worked and
rehearsed in conjunction with everyone except the marines with whom
they would actually be fighting.[35]

Designated as the operation's floating reserve, the 27th ID had no
idea when and where it might be called on to land. As a result, the staff
drew up 21 separate plans of action. The three most likely, and therefore
the most detailed, plans concerned supporting the landings on Saipan or
Guam or leading the assault on Tinian. However, throughout the division's preparation period, the uncertainty as to where it would find itself
employed not only complicated training activities, but also made the
combat loading of the ships a guessing game, since what equipment a
landing force would need first depended on which beach they landed.[36]
Furthermore, the division's operational planning was conducted largely in
an informational vacuum. As of 12 May, the division had still not received
any hydrographic information or a detailed map of the island. Indeed, the
division did not receive any photos of the potential landing beaches until
26 May, just days before it set sail.[37]

Even more difficult was the attitude the division faced from the
operational commander, Holland Smith. He later stated, "After my
experience with the 27th at Makin and Eniwetok, I was reluctant to use
them again in the Marianas, but . . . they were the only troops available and I had to take them."[38] He also made claims that "except for
his own personal leadership of front line elements at Makin, the attack
of . . . the 27th Division would have been unsuccessful."[39] Considering
that he only landed the day before the 27th secured Makin, it is doubtful his presence or leadership had any bearing on the outcome. General
Sanderford Jarman, who was slated to be the garrison commander once

Saipan was secured, observed, "H. M. Smith on various occasions indicated . . . that he did not believe the 27th Infantry Division would fight, that he had no confidence in their ability to do a job."[40] This makes the aforementioned failure of Holland Smith and his staff to visit the unit training even more remarkable.

So it was that the 27th ID departed for Saipan on 1 June, without any clear idea of where it would land or what was expected of it, and saddled with a staff and senior leadership that if not quite incompetent, was not of the highest quality. Moreover, they were going to fight under a corps commander who had no faith in their combat ability. It also had escaped the corps staff's notice that the division's training had been rushed and, given their nebulous mission, was not as focused as that of other units scheduled for the operation. This would show especially in the 105th Regiment, which was in combat for the first time and had never conducted a landing. Their slow landing and unloading of equipment resulted in congestion and the temporary loss of their equipment. Finally, it was not until the division was at sea that the leadership revealed the ultimate target and began briefing the soldiers on the particulars of the operation, at least, as much of the particulars as possible, given that the division leaders still had no idea how Holland Smith would employ the unit on reaching the Marianas. The combination of these factors greatly increased the possibility that the 27th ID was a fiasco in the making.

OPERATIONS

Enemy Operations

The Japanese also understood the strategic importance of the Marianas, and the Commander in Chief of the Combined Fleet, Admiral Koga, chose Saipan as his northern headquarters (his southern headquarters were in the Philippines). He vowed to stop the Allies east of the Marianas-Carolines line.[41] Along with a buildup of troop concentrations on Saipan, the Japanese undertook an ambitious plan to construct airfields and fortifications, the latter focused on the beachheads, as they had on earlier, smaller islands.

In keeping with the Japanese strategy of doing everything possible to defeat invaders on the beach, they built the majority of the defensive positions on probable landing sites. As in the past, they covered the beaches by machine guns, anti-boat and anti-tank guns and mortars while emplacing most of these weapons in natural caves and coral formations as well as concrete pillboxes typical of what the marines had encountered on other islands. However, there were also a large number of hastily constructed positions, included some made of sandbags.[42]

Unfortunately for the defenders, these beach defenses were inadequate for the defense of an island the size of Saipan, as they did not extend far inland. Once the Americans punched through the beachhead, all of the carefully laid-out defensive works were for naught. When the Americans broke through the crust of defenses, the defenders scattered and were forced to use hastily improvised shelters in the numerous caves on the islands. This scattering was the primary reason the Japanese were never able to launch a large coordinated counterattack, but rather had to fall back on small unit attacks.

The original defensive plans had called for various layers of defenses. Unfortunately for Japanese prospects, the layers beyond the beach were never constructed. A Japanese officer later confessed that the inadequate defenses were a result of the various ships carrying concrete and steel for this purpose being sunk en route to the island. Furthermore, the Japanese did not expect that the Americans would land before November, so the island commander thought he had five more months to work on the island's bulwarks.[43]

There were attempts to hamper the American advance through the use of land and sea mines, coupled with crude booby traps, although the latter proved to be more nuisances than anything else. The Japanese emplaced the mines on the landing beaches "by the book" in terms of pattern and density, but failed to arm the majority of them before the Americans' surprise arrival and landing. The sea mines, which the Japanese placed after the UDT reconnaissance, were numerous, but most suffered seawater damage and failed to detonate. Further inland, obstacles were more haphazardly placed, barely concealed, and poorly improvised.[44]

The most formidable obstacle on the island turned out to be the terrain. The cane fields, marshes and mountainous topography slowed down dismounted troops and canalized vehicles onto the island's few, poorly constructed roads. Many times, American tanks were slowed to a crawl and unavailable to support infantry attacks.[45] Nevertheless, because the cohesion of the Japanese units collapsed after the Americans established themselves and broke through the beach defense, they were never able to make full use of the terrain. Unable to coordinate defenses and establish a coherent line that could make use of interlocking fields of fire and pre-planned fire-support from mortars and artillery, the Japanese defense degenerated into a series of individual holding positions. Of course, given the Japanese commitment to fanatical defense, these proved a brutal enough obstacle when the Americans encountered them.[46]

Indeed, within a week of the American landings, it became obvious to the defenders they were not going to be reinforced, resupplied, or evacuated. Realizing that all that was possible was a postponement of the inevitable, the Japanese accepted that their only option was a slow, grinding battle of attrition, in the hope of killing as many Americans as possible. However, the Japanese military leadership recognized that its rigid adherence to outdated tactical rules was affecting the ability of their soldiers to counter the Americans. An enemy paper captured on Leyte later in the war referenced lessons learned from Saipan and admonished, "If we persist in employing the inflexible and stereotyped methods used up to now, the enemy will have the upper hand."[47] Despite this acknowledgement, the Japanese commanders seemed unable to deviate from the norm and time and again they veered back to familiar, if unsuccessful, tactics.

Saipan did present the Americans with one more major complication and the ruthless Japanese occupiers with one great defensive advantage: Saipan was the first contested island in the Central Pacific that had a large civilian population. As the Japanese had no compunction in using civilians as human shields and preventing them from surrendering, they were able to use American concerns over the fate of noncombatants to hamper U.S. fires and maneuver significantly. Many times, entire amphibious tractor battalions were removed from their combat duties to rescue civilians holed up in caves that were only accessible by water.[48] Despite repeated announcements by interpreters assuring them of their safety, the Japanese brainwashing of the population resulted in one of the most shocking and horrifying episodes of the war—one that would haunt even the most hardened veteran.

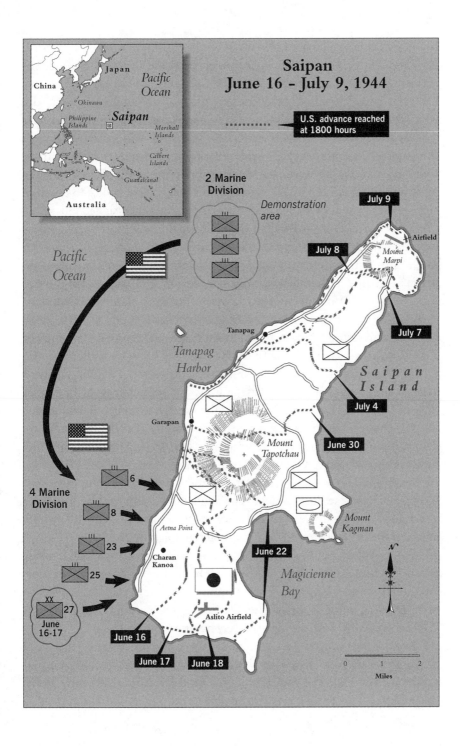

Saipan
June 16 – July 9, 1944

Landing Operations [49]

As the convoys sailed from Hawaii, over 300 men from the underwater demolitions teams (UDT) swarmed the reefs to look for underwater obstacles and determine their topography. Not only did they verify the lack of obstacles, but the UDTs determined the reefs were relatively flat and two-to-four-feet underwater. This meant the various landing craft such as the DUKWs and LVTs could easily cross the reefs without track or by gaps blown by explosive.[50] Having gained such familiarity with the underwater terrain, the UDT members were the logical choice to pilot the control vessels that guided assault boats through their assigned lanes.

Meanwhile, four days before the scheduled landings, the naval bombardment began, with focus on the aircraft and Japanese facilities on the islands. The bombardment actually commenced a day earlier than planned thanks to excellent sailing weather that brought Admiral Marc Mitscher's TF-58 in range of the islands earlier than planned. Despite his early morning arrival in attack position, Mitscher waited until afternoon to launch his first air attack, hoping to surprise an enemy accustomed to American air armadas hitting them at dawn.

The surprise was total. The first sweep destroyed over 200 Japanese aircraft sitting on Saipan's, Tinian's, and Guam's airfields against a loss of only twelve American aircraft. In this, the Japanese were actually lucky—just ten days earlier there had been over 500 aircraft on the three islands. The other 300 aircraft were temporarily spared destruction when the high command ordered them to New Guinea to support operations there. However, the loss was still devastating, both in terms of equipment and morale. A Japanese diary noted, "For about two hours the enemy planes ran amuck and finally left leisurely. Amidst the unparalleledly inaccurate antiaircraft fire. All we could do was watch helplessly."[51]

It is doubtful that the ensuing naval fire that day did as much damage for several reasons. Not only had new fast battleships and their target spotters not received training in proper shore bombardment, but, in order to stay out of the range of shore batteries, the ships were forbidden to come in closer than 10,000 yards, which severely hampered their accuracy.

For the next several days, the air attacks continued against Saipan and all the nearby islands, ensuring that there would be no Japanesee aircraft replacements. Thus the Americans possessed air dominance throughout the landings, a luxury not always available in the past. Although protecting the landings and softenening up the Japanese defenders remained a top priority, the naval air forces scored their biggest coup when they sighted two convoys leaving the area. They promptly sank twenty Japanese ships and 30,000 tons of supplies. Despite several days of intense pounding, however, aerial photographs revealed that the naval bombardments still had not destroyed a number of big defensive positions. Saipan's sheer size, the lack of time, superb Japanese camouflage, and the mobility of the enemy's major weapons all conspired to negate the hoped-for effects of the American bombardment. When the marines came ashore they would find most of the defenses still intact, particularly the sturdy coconut log and concrete shelters that appeared untouched. On the positive side, the bombardment had cut most of the communications lines between Japanese positions, making it impossible to coordinate their actions. It also forced the defenders to move their mobile artillery pieces off the beach and place them on the reverse slope of the nearest hill, where they were less effective against the landing troops and their ships.[52] As a bonus, the large naval shells obliterated most of the fixed anti-aircraft sites.

Despite the relative lack of physical damage, the naval bombardment took a significant psychological toll on the defenders. One of the Japanese soldiers wrote in his diary, "I have at last come to the place where I will die . . . Naval gunfire supporting this attack is too terrible for words." Many commanders worried that their troops' nerves could not stand up to the constant shelling and ordered them to withdraw back to caves dotting the interior hills. A prisoner of war later admitted that the original plan called for a beach defense supported by artillery and mortars, but that the naval shelling had been too heavy and had forced the troops to move east. A Japanese commander noted, "Only thoroughly trained troops can be expected to withstand resolutely the fierce enemy shellings and bombings . . . It is regrettable that very many of the troops now scatter and get out of hand in these situations."[53]

In order to divert Japanese attention from the actual landing sites, the 2nd Regimental Combat Team (2nd MARDIV) and 1st Battalion, 29th Marines conducted a mock landing north of the actual landing beaches, near the town of Garapan. The marines embarked in boats, went to within 5,000 yards of the beach and circled for ten minutes. They received no enemy fire and soon returned to their ships. A captured Japanese intelligence officer admitted that there was a Japanese regiment in the area, but the commander did not think the landing would actually be there and so did not commit his troops. In fact, the concentrated shelling, UDT surveillance, and propaganda leaflets dropped near Charan Kanoa told the Japanese where the landings were likely to occur (as indicated by the artillery target flags the Japanese placed on the reef). However, since the Japanese considered the beaches of Magicienne Bay on the northeast side of the island to be the best and most likely landing site, the command split its forces and positioned a signficant amount of combat power overlooking those beaches, just in case they had guessed incorrectly.[54]

In the meantime, in the early morning of 15 June, the actual landing forces sat in their LSTs approximately 4,250 yards from the landing beaches and waited for the signal to commence landing operations a few minutes past 0800. For thirty minutes over 150 planes drenched the beaches with harassing fire intended to demoralize the enemy. The plan called for these strafing attacks to move inland as the troops landed. Naval fire had been landing since 0530 that morning. At 0730 the ships would shift from pre-planned inland targets to providing close fire support for the landing forces. The plan called for heavy guns to fire until the landing forces were 1,000 yards from the beaches and smaller guns would continue until the troops were 300 yards offshore.

The first wave of landings began, just 10 minutes behind schedule and under moderate gunfire, in an orderly fashion. From north to south, in the 2nd MARDIV area the 6th Marines hit RED beach and the 8th GREEN beach; in the 4th MARDIV sector the 23rd Marines landed on BLUE and the 25th on YELLOW. As soon as the LVTs crossed the reef, the Japanese opened up with automatic weapons, artillery, and mortars and sent the orderly formations into chaos.

Throughout the 2nd MARDIV area all formation integrity further broke down when a navy guideboat went off course and forced the entire line to shift north, causing the center to become badly crowded. The reason for this drift has been variously attributed to compass error, strong currents, and heavy gunfire from the south, although none of these can be definitively proved as the cause. Adding to the problems, the landing craft that put the first wave ashore became entwined with the following wave in its run for shore, throwing them into confusion. By the time the final wave came ashore at 1105 AM—two hours late—6th Marine casualties had already reached 35 percent.

The dividing line betweent the two divisions was Afetna Point. However, due to the drift north by the 2nd MARDIV a wide gap developed between the two divisions that would not be closed for three days. The 8th Marines were supposed to capture the point on the first day, but when they landed, the troops equipped with short-range weapons such as flamethrowers and bazookas were scattered and unable to form up until the next day to capture the point. Matters were less chaotic on the 4th MARDIV beaches, the area of which included the town of Charan Kanoa. Although opposition from the town itself was surprisingly light, overall resistance was sufficiently stiff to prevent a coordinated marine advance. Soon after coming ashore the advance broke down, as a number of small units engaged in their own isolated fights along the line.

As night fell, more than 20,000 marines had landed, occupying a beachhead 10,000 yards long and 1,000 yards deep. Although the landing forces had sustained over 2,000 casualties and occupied only two-thirds of their objectives, the landings were still judged sucessful as the marines were ashore to stay. Part of the floating reserve from the 2nd and 25th Marines had landed as did Watson and Schmidt, who were now directing tactical operations for their respective divisions. Although it would be six days until the marines totally secured the beachhead, the landing forces had a toehold. Over the next weeks a continuous stream of men and equipment would flood onto that beach as the marines pushed slowly forward. Turner observed, "The Saipan landing . . . was the most difficult of any I personally witnessed during the war. The men who made it . . . were, on the whole, better organized and better trained than for any other landing."[55]

Battle Summary[56]

All through that long first night the various units braced for a Japanese counterattack. No two battalions faced the same conditions, so defensive plans varied widely. For example, the units in Charan Kanoa conducted patrols throughout the night to ensure that no Japanese could infiltrate the gap between the divisions. On the extreme right flank of the 25th Marines where Agingan Point remained in Japanese hands, the marines had to worry about being flanked, so they set up a strong defensive perimeter. By contrast, the front of the 23rd Marines revealed an open plain with no Japanese infantry in sight, which allowed them to mark their fields of fire and get more rest than other regiments. In the 2nd MARDIV sectors, small unit attacks came every hour, which the marines believed were probing attacks searching for weak points in the line. But at 0300, a full-scale attack with supporting fire struck the 2nd Marine sector. The attack lasted for several hours until it was finally broken by crushing American artillery fire. Daylight showed more than 700 Japanese bodies along the line. Other than some small infiltrating groups, which were soon mopped up, no large unit of Japanese had broken through. On that first full day after the landings, the marines concentrated on consolidating their gains and achieving the objectives left undone during the landings. By the evening, the units straggled along the line designated O-1 (Objective-1).

Holland Smith remained offshore in his command ship, trying to piece together a picture of the battle from reports and air observers. Added to his stress were submarine reports of a large force of enemy ships moving towards the Marianas that would be in position to attack by D+2 (17 June). In light of this, Spruance indefinitely postponed the landings on Guam scheduled for D+3 and halted unloading of supplies on Saipan at dusk of 17 June. The majority of the transport vessels were then ordered to move east of Saipan, out of harm's way. Additionally, portions of the Saipan bombardment group moved west to confront the advancing Japanese, while Spruance ordered Mitscher to discontinue air operations over Saipan in favor of night searches.

The crucial question was what to do with the 27th Division, which had arrived on 16 June. It was resolved in favor of landing two of its regiments immediately. The final regiment—the 106th—would remain in floating reserves in support of the postponed Guam invasion. Ralph Smith sent one of his remaining two regiments, the 165th, ashore near Charan Konoa. From there the soldiers moved into the line on the right flank of the 4th MARDIV.

The 165th came ashore in total darkness on the night of 16 June. The soldiers found the 4th MARDIV rear area in a confused state, which they promptly worsened. The regiment had landed in scattered packets all along the beach and it was slow work gathering the soldiers while trying not to interfere with ongoing 4th MARDIV operations. However, even after he had his forces assembled, the regimental commander, Colonel Gerard Kelley, had no idea what their mission was. It was not until 0330 that the 4th MARDIV chief of staff informed Kelley that he was expected to be ready to attack and seize Aslito Airfield at 0730. Fortunately, the Japanese attacks in this sector had been relatively light that evening, allowing the regiment to move into line relatively undisturbed.

It had not been a quiet night, however, in the 2nd MARDIV sector. That night, the Japanese launched 44 medium tanks to attack from the east, while a second force attacked on foot along the road from Garapan. The objective of both elements was the Saipan radio station, about 400 yards behind the 6th Marines. Given that the 2nd Division was still recovering from the losses and trauma of the landing, the Japanese stood a fair chance of success had their attacks not been so disorganized. Instead of a large massed attack, the Japanese attacked in piecemeal fashion, which allowed the marines, who made liberal use of supporting artillery and naval gunfire, to repel each attack in turn. When dawn broke, at least 25 enemy tanks lay smoldering.

With that same dawn the 165th Infantry moved out to capture Aslito Airfield, which lay about 1,600 yards away. However, along those yards lay a small village, several cane fields and a ridge that reached 180 feet in height. Japanese entrenched along that ridge could cover every step of the advance with murderous fire. Despite these conditions, by the end of the day, the 165th had closed to with 200 yards of the target. Although it appeared unoccupied, Kelley decided to wait until morning to sweep across the airfield. He was afraid that an immediate assault would spread his battalions too thin and place him in a poor position to fend off possible Japanese counterattacks during the night. In contrast, the 25th Marines to the immediate north had a much easier time during its advance, although Japanese resistance grew stronger even further north along the line of advance. As a result of the uneven advances, the evening began with a narrow gap between the 165th Infantry and the 25th Marines and a large one between the two marine divisions' sectors.

The next day, Holland Smith landed, as did Ralph Smith and the 105th Infantry. However, due to slow unloading, an air raid warning, and the anticipated arrival of the Japanese fleet, the transport ships quickly moved to the east side of the island, where they would remain until 25 June. Only then would they finish landing all of the regiment's personnel and equipment. Thus, the 105th had to make do for over a week with almost no communications equipment and without much of its regimental staff, which was trapped on shipboard when the fleet weighed anchor.

On a happier note, by the time the 105th was ashore its sister regiment, the 165th, had seized the abandoned Aslito Airfield, which they immediately rechristened "Conroy Field" in memory of their former regimental commander who had fallen at Makin.

By the evening of 18 June, the Americans occupied most of the island's southern part, save Nafutan Point, and had effectively cut it in half. The plan now called for the marines to pivot north, while the 105th and 165th completed mopping up operations in Nafutan. The night was relatively quiet, other than an attempted Japanese counter-landing north of Garapan. As the 35 boats approached the beach, American artillery and naval fire opened up, sinking 13 of them. The rest turned back and did not make a second attempt.

On 19 June a Japanese air patrol spotted the ships of Mitscher's Task Force 58, consisting of four carrier groups, which had been slowly moving southwest in search of the Japanese fleet, which intelligence estimated was only 350 miles away. Mitscher planned to move quickly into position for a dawn surface attack, but Spruance overruled him. Fearful of the Japanese doing an "end run" around the fleet, Spruance decided not to risk the enemy cutting the fleet off from the ground troops. Instead, Mitscher was told to wait and let the Japanese come to him.

In the morning they came. For five hours the Japanese threw wave after wave of aircraft at the American fleet. Their only success was to lightly damage one ship. By contrast, the American pilots had a field day attacking Japanese. They shot down 430 Japanese aircraft against a loss of only 30 of their own. What became known as the "Great Marianas Turkey Shoot" effectively broke the back of Japanese naval airpower for the remainder of the war. As the carriers chewed up the Japanese air armada, the surface fleet subjected the islands of Guam and nearby Rota to a steady bombardment.

By the conclusion of the naval battle, the Americans had sunk two Japanese carriers and forced the Japanese fleet to turn and flee for home. Mitscher pursued and the next afternoon destroyed 65 of the remaining 100 Japanese carrier planes, sank another carrier and two precious oiler tankers, and damaged yet a fourth carrier. Although Spruance did not allow Mitscher to continue the pursuit, the damage had been done. The Americans would have uncontested air dominance for the rest of the Marianas campaign; the damage inflicted on the Japanese fleet crippled its efforts for the rest of the war. Even worse, as far as the defenders of Saipan were concerned, the Japanese defeat in the Battle of the Philippine Sea sealed their fate. They were a doomed force that would have to fight on without hope of resupply or further aid.

As the battle raged at sea, the 27th Division made slow progress against the defenders of Nafutan Point. Jagged terrain, cane fields, solidly dug-in enemy and a lack of communications equipment added to its cautious fighting style and reduced daily progress to a matter of yards. This slow movement by the 27th held up the marines and caused gaps between the coordination lines. Additionally Holland Smith grew steadily more impatient, since he wanted the point taken immediately so that the 27th could join the marines in the northward sweep.

By this time, the 106th Infantry had landed and taken over as the corps reserve. In order to start the northern sweep, Holland Smith ordered two battalions each from the 165th and 105th to mop up Nafutan Point, while the rest of his corps pivoted and moved towards the north. Soon he changed his mind, claiming that there were few Japanese left on Nafutan Point and a single battalion should be sufficient. According to him, there were only 200 enemy soldiers left in the area, although later events would show that there had been approximately 1,250.

Holland Smith did not specify where the battalion should come from. As Ralph Smith and Holland Smith had previously discussed using the 105th Infantry for mopping operations, the former ordered its 2nd Battalion to undertake the mission. There was one problem with these orders: the 105th, which had been the corps reserve before it landed, had not yet been released from corps control. Despite the fact that Holland Smith gave the exact same instructions only a short time later, he was enraged that Ralph Smith would issue orders to a unit not under his command.

Holland Smith found the 27th ID's actions during the attack north on 23 June even more infuriating. First, the division was late crossing the line of departure, forcing the entire attack, including the marines, to start more than an hour late. Then, positioned in the center of the line, the 27th moved more slowly than its marine counterparts on the flanks. As a result, a deep "U" developed in the line. Although all three divisions faced tough terrain, the army's line stretched through an area the Americans had christened "Death Valley." Afterwards, the 4th MARDIV commander noted that no one on the island had a tougher job than the 27th

Division in Death Valley, but Holland Smith was not listening to explanations. On the left, the line between the 27th ID and the 2nd MARDIV was on the slopes of Mount Tapotchau. Since the lines had been drawn using maps rather than scouting reports, the corps staff did not realize that the right side of the mountain fell off abruptly, so that the 106th had to divide its force between the high ground and the low ground. On the right was a line of hills dubbed "Purple Heart Ridge" due to the withering fire that came from the Japanese ensconced there. The whole area was dotted with caves and cliffs, which the soldiers were reluctant to bypass without clearing, since bypassing would leave the unit's rear and flanks vulnerable to Japanese counterattack. By nightfall, the 165th had moved barely 700 yards, while the 106th went a mere 100 yards. In contrast, the marines had advanced over a mile. Even worse for the 27th, a lucky hit by an enemy shell exploded an ammunition dump behind the 106th, forcing its soldiers to retreat and lose what little they had gained.

This slow progress and the apparent stalemate on Nafutan Point caused Holland Smith to reach his breaking point with the 27th. He had, of course, had issues with the division and Ralph Smith since Makin. This disdain made his decision to employ the 27th ID in the center, along the most rugged terrain and vicious enemy resistance, puzzling. Now he believed his suspicions confirmed. As far as he was concerned, the 27th Division would not fight and that reluctance was jeopardizing the entire mission. He visited Turner and Spruance to seek permission to relieve Ralph Smith from command on two premises. The first was the taking of a battalion from the corps reserve without authority. The second was that the 27th was late in launching its attack on 23 June, thus holding up the marine advance on its flanks. Spruance approved the relief, thus touching off a controversy (covered in detail later in the chapter) that would define and threaten to poison army and marine relations for the rest of the war and beyond. And so Jarman, who had been scheduled to take command of the garrison after combat operations were completed, took command of the 27th Division. A few days later, he too was replaced by General George Griner and Jarman moved back to assume his garrison command.

By this point the troops had devised a way to clear out the entrenched Japanese, using a combination of artillery, mortars, and flamethrowers and by maneuvering around the flanks to clear out the cliff emplacements.

In fact, they were using a plan that Ralph Smith had devised immediately before his relief.[57] By 27 June, the army cleared Nafutan Point and by 30 June, the rest of the corps had pushed the surviving Japanese north to Marpi Point, from which they would launch one last suicidal counterattack on 7 July. Oddly, Holland Smith even complimented the 165th Regiment on a visit to their command post on 29 June, telling the commander, "Tell the regiment they are doing a swell job."[58]

Just before committing suicide on 6 July, General Yoshitsugu Saito, the Japanese commander, sent orders for every man to take "seven lives to repay our country." After nightfall an initial wave of between 3,000 and 4,000 Japanese swarmed the 1st and 2nd Battalions of the 105th Regiment. American artillery fell at the rate of 40 shells per minute and still the Japanese came on. As the two besieged battalions struggled in desperate hand-to-hand combat, a group of Japanese poured through a seam between the two units and overran the 10th Marine artillery positions. The breakthrough caused the American lines to fall back into Tapanang village on the western edge of the island. There the fight devolved into vicious house-to-house combat, which lasted throughout the day. Relief finally came in the form of American tanks and two battalions of the 106th Infantry. The fighting finally ended just before midnight. The two American battalions had suffered 406 killed and 512 wounded. Around them lay more than 4,300 enemy dead. Holland Smith relieved the battered regiment and used the relieving units to mop up remaining Japanese resistance by ferreting out the defenders from caves and gullies around Marpi Point. On 9 July Turner declared the island secure.

However, there was one final act of horror awaiting the men on Saipan. The Americans gave bullhorns to civilians who had already surrendered and the division interpreters so that they could beg non-combatants to come out of the caves around Marpi Point. To the shock of the marines, Japanese soldiers still holed up in those caves shot those trying to escape. Astoundingly, many more—men, women, and children—rushed out of the caves and flung themselves off the cliffs rather than surrender to the Americans. Several hundred died this way, as the Americans looked on helplessly. One marine said of the carnage, "It makes one wonder at just how good the propaganda the Japanese had been telling the people [about the Americans] was."[59] After this last orgy of death, the island lay largely quiet although almost 2,000 Japanese still remained holed up in caves and hideaways. The marines departed for Tinian, leaving the 27th to finish mopping up the island, which would take another month.

ANALYSIS

Planning

There were some advantages in having divided planning staffs. Since the two staffs had conducted the initial planning together, both sets had a clear understanding of the entire operation, but were able to focus on their individual slice of the campaign. A large portion of the V Corps staff had been involved in the planning and training of operations in the Central Pacific since September 1943 and they had an unparalleled understanding of amphibious landings and island warfare. However, this advantage was balanced by the fact that the staff was already small for a corps-level staff and, by dividing it, both were extremely short-handed.[60]

This G-3 (operations) staff came up with a novel solution to this problem by detaching observers from Turner's staff to revolve through the corps and frequent conferences with the divisions ensured that the flow of information went both ways. This allowed the higher headquarters to have a more intimate view of the plan as it developed.[61] Not only did the corps have their plan virtually complete by the time that their higher headquarters forwarded their final plan, but the two were completely synchronized. Holland Smith was able to release his plan by 1 May. However, the plan showed the relative inexperience of his staff as the few objectives would prove to be too ambitious and did not take into account conditions on the ground. Furthermore, since Holland Smith thought that he would be able to conquer the island in just a few days, the plan did not go much beyond that. All of this, combined with his natural stubbornness, would make it difficult for him to adapt his tactics to the reality on the ground. The only thing he understood was lightning-quick frontal attacks, even when the events on the battlefield called for creative thinking.

However, despite the corps' attempt to maximize planning schedules, time was indeed the limiting factor. In the case of the 27th ID, the division had to make 21 separate contingency plans and work in rehabilitation and training in just two short months.[62] For the 4th MARDIV, there were times when the plans and guidance its staff provided to its regiments were often inadequate and incomplete.[63] This is something that all echelons strove to improve and, by the time operations began, the corps was able to get updated orders prepared and sent to their subordinates in four hours.[64]

Intelligence

As the Americans had found in previous operations, the maps and photographs provided for the operation proved inaccurate and failed to give a true representation of the actual terrain.[65] The G-2 provided maps at a scale of 1:20,000, which the troops found nearly worthless, as they did not accurately depict terrain details. Instead, they requested 1:10,000 in future operations. On the maps provided, cliffs and various topographic elevations were poorly marked, leaving the units with almost no idea of what terrain lay in front of them.[66] As a result, regimental lines, particularly for the 27th ID, often had units split between topographic features. As the headquarters typically made tactical decisions off faulty maps, operations were unnecessarily hampered and higher commands often had trouble understanding why advances were so slow over ground that, at least on the map, seemed relatively easy to cross.[67]

As in earlier operations, the number of interpreters was inadequate, although the capabilities of those that were available were excellent.[68] They were put to good use gleaning information from the sizable civilian population. Unfortunately, the civilians had been so well conditioned to fear the Americans that many committed suicide rather than surrender. Some of these fatalities could have been alleviated if the Americans had known that a significant number spoke a local dialect and therefore could not understand the leaflets in "correct" Japanese and Korean dropped on the island.[69]

However, the major failure of intelligence, at both the corps and division level, was in missing or ignoring hints about preparations for the Japanese banzai attack on 7 July. A POW had warned the corps G-2, an army officer, that a suicide attack was impending. Nevertheless, the corps did not deem it an imminent threat. Although the division had been informed of the threat, it was not conveyed as an immediate threat and so no action was taken to strengthen the line. Even after the attack, the corps acted on the assumption that the 300 Japanese that overran the marine battalion was the main force and wasted several hours before sending reinforcements to the 105th.[70] As one officer put it,

Both the corps and division failed in their estimates of the situation—corps insofar as it disregarded important G-2 information and division by not taking proper action on G-2 information in its possession. Division G-2 passed information back to the corps about Japanese massing . . . but neither corps or division took any positive action to guard against a threatening counterattack.[71]

Training

Between the staff shortage and the need to train the corps staff itself (since most of the staff had no actual combat experience), the corps neglected its oversight role of divisional training. This was justified by the fact that the units participating all had combat experience and the G-3 claimed that

> It is obvious that the divisions making the assault landing had sufficient previous experience so that training presented no particular problem other than working replacements into teams, training special units such as amphibian tractors units and JASCOs and conducting a rehearsal[72]

This hands-off approach was probably not necessarily the best decision. Lower echelons complained that the lack of information from the corps resulted in a haphazard approach to training by the divisions. While the divisions did not require details about the objective, knowing the general task organization, terrain, and type of operation would have allowed the units to focus on mastering specialized equipment or tactics as needed.[73] As the corps did not insist on the units training or conducting exercises together no one knew the strengths and weaknesses of others. The trust that binds organizations together into a superior fighting force, and which only comes from long familiarity with each other, was never formed. Moreover, the corps' hands-off approach meant that the senior leadership had no grasp of the true capabilities of subordinate leaders or organizations. While this may not have been an issue on parallel operations, in protracted joint operations it was essential to address these differences in training and not on the battlefield.

A later study of the operation determined that this disjointed approach led to "petty tactical differences which combat later magnified into such strategically different monumental disagreements that ground operations were not only thereby hampered, but casualties were materially increased."[74] A company commander in the 27th Division whose company relieved a marine unit remarked, "A mutual understanding between the various services is necessary to recognize and understand the different methods used by each in their training and use of arms in combat."[75] Combined training would have also revealed equipment differences between the services. For example, the army and marine LVTs employed different radios, which, as they could not talk to each other, severely hampered command and control. Even a short exercise would have revealed this mismatch and allowed the same radios to be put in each LVT.[76]

Finally, the divisions felt that their men, most of whom had already conducted at least one landing, did not need as much time on ship-to-shore training. Instead, they wanted more time allotted to train for actual tactical operations on land. Since most of the earlier operations had lasted less than a week, unit capabilities for sustained operations had degraded.[77] However, they were not given the equipment or space to do such training.[78]

As with earlier operations, the divisions considered training time inadequate. Moreover, although they considered the rehearsals valuable, the lack of similarity between the practice and actual landing beaches, coupled with the lack of ability to use live ammunition, blunted realism. Army units in the area had priority for training areas and often bumped marine units, something that did not help engender good relations between the services. More importantly, the marines complained they were denied a chance to conduct "progressive training" that built from the individual to larger unit tasks. Instead they had to perform limited small-unit training at whatever facilities were "left over." In general, the marines judged that their leaders did not fight hard enough to get them priority in training.

Finally, over 4,000 of the American casualties (one-fourth of the total) occurred during the first two days of the operations. These were mainly the result of enemy artillery fire from guns that had not been located and destroyed by naval gunfire. This went directly back to concerns V Corps had earlier expressed about the lack of training received by spotters on the fast battleships. As such, they recommended once again that the schools for all air observers focus on identifying and destroying enemy artillery emplacements.[79] Just as important, they recommended that all naval fire control officers become well-versed in infantry tactics to best advise ground commanders on the use of naval fire.[80]

Casualties[81]

The total American casualties came to 3,591 soldiers and 12,782 marines killed, wounded, or MIA out of a total number of 67,545 personnel.[82] This total, 19.8 percent, was far lower than casualties at Tarawa, although higher than other operations. The only other long-term operation—Guadalcanal—had a casualty rate of about 11 percent, although that number does not include the malarial patients that continued the fight. However, one needs to break down these numbers further. The percentage of casualties sustained during the landing was only 10 percent of the landing force, far below those at Tarawa, the only other landing that encountered the same level of enemy resistance.

Experience, amphibious training, and better equipment all contributed to lowering this number. American leaders had taken to heart the suggestions from earlier operations and provided the landing forces with much of the specialized equipment requested and in the numbers required. For instance, experience showed that flamethrowers were the best equipment for clearing caves and pillboxes, so each platoon received at least one of these.

During the battle, the Americans had wiped out virtually the entire Japanese garrison of 30,000 soldiers, a casualty ratio of 2:1, a major improvement over previous operations. The Americans had not only become adept at employing their own tactics, but they had adapted to the Japanese style of fighting. When Holland Smith relieved Ralph Smith, one of his complaints was that the army's hesitation was endangering the lives of "his" marines and that the low number of army casualties was indicative of the cowardice of the 27th.[83] One of the army officers attached to the V Corps Headquarters wrote a memorandum to Griner stating his impression that "General Smith's idea of a good fighting division depended entirely upon the number of casualties they sustained."[84] At first glance, it appears Holland Smith was correct: 25 percent for the marines versus 22 percent for the army. However, when the casualties from the landing are subtracted (since the army did not participate in that operation), the numbers are virtually identical: 21 percent casualties for the marines versus 22 percent for the army. If Holland Smith wanted to measure fighting spirit and capability by casualties, then the army was equal to the marines. Furthermore, of the 6,500 Japanese killed, approximately 35 percent of the total died along the 27th Division's front. This was an impressive number, especially considering that the army arrived in battle four days after its marine counterparts.[85]

As with all Pacific battles, combat was not the final arbiter of the number of casualties. Mosquito-borne diseases, especially dengue fever, once again became an issue due to Saipan's climate and the duration of the operation. In order to combat these diseases, the Americans developed and instituted the use of airplane spray for the pesticide DDT. This proved successful in decreasing the mosquito population and the number of dengue fever cases dropped precipitously in the three weeks following the spraying.[86]

Commanders

There were some hints in various observers' after-action reports that leadership throughout the campaign was inadequate, especially in the 27th. One company commander recommended that morale would certainly increase if the army had permitted the wholesale replacement of the division's leadership. "Capable, energetic and inspirational leadership on the part of the officers in command [is necessary] . . . especially during periods when casualties are high and units are temporarily set back by heavy enemy opposition. No adverse quality is more reflected in troops than a defeatist or futile attitude on the part of the officers."[87] The commander got his wish. When his regiment—the 106th—found itself mired in an area called "Hell's Pocket" a couple of division staff officers visited it. They found the regiment's battalions at a standstill and in a demoralized state from the heavy Japanese fire and high casualties. They recommended the relief of the regimental commander, Colonel Russell Ayers, and he was soon replaced by the division's chief of staff who got the regiment moving again.

Ironically, Ralph Smith had considered relieving Ayers after his regiment landed on Eniwetok in February 1943. During the battle, Ayers stayed offshore and, in the words of Admiral Hill, "showed no desire to go ashore and take command of his troops and was finally ordered by General Watson (then commanding the operation as commander of the 22nd Marine Regiment) to do so."[88] After the battle, Watson omitted Ayers from the list of meritorious awards, but was pressured to award him something. At some point he was given a direct order to submit Ayers for the Navy Cross (second only to the Medal of Honor). It is not known who gave Watson the order and, although he initially protested the award, Holland Smith flew to Hawaii and personally presented the medal to Ayers. Thus, even if Ralph Smith wanted to remove him, it would be awkward to remove a commander for incompetence in an operation for which he received the Navy Cross. As the 27th Division historian observed, "This was absolutely the most foolish miscarriage of justice I have ever seen . . . [Ayers] was a lost soul and then for H. M. Smith to come up there and give him the second highest award for his incompetent performance, what kind of spot did that put Ralph Smith in?"[89]

However, even at corps level the leadership was not all that Holland Smith later claimed. Despite his obvious talents and success as a trainer and staff officer, Smith had never before commanded men in combat. He often had an image of how the frontline looked—without ever visiting it—and made his decisions based on these preconceived and inaccurate notions. In fact, Smith only visited the division command post once, on 18 June, immediately after the division had captured Aslito Airfield. Moreover, members of his staff only visited the division twice more.[90] After the war, Smith's chief of staff, General Graves Erskine, suggested that no one on the corps staff had any idea of the true situation on the front line, especially in the 27th's area.[91]

The one episode that defined and continues to dominate the operation is the relief of Ralph Smith. At the time, all involved assumed that Ralph Smith's relief was the final word on this potentially debilitating interservice squabble. After all, three other division commanders had been relieved in the Pacific theater—two of them by naval commanders—without threatening service relations.[92] However, Smith's relief became the opening salvo of a battle that raged throughout the remainder of the war and beyond. At the time, no one was angrier than General Robert Richardson, the commander of Army Forces in the Pacific. Much like Holland Smith's earlier role, he oversaw only training and administrative issues and had no combat responsibilities. Also like Holland Smith, he was hyperpartisan and always concerned about the army getting its proper share of recognition in the Central Pacific. Collins, who had served as his chief of staff in 1941, noted that Richardson's cadet nickname "Nellie" suited him perfectly, recalling, "he had the aura of a staff officer rather than a troop commander . . . [he] was unquestionably an able man, but he was also finicky, a stickler for protocol, and, at times, inordinately sensitive."[93] He had been slated for command of I Corps, but Marshall had pulled his name after Richardson's actions and statements made him question Richardson's judgment.[94]

It was Richardson who fired the first shot in the Smith versus Smith controversy. On 4 July he convened a board of inquiry into Ralph Smith's relief. The board was headed by General Simon Bolivar Buckner, who limited testimony to only army officers and the official campaign records. As expected, officer after officer testified as to Holland Smith's prejudice against the army.[95] Unsurprisingly, the board found that while Holland Smith possessed the authority to relieve Ralph Smith, the relief was not justified and should not adversely affect Ralph Smith's career. To add to the insult, a week after hostilities on Saipan ended, Richardson, without Holland Smith's prior permission, landed on Saipan and presented commendations to the 27th Division. This was a breathtaking breach of military etiquette since Richardson had no authority to present awards to soldiers not under his command, nor had he cleared his trip through the proper channels. He had obviously designed his actions to send a message to Holland about how the army viewed the 27th Division's performance.

While, in the interests of interservice harmony Spruance decided to ignore the insult, Turner felt no such compunction and unleashed a tirade on Richardson. Spruance tried to mollify Richardson's fury, telling him "That is just Kelly Turner's way." Turner followed up his outburst with an angry letter to Nimitz via Spruance about Richardson's unlawful assumption of command. Nimitz not only ignored the letter, but deleted any references to Smith's relief from the final report.[96]

This did little to diminish the army's anger over Ralph Smith's relief. Service relations became so strained that several army commanders—including Jarman and his replacement Griner—wrote letters stating that army units should never serve under Holland Smith again. Griner argued that his soldiers were so demoralized that he would not be able to lead them into combat again unless army leadership acted to clear their unit reputation.[97] Even Marshall's assistant chief of staff, General Thomas Handy, recommended that it would best if both Smiths left the theater, but acknowledged that the army could not recommend Holland Smith's relief without appearing vindictive.[98] Back in Washington, Marshall and King expressed concern that relations between the two services had deteriorated beyond normal rivalry, but decided not to take official action in the hope that the controversy would die down on its own. Marshall did, however, send King a memorandum suggesting that they send identical telegrams to Richardson and Nimitz, instructing them to take steps to ensure interservice harmony.[99] For Marshall's part, he recognized that as the U.S. moved closer to the Japanese homeland, the size and duration of upcoming battles meant that they would necessarily have to be led by the army.

Ironically, the final V Corps report credited the success of the operation to "all-around cooperation and understanding and cemented by mutual respect and confidence, which has developed through a series of operations and has welded one experienced team from many varying elements."[100] However, Holland Smith could not refrain from taking one last shot at the 27th Division in this report:

> The decisive factor, without which all support and amphibious technique would have been futile, was the character of the troops employed. Leadership and aggressiveness of the highest order were called for, coupled with experienced teamwork . . . The 2nd and 4th Marine Divisions fought through most difficult terrain and vegetation against determined resistance suffering severe casualties . . . They expected an equally high performance by the 27th Infantry Division employed with them. This less experienced unit lacked leadership and training to conform to such demanding standards.[101]

Not satisfied with this, Holland Smith also launched a personal attack on Ralph Smith. In a letter to Vandegrift, now the Commandant, he claimed, "R. Smith is a weak officer, incapable of handling men in battle, lacks offensive spirit and tears would come into his eyes on the slightest provocation."[102] Given that Ralph Smith had won two Silver Stars in World War I, it is hard to believe that harsh words would make him cry. However, as will be seen later, this was typical of the personal attacks Holland Smith launched at anyone he considered a foe.

After the service chiefs had effectively ordered a "cease-fire" between the army and marines, it remained for the media to continue the fight. Almost as soon as the battle on Saipan finished, the Hearst newspapers fired a public salvo, castigating Holland Smith as a butcher who measured fighting spirit by casualty numbers. In response, *Time* and *Life* magazines, led by correspondent Robert Sherrod, who had landed with the marines at Tarawa, Saipan, and (later) Iwo Jima picked up the gauntlet for the marines. Sherrod, possibly aided and abetted by Holland Smith, played a large role in stirring controversy between the two services. First, in September 1944 he wrote an unsigned article for *Time* magazine, in which he claimed that the men of the 27th Division "froze in their foxholes." Even more damning, he claimed that the banzai attack of 7 August was only stopped by the 10th Marine Artillery Battalion.[103] Since, according to the division staff, Sherrod had never once visited the 27th Division's command post or walked the terrain, it is hard to believe that he was making an objective report of the facts on the ground. In fact, while most of the 10th Artillery had fought bravely, the unit had been overrun so quickly and unexpectedly that dozens of the marines were slaughtered in their hammocks and the battery had not fired any artillery during the battle.

Ed Love, combat historian for the 27th Division, and Richardson both wrote letters rebutting the maligning article, but Nimitz, perhaps still hoping the issue would fade away, refused to release them. Ralph Smith's relief from duty might have remained a footnote in the Central Pacific if not for one man: Holland Smith. The publication of *Coral and Brass* in 1948 was a grenade lobbed into the middle of the Pentagon. The navy and marine leadership had just completed the acrimonious unification battle following the war, during which the army had proposed curtailing or outright eliminating the Marine Corps. They had no desire to stir up an ancient controversy.

In private letters, however, several of his contemporaries questioned Smith's stability and his motives for publishing a book filled with such easily disproved fallacies.[104] Admiral Harry Hill, who had worked closely with Smith on many landings, even threatened to sue him if certain statements attributed to him were not removed from the book before publication. He also sent a note to Turner lamenting, "Poor old Holland . . . I hate to see him throw away what he gained in his whole career just for the sake of getting all of this off of his chest . . . he was a very bitter individual."[105] Holland Smith wrote his own legacy, one that overshadowed his considerable achievements.

LESSONS LEARNED

Decentralized planning may have worked during earlier landings when each division landed on its own island and conducted independent operations, but they did not work for large-scale operations such as Saipan. Here, divisions operated in tandem and the tactical decisions of one inevitably affected adjacent units. Therefore, foremost amongst the lessons taken from Saipan was the requirement that preparations and planning for large operations needed centrally directed control by the highest ground command, whether it be a corps or an army. Only in that way could senior commanders resolve interservice difference in tactics, equipment, or personality and resolve issues prior to launching an operation. Everyone became painfully aware that if army and marine units were going to fight effectively together, they would have to plan, train, and conduct exercises together.

Tactically, the plan to use the LVT(A)s to move inland and cover the first wave's advance to its first objective, approximately 1,500 yards to a mile off the beach, proved a dismal failure. The LVT(A)s did not have sufficient armor or firepower to withstand the combined effects of enemy artillery and mortars. They were also clumsy and slow compared to medium tanks, while minor obstacles such as sand, trenches, shell holes, and trees easily stopped them.[106] However, observers did recommend exploring the feasibility of using the LVT(A)s as mobile field artillery in the early stages of landings.[107]

In light of the inadequate identification and destruction of enemy artillery emplacements, V Corps recommended that the fire planners be located with the fire direction center of the highest landing force headquarters during the landing. This would allow for maximum coordination of all supporting fires during the critical landing phase.[108] Furthermore, the preparatory fire should also cover the high ground behind the beach, which proved the most likely location for the emplacement of enemy artillery pieces. Even more important, on the day after the initial landing, all spotter planes should be out at dawn to determine where the enemy moved the guns during the night.[109]

Based on recommendations from the Marshalls operations, the JASCOs remained on the division command ship until the beachhead was secured in order to stay out of the way of the assault troops. After Saipan, the divisions recommended that the JASCO become an organic divisional unit as opposed to a corps unit and that there be a liaison in each regiment. They also recommended that each JASCO have organic radio capabilities and a naval gunfire officer. The final recommendation was that army and marine JASCOs train together under one headquarters in order to ensure that they were interchangeable during operations.[110] The DUKWs proved their value once again, particularly for landing artillery and ammunition. More than that, they also provided support and rescue to soldiers cut off and trapped against the sea during the attack on 7 July.

Remarkably, despite all the attention given to the previous failure between infantry-tank communication, this remained a problem on Saipan.[111] Units now requested a two-way speaker at the rear of the tank in lieu of the improvised phones that had been installed on the tanks.[112] Moreover, because tank team assignments changed daily, there was little chance to develop a rapport between the tankers and the infantry they supported. This constant changing also made it impossible to make use of precious training time to rehearse standard procedures for actions during combat. Even more detrimental, during the fighting, the tanks departed each evening to position themselves several miles to the rear for servicing. This meant that were they were often not available at the beginning of a Japanese attack when they were most needed.[113] Finally, during the banzai attack on 7 July the inability of the infantry and tanks to communicate resulted in tactical chaos and the loss of several crucial hours before the defense of Tapanang could get itself efficiently organized.

While Holland Smith's accusations of lack of fighting spirit related only to the 27th, the marines noticed the same thing in their units. The rapid operational tempo resulted in little time to focus on and prepare for the attacks on individual objectives. Commanders noticed instances of "lack of initiative, misunderstanding of orders and a let down in the spirit to attack vigorously."[114] What Holland Smith dismissed as a natural byproduct of battle fatigue in marines, he viewed as proof of cowardice in army units.

A complaint from all the units was the fact that they were stretched too thin throughout the campaign. On Nafutan Point, a single battalion was stretched across a front approximately 3,000 yards wide, a frontage generally manned by a full division.[115] This stretching made it difficult for the units to maintain contact and often the unit had to deplete its reserve to plug up the gaps, leaving an inadequate reserve to meet a crisis, if one developed.[116]

The weapon most dreaded by the Japanese was the flamethrower, especially the tank-mounted ones.[117] As stated earlier, under the new marine organization structure, the authorization for this weapon increased ten-fold, including some that could be mounted on tanks. These proved invaluable against the caves and in clearing out the impassable cane fields. However, the resupply of napalm was difficult and units often relied on the less effective diesel fuel.[118] Moreover, while each squad had a flamethrower, they did not receive a trained operator with it, meaning that they had to assign one man to transport the 67-pound weapon, which slowed down squad movement. Since each squad also had to assign a man to carry the bazooka, these new weapons effectively reduced the squad manpower by one-sixth. Units recommended that the flamethrowers, along with personnel and transport carts, be assigned at the platoon rather than squad level for maximum flexibility of use.[119]

EFFECT ON FUTURE OPERATIONS

Despite the importance of the Marianas campaign, it has been often overlooked in favor of the D-Day landings that were happening on the other side of the world. The loss of Saipan meant that Japan had one less layer of defense around the home island and the loss of two carriers and hundreds of aircraft and pilots was an even bigger blow to Japan's strategic position. In fact, so critical was Saipan to Japan's defensive plan that after its loss the Japanese Prime Minister, General Hideki Tojo, and his entire cabinet resigned. The naval advisor to the emperor confessed, "Hell is upon us." This indicated that, perhaps for the first time, the Japanese military understood that defeat was not only possible, but probable.

For their part, the Americans realized that operations on larger islands demanded a different training focus. Not only did the divisions participating in large island operations need to rehearse the landing phase, but they also needed time to focus on basic infantry skills, something they had not needed in the small island battles. Additionally, the leaders realized that despite three years of fighting in the Pacific, the army and marines still had a fundamental mismatch in ground operations doctrine and only joint training could mitigate this issue. The Smith versus Smith controversy made this more difficult as the men of the two services now distrusted one another, with marines believing soldiers were weak and the soldiers believing marines were reckless. It would take a long time for this mutual distrust to dissipate.

Never again would Holland Smith command army troops. When Nimitz recommended that Sherrod's credentials as a war correspondent be revoked in response to his malicious articles about the 27th Division, Smith saw it as a personal betrayal and a rebuke of his actions and his long friendship with the admiral began to crumble. Perhaps most galling, when planning began for the landings at Okinawa, the Tenth Army was given to the man who had exonerated Ralph Smith—Simon Bolivar Buckner—while theater leadership moved Holland Smith out of the combat zone following the landings on Iwo Jima.

Lost in the fog of the Smith versus Smith controversy was the fact that the Americans no longer had to worry about equipment or tactics. Both had been amply validated. Instead, as they looked forward to the landings on the Japanese home islands, the various services would have to put personal issues aside as they synthesized three years of cooperation and lessons learned. With Holland Smith out of the picture, the tension between the army and marines dissipated somewhat and the new commander brought in to lead the force would come in with a relatively clean slate.

— CHAPTER 5 —

OKINAWA:
The Final Victory

After the victory at Saipan, American forces continued their steady progress across the Pacific, tightening the noose around the Japanese homeland. By early April 1945, U.S. forces were poised to launch the largest amphibious operation of the war, aimed, for the first time, directly at one of the Japanese prefectures—Okinawa. This operation was the capstone of three years of brutal warfare and presented the ultimate test of everything the army and marines had learned about joint operations. At Okinawa, the lessons of cooperation and coordination, the techniques of amphibious operations, and a thorough knowledge of Japanese tactics and the methods of countering them culminated in one colossal push into the final circle of Japanese defenses.[1]

To do so, America assembled the largest amphibious force ever seen the Pacific. A full army, consisting of seven divisions organized under two corps headquarters, prepared to storm the island. In support were over fifty carriers and their escorts, organized in five naval task forces, including one British carrier task force. When one considers that only two years before, the navy had to send a barely patched-up USS Yorktown to Midway to meet a Japanese invasion with three carriers, the quantity of materiel commanders now had at their disposal must have appeared miraculous. America was now sending almost seventeen times the number of carriers they possessed at Midway just to capture a single Japanese island. Despite this preponderance of materiel power the Battle of Okinawa proved to be a test of endurance, only won because U. S. commanders had absorbed the lessons of past engagements and learned the intricate art of coordinating all of the various arms and branches of each service into a single power-ful joint fist. Creating such a dynamic and successful synergism dem-onstrated that the operation's senior leaders had mostly put aside the lingering bitterness from the events on Saipan, and gotten on with the business of winning the war.

Given the relative swiftness of the other island battles and taking into account what they had learned in three grueling years of cam-paigns, American commanders had no doubt as to their eventual vic-tory. Their greatest concern was over the possible cost of that victory. In the end, the 84-day battle for the island was more costly in men and materiel than anyone had imagined. Why? Mostly because U. S. planners had failed to anticipate that Japanese tactics had also evolved. Moreover, if the Americans thought that previous cam-paigns had given them an understanding of Japanese fanaticism, the fight for Okinawa disabused them of that notion. In defense of their homeland the Japanese ratcheted up their resistance to a degree that bewildered Allied commanders. As a result, the campaign dragged on and casualties mounted, both on land and at sea. American com-manders and planners realized that what they were experiencing was a preview of the horrendous fighting and losses they could expect when they struck at the Japanese mainland, a battle that loomed in the not very distant future

STRATEGIC SETTING

A scant month after operations concluded in the Marianas, the 1st and 2nd Marine Divisions launched an attack on Peleliu in the Palau islands, in support of MacArthur's Philippines attack. As this battle raged, Nimitz met with King to discuss the next step in the Central Pacific Campaign, this one aimed at the Japanese home islands. King had long favored an attack on Formosa (Taiwan), off the southeastern coast of China, which he saw as a perfect airbase both to support future amphibious operations against Japan and to pound its cities into rubble and ash. Nimitz, however, in a rare occurrence, favored a plan put forward by MacArthur. Nimitz proposed that MacArthur retake Luzon and Manila, while the forces intended for Formosa shift to assaults on Iwo Jima and Okinawa. Both Buckner, now the designated commander for the Formosa operation, and

Harmon, the commander of the Pacific Army Air Forces, supported the Nimitz plan, as did Spruance, Halsey, and Turner.[2]

Their reasons for the new plan were three-fold. First, the Japanese had a full field army—more than 170,000 soldiers—dug in and well supplied with munitions defending Formosa. Assured success against so large a force would require more Americans than were available in the entire Pacific theater at that time. Second, estimated casualties in such an operation were in excess of 150,000, a number all found unacceptable. Finally, the operations Nimitz was proposing (Iwo Jima and Okinawa) would sever Japanese oil sources and provide a superior location for bombing operations against the home islands than Formosa.

To their surprise, King offered no disagreement. In fact, after studying a series of logistics reports on the proposed Formosa operation, he had been inching towards the same conclusion. And so, with a minimum of fuss, the theater commanders adopted a new operational focus: they would bypass Formosa and have the marines attack Iwo Jima, followed by a joint army-marine attack on Okinawa. Detailed planning for the invasion of Okinawa—Operation ICEBERG—began immediately.

OPERATIONAL PLANNING

As this was the biggest and most complex operation in the Pacific, the chain of command differed from that of past operations. As each phase of the operation played out, command passed successively from Spruance to Turner to Buckner. From the point of departure until the fleet arrived at Okinawa, Spruance was in overall command. Turner would command the amphibious operation itself and Buckner would report to him until the amphibious assault was completed and ground operations begun. At this point Turner's TF 51 would come under the operational control of the Tenth Army and Buckner would report directly to Spruance. At some point, Nimitz would assume direct command of operations and put Buckner in command of all aspects (ground, air, and naval garrison) of the joint task force. In this role, Buckner would answer only to Nimitz.[3] Spruance argued vehemently against this change, asking Nimitz to keep the command relationship "used heretofore in the Central Pacific and understood by all hands."[4] However, Nimitz reasoned that the amphibious phase would be a relatively short phase of the operation and that the size and scope of the ground operations, combined with its location so close to the main Japanese bases, warranted the need for him to directly oversee the campaign.[5]

In addition to the tactical air and naval forces, Buckner had two corps under him: XXIV Corps commanded by army General John Hodge, consisting of the 7th and 96th Infantry Division; and III Corps commanded by marine General Roy Geiger, consisting of the 1st and 6th Marine Divisions. Moreover, Buckner had the 2nd Marine Division (Demonstration Force) and the 27th (Floating Reserve) and 77th Infantry Division (Western Landing Force). Nimitz retained the 81st Infantry Division on New Caledonia under his command as the area reserve.

The Ryukyu chain, of which Okinawa is a part, lies barely 375 miles from the Japanese home island of Kyushu and 500 miles from Formosa. The chain is almost 800 miles long and the Okinawa group stands at it center. The largest island, Okinawa proper, is 60 miles long and varies from 2 to 18 miles wide—over 485 square miles in area. The Japanese annexed and colonized the Ryukyus in 1879, but had never assimilated the indigenous population. The 500,000 Okinawans, a peaceful race with no history of war, spent their days farming and building elaborate tombs for the bones of their ancestors. The Japanese, with their customary lack of regard for other cultures, thought these tombs excellent locations for artillery and machine-gun emplacements.

As on Guadalcanal and Saipan, the biggest advantage Okinawa afforded the defenders was its terrain. In the south, the ground was rolling, growing more mountainous as one moved north. Mountain peaks ran east-west, bisecting the island. This forced attackers to go up and over successive peaks as they advanced north. As will be seen later, the Japanese propensity to heavily defend the reverse slope of these peaks, where they were immune to the worst of American shelling, made taking these mountain chains hugely expensive. Caves and coral overhangs, which provided superb defensive positions, dotted all of these peaks. The Japanese greatly improved on these natural strongpoints by connecting them with tunnels, which allowed their soldiers to move about, safe from even the heaviest naval and artillery bombardments.

Although a series of roads and paths crisscrossed the island, most were incapable of supporting heavy American vehicles. Moreover, the only decent north-south road became impassable in heavy rain, which was a frequent occurrence. As one soldier observed, "Okinawa had an excellent network of bad roads."[6] Finally, there were four fully operational airfields, although the Japanese had started and abandoned several more.

Since the terrain in the north was so rugged, the majority of the population lived in the southern half of the island and this is where the Japanese concentrated their defenses. The centerpiece of these defenses was at the ancient capital of Shuri, which rose almost 600 feet above sea level. It lay in the middle of southern Okinawa, positioned between the island's two largest cities: Naha on the western coast and Yonabaru on the east. Because of its elevation, Shuri provided a commanding view of the surrounding beaches and farmlands. As it also possessed an extensive and fully developed tunnel system it was a formidable fortress with which the assault force had to contend.

In addition, the feature that made Okinawa an attractive target—its proximity to the Japanese mainland—cut both ways. Just as land-based American aircraft could hit Japan from Okinawa, Japanese planes could reach the attackers from their home islands. Fortunately for the Americans, the near-total destruction of the Japanese air power in October 1944 prevented the enemy from taking full advantage of their mainland air bases.[7]

The original plan called for a three-phase operation. The first phase consisted of capturing the small adjacent islands of Kerama Retto and Keise Shima, in order to provide anchorage and naval repair facilities as well as long-range artillery support. Once these islands were secure the main landing on southern Okinawa would immediately proceed. Phase II called for an advance that would overrun northern Okinawa and Ie Shima. The final phase was the occupation of further islands in the Sakishima group in the southeastern Ryukus.[8]

PRE-COMBAT TRAINING

Tenth Army

When the time came to choose a ground commander, Spruance and Turner favored using Holland Smith, with whom they felt comfortable after so many operations together. However, not only did the operation consist primarily of army units, but the plan called for the type of prolonged land operations at which the army excelled. Moreover, the specter of the Smith versus Smith controversy still hung heavily over the Pacific, and Nimitz felt that putting Smith in charge of not one but up to five army divisions, including the 27th ID, would just add fuel to the interservice fire.

Furthermore, Nimitz privately believed that the division had been treated unfairly, especially by Sherrod's article, which had accused the division of mass cowardice. In fact, when he had forwarded Richardson's complaints about the article to King, Nimitz included a note saying, "I am in complete accord with the objections raised by . . . Richardson."[9] On a personal level, despite his public neutrality on the Smith versus Smith issue, he had become progressively more displeased with Holland Smith on a number of other issues. He even went so far as to mark him as only "Fair" in the loyalty section of his fitness report. Typically, this was a kiss of death for any military career. For all of these reasons, Nimitz felt that not only should the Tenth Army commander be an army general, but that he should be someone from outside the theater. In July 1944, Marshall brought Simon Bolivar Buckner down from the Alaska Defense Command to help organize the Tenth Army. However, he was not officially given command until October, possibly because of his heading of the commission looking into the firing of Ralph Smith.

To Richardson's displeasure, Buckner approached the evidence given to the board in an even-handed manner and refused to demonize the marines. During the board proceedings, Richardson invited Buckner and other members of the board to dinner—ostensibly to celebrate Buckner's birthday, but really to rail about the marines and navy conspiring to push the army out of the Pacific. Buckner listened without comment, but privately noted, with some scorn, "It seems not unlikely that Richardson invited us to indoctrinate us along these lines."[10] The indoctrination did not take, and Buckner, while finding that the relief was probably unwarranted, refused to find any faults with the marines or their commanders. Sticking to the facts before him Buckner took particular care to insure that the debate did not devolve into a battle over which service's tactics were superior. He even commiserated with Nimitz about the fact that Richardson had sent a copy of the report to Marshall in Washington, when all had hoped the commanders could resolve the issue in theater.[11]

This fair-mindedness was enough to satisfy Nimitz that Buckner was the right man to lead the Tenth Army. A month later, after completing the commission report, Buckner noted his new assignment with the same even tone as he noted the outcome of unit softball games.

> Admiral Nimitz, after sounding out my attitude on the Smith vs. Smith controversy once more and finding that I deplored the whole matter and harbored no interservice ill feeling, announced that I would command the new joint project.[12]

At 58 years old, Buckner was a tall, ruddy, white-haired officer and for reasons unknown, his soldiers referred to him as "The Old Man of the Mountain." He was the son of the famous (or infamous, depending on which side of the conflict you fell) Civil War general who surrendered Fort Donelson to Ulysses S. Grant, thus becoming the first Confederate general to surrender a field army. Much as Holland Smith was an acknowledged expert on amphibious doctrines, so did Buckner's contemporaries consider him the "leading army schoolmaster." He had spent the years before the war teaching battle tactics at the Command and General Service Schools, the Army War College, and the United States Military Academy.[13] However, despite his grasp of the theory of war, Buckner had virtually no combat experience. He had spent World War I training aviators and the sum of his experience thus far in World War II consisted of shoring up the defenses in the Aleutians, while his contemporaries slugged it out across Europe and the Pacific. Moreover, his years of teaching theory had left him a conservative, rather unimaginative leader. Temperamentally the opposite of the slashing Holland Smith, he made clear that his intention was to slowly and steadily grind down the enemy. He shared his opinion with reporters, "You will see many Japanese killed. You will see them gradually rolled back . . . but you won't see spectacular advances because this isn't that kind of fighting."[14] One of his deputy commanders summed him up as, "General Buckner was a fine gentleman. I don't know if he was brilliant mentally, but he had character, he was solid."[15]

Despite the fact that Buckner was supposed to be a non-controversial choice, not everyone was pleased with this decision. Buckner's animosity with Admiral Robert Theobald, the naval commander for the Northern Pacific force, was acrimonious, to say the least. At one point, Buckner wrote and distributed a poem mocking Theobald's cautious manner and Marshall nearly removed Buckner from command to keep the peace with the navy. Fortunately for Buckner, he got along famously with Theobald's successor, Admiral Thomas Kinkaid.[16] Similarly, he and Turner got off to a rocky start when he visited Turner in Saipan and the latter derided the army divisions as "National Guard divisions" and implied that only the marines were competent in amphibious operations. Buckner did not let the slight to his soldiers' competence pass and casually pointed out that the army was conducting amphibious operations in the European theater just fine without any marine assistance. As Buckner noted, "his attitude improved and he asked me for a good [brigadier general] for his [assistant Chief of Staff]."[17]

Like all of the earlier assault teams, the Tenth Army consisted of a hodge-podge of available units, with little thought as to prior experience, location, or training. Fortunately, all of the divisions had had some combat experience. In fact, as was true of Holland Smith's corps staff in Saipan, Buckner's army staff probably had the least combat experience relative to the corps and division staffs below them. This was due in part to Buckner's decision to bring in officers who had served with him before, most of whom had been tucked away in the Aleutians. General Oliver (O. P.) Smith, Buckner's marine deputy chief of staff, remembered,

> The only trouble in that Tenth Army setup was that the Tenth Army was made up of two veteran corps . . . that had plenty of combat experience and General Buckner had a staff that, as far as Leavenworth staff work went, was highly qualified, but had no combat experience. And of course, these two veteran corps weren't happy about getting orders from a staff that had no combat experience.[18]

However, Smith also noted that not only did Buckner bend over backwards to get a joint staff, but that he might have gone too far, padding his staff with 60 marine and naval officers. When Smith arrived, he found the staff horribly bloated by these additions and was dismayed to find marine officers being used as clerks. He managed to get one-third of them released and the remaining officers assigned to functional billets.[19] Smith found that interservice relations were "friendly, except that, my goodness, sometimes you were aghast at what people without combat experience could do. . . . [for instance] they'd laid out the staff according to the book for the army and found it scattered across the countryside and there weren't any roads there [on Okinawa] . . . eventually it was stripped down."[20]

Buckner was ahead of his time in that he was a fitness fanatic and tried to walk several miles a day and pitched for his staff softball team. He noted his daily exercises in his diary and expressed frustration when other duties prevented him from his long walks.[21] He believed that conditioning of the troops was of paramount importance, followed by weapons training with tactical training third. Turner expressed irritation at this attitude, fuming

> We are having a hell of a time trying to train General Buckner and his Tenth Army staff to be amphibious minded . . . because General Buckner makes [his staff] walk over a mountain once a week, and on the other days to qualify in rifle and pistol shooting. Apparently there is no room in the Tenth Army for thinking; there is only room for soldiers.[22]

Oliver Smith agreed with this, noting after the war that while the physical training regimen was suitable for battalion commanders, most of the staff officers were over fifty, under severe mental strain already, and the exercises resulted in "broken collarbones, broken arms, charley horses [leg cramps] and sprained ankles."[23]

Despite any staff doubts about his training methods, Buckner was conscious of the fact that his scattered command was almost too big to get his arms around and that the army would not come together as a group until right before the invasion. Indeed, parts of his command were still engaged in combat in the Philippines and on Saipan. In an attempt to assess the status of training, he initially made each division submit a monthly training report. He eventually abandoned this requirement when Oliver Smith pointed out that he was making veteran combat units submit training checklists more appropriate to newly formed divisions.[24] He then embarked on a tour of the various divisions, along with key members of his staff, at the end of January 1945. This allowed him to observe their training first-hand and discern where his staff could best assist.[25]

He was encouraged by what he observed, noting time and again just how well-trained and disciplined each unit appeared. After Buckner had made visits to all of his assigned units and was satisfied that his subordinate commanders were following training directives, he gave them the autonomy to determine their own training plans, with the Fleet Marine Force supervising the marine division training. This showed just how much trust he placed in his subordinate commanders, and with good reason. The division staffs not only had copious combat experience, but had grown used to planning and training independently. As in the past, the main drawback of this lack of combined training was that the units had no opportunity to build esprit or to provide objective assessments of one another. This could have had deleterious effect on the operation, as it had on Saipan. In fact the opposite proved true and the entire operation was remarkably free of the interservice sniping that had marked earlier battles. It is hard to say whether this was due to the fact that the services had become accustomed to one another's tactics or the lack of Holland Smith's constant instigation. Either way, this operation demonstrated that it was possible for the army and marines to fight side by side amicably.

Because of the limited training time available, Tenth Army staff quickly finished its final plan so that the divisions could focus their training. They tasked the 77th Infantry Division, under the command of General Andrew Bruce, with conducting the initial landings on Kerama Retto and Keise Shima. Once it had secured the islands, the division would provide security for the UDTs and provide artillery cover for the landings on the main island.[26]

The main landing plan called for two divisions from each corps to land abreast on the southwestern beaches of Okinawa and then drive east across the island, cutting it in half. Then the marines (the 1st and 6th Marine Divisions) would take the Yontan Airfield and swing north to the Motubu Peninsula, while the army (the 7th and 96th Infantry Divisions) would take the Kadena Airfield and swing south to occupy the town of Naha and the Shuri Castle stronghold. At the same time, the 2nd MARDIV would execute a diversionary landing on the southeastern tip of the island. While all of this was going on the 27th ID would remain as the floating reserve, ready to land wherever they would be needed the most. With their orders in hand, the corps and divisions were ready to start their training.

XXIV Corps

Hodge had bounced around during the war and, as a result, saw a greater variety of operations in the Pacific than almost any other commander.

He certainly had quite a bit of combat experience and had worked closely with the navy and marines on a variety of occasions. He started as VII Corps chief of staff and then became Collins' assistant division commander during Guadalcanal. He followed this with command of the 43rd Infantry Division on New Georgia and then the Americal Division on Bougainville before leading the XXIV Corps—which consisted of the 7th, 77th, 32nd and 96th Divisions—on Leyte. In fact, the corps was still engaged in operations on Leyte when it received the warning order for Okinawa. However, MacArthur, apparently still smarting from being passed over for the Okinawa operation, refused to release the corps until mid-February and even then, each of the three divisions earmarked for Okinawa was short hundreds of men.[27]

Buckner was concerned about the army divisions, not because of their lack of ability, but because they were just coming out of three months of combat and were understrength, underequipped, and would have no recovery time. When the divisions finally moved to Dulag, they had less than six weeks to recover from the previous operation, incorporate fresh troops, and train for the Okinawa invasion. In addition, the units not only had to load and unload their own equipment during the move from Leyte, but had to construct their own camps for billeting and training, which left precious little time for actual progressive training.[28] During that time the two divisions managed to train in the use of the newly introduced sniperscopes and the indispensable flamethrowers and focus on getting their replacements integrated into their teams. However, the corps did manage to carve out enough time to conduct a full-scale four-day landing rehearsal during which its divisions practiced landing abreast and moving inland, which turned out to be close to the actual landings on Okinawa.[29]

7th Infantry Division "The Bayonet"

After their conquest of Kwajalein and Eniwetok in February 1944, the 7th ID participated in the battles for Yap Island and Leyte, both of which left it scant time for training. Indeed, due to the latter operation, much like the 77th ID, the division staff had scarcely six weeks to conduct planning and training before departing for Okinawa.[30] After Kwajalein, Corlett had departed to take command of a corps in the European theater and was replaced by his deputy General Archibald Arnold, a stalwart officer once described by S. L. A. Marshall as one of the finest division commanders in the war.[31]

With little time and little information about their proposed mission, the division had insufficient time for rest and recuperation, as MacArthur had not released them from his control until mid-February and the unit had to conduct training there on Leyte. One replacement noticed how life in the jungle had taken its toll on the veterans. "There weren't many healthy bodies . . . The medics on Leyte didn't seem to be able to do anything for the many cases of jungle rot, dengue fever and the parasitical diseases of the stomach."[32]

While the division might not have been healthy, it was experienced and it had to use that experience to train new soldiers. With little time for broad training, the leaders focused on correcting deficiencies noted in the Leyte campaign with special attention given to demolitions, new weapons, and perimeter and night defenses. To help with the latter, the army fielded sniperscopes and each battalion trained a team in the use and maintenance of this new equipment.[33] The division staff also came up with a novel approach to solving the issue of tank-infantry communication that had plagued every operation, by outfitting a mortar platoon from the tank battalion with radios and creating two-man liaison teams that they then attached to each tank platoon.[34]

The need to use the troops to load the ships for the operation further degraded the men and hugely reduced the time and equipment available for training. Moreover, the division was critically short of individual weapons and, despite receiving a shipment shortly before sailing, they found that many of these weapons were barely serviceable. Finally, the unit embarked for Okinawa was short over 1,000 soldiers and would not receive the rest of its replacements until D+10.[35]

96th Infantry Division "Deadeye Division"

The 96th Infantry Division was originally activated during World War I. Unfortunately, the war ended just three weeks after it was established and its assigned troops never even underwent basic training before being deactivated. In 1921, the division received a new life when it was reconstituted as a reserve unit in Portland, Oregon. However, by the time World War II started, almost all of its reserve soldiers had been called to active duty and moved to other units. Under the command of General James

Bradley, and with a cadre taken from the 7th Infantry Division, the army reactivated the 96th ID in August 1942 at Camp Adair, Oregon, and began filling it with recruits.

Arguably the most influential officer in the new 96th Division was not the division commander, but the assistant division commander, General Claudius Easley, who, before the war, had spent seven years as a weapons instructor and was captain of the army's infantry rifle and pistol teams. As a result of his emphasis on marksmanship, the division was soon nicknamed "The Deadeyes." Easley would also have the dubious honor of being the second-highest-ranking officer killed on Okinawa, when he was cut down on 19 July while directing fire on one of the last remaining enemy positions.

In February 1943, the army split the division in half to form the cadre for the 69th Infantry Division. As new recruits continued to make up the losses, the division spent the next eighteen months training along the West Coast. It ultimately moved overseas and concluded its amphibious and jungle training in Hawaii before departing for operations on Leyte in October 1944.[36]

After 115 days of combat, the division received notice to begin planning for the operations on Okinawa. Thus, the unit commenced preparations for its next mission while still conducting mopping-up operations in the Philippines. As a result, training for the Okinawa operation was negligible and made particularly difficult as any spare equipment that otherwise would have been available for training was packed for shipment to Okinawa.[37] However, the 96th ID was luckier than the other army units on Leyte since it had received an influx of replacements during the final phase of the operation. As a result, these new soldiers took part in "combat and reconnaissance patrols, gaining valuable battle indoctrination through physical contact and skirmishes with small isolated groups of Japanese."[38]

Despite severe time constraints, the division managed to conduct some Okinawa-specific training, including a full non-firing rehearsal with the 7th ID and the XXIV Corps headquarters that included amphibious landings and breaching of beachhead obstacles, such as sea walls.[39] The practice landing was useful for coordinating and testing ship-to-shore movement and navy-army communications during landing operations.[40] The rehearsal, however, was of dubious value to the soldiers, as the beaches around Leyte were sandy and had no reefs like those they would encounter on Okinawa. Fortunately, there were no repercussions from this lack of realistic landing rehearsals as the Japanese allowed them to land unopposed. Finally, now that the division leaders understood the toll that casualties could take on unit effectiveness, they had all soldiers trained on several tasks outside of their normal assignment in order to insure that there were internal replacements for any losses.[41]

On 27 March, the now-veteran and battle weary 96th Division departed the Philippines bound for Okinawa. During the trip, the division continued intensive training, focused on orienting the soldiers to conditions they would meet on the island. For the first time, the operational forces had excellent intelligence on their target. Not only did they have relief maps and models of the landing beaches available, but all the personnel took four tests on geography and various aspects of the operational plan to ensure that they understood it. By the time the division loaded into the landing craft for the run to shore, the island was familiar territory to the soldiers and landing craft operators alike.[42] This multidimensional training method proved its value during the initial days of the battle when the units moved seamlessly from the landing beaches to their assigned objectives.

III Amphibious Corps

Geiger was unique among the marine commanders since he was first and foremost an aviator. In fact, in 1917 he became only the fifth marine to earn his flight wings. As a result of his early conversion to the importance of aircraft to future warfare, within five years of joining the Marine Corps he was commanding a squadron of the First Marine Aviation Force during World War I. He then spent the interwar years helping to expand and develop marine aviation. During the invasion of Guadalcanal he was the natural choice to command the joint "Cactus Air Force," which was credited with shooting down almost 300 Japanese planes, damaging about the same number and sinking or damaging 24 enemy ships.[43]

Once the island was secure Geiger rotated back to the United States and settled into a position on the Marine Corps staff as director of marine aviation. When General Charles Barrett died just prior to the landings on Bougainville, Geiger assumed command of the I Amphibious Corps, thereby becoming the first marine aviator to command such a large ground force. He stayed in charge as I 'Phib became III 'Phib and led

them through the invasions of Guam and Peleliu. The operations on Peleliu had barely concluded when the Tenth Army tapped the corps to take
part in the invasion of Okinawa.

Because the composition of the III 'Phib changed with each operation, Geiger had already worked with many of the units and commanders
scheduled for Okinawa. During the Bougainville operation, Geiger had
under his command the 3rd MARDIV, the 37th Infantry Division, and
a New Zealand Infantry Division. In Guam, he once again had the 3rd
MARDIV, with the addition of the 1st Marine Provisional Brigade (which
became the core of the 6th MARDIV) and the 77th Infantry Division. At
Peleliu, he had the 1st and 2nd MARDIVs plus the 81st Infantry Division. In fact, the operation on Okinawa marked the first time that Geiger
would command a purely marine corps.

Command relationships were further eased by the fact that Geiger
and Buckner had been friends ever since they had attended the Army
Command and General Staff College together in 1924–25.[44] They even
resembled each other physically—tall with gray hair and bright blue
eyes. As a result of their long association Buckner trusted Geiger implic-
itly. Furthermore, despite his long years as an aviator, Geiger had proved
through three operations that he had not lost his ability to conduct
ground operations. It also helped that Geiger had previously worked with
and fought alongside five of the eight division commanders, including
two army divisions, in three previous campaigns without the slightest
hint of interservice issues. If Buckner had been possessed of any doubts,
they were dispelled when Geiger briefed his initial plan for the invasion.
Buckner must have been impressed with the thoroughness of Geiger's
plan, as he found little to criticize or even add.

This was one reason that Buckner tapped him to be his successor in
the unlikely event that he was killed or incapacitated during the operation.[45] The other was Geiger's experience as an aviator. As a fellow aviator, Buckner understood the importance of the tactical air portion of the
operations plan and as the majority of the air support was marine aviation,
he believed that Geiger was the best person to integrate air with ground
operations.[46] As this meant skipping over General Fred Wallace, the next
most senior army commander and designated garrison commander,
Buckner sent this request up through Richardson. This was a mere cour-
tesy since Richardson was technically in charge of all army forces in the

theater, but had no actual command authority over the operation. Buckner noted in his diary, "Sent letter through Richardson to Admiral Nimitz asking that Geiger take over the Tenth Army should I become a casualty. His reaction will be entertaining since he mortally fears and distrusts the marines."[47] However, when Richardson frostily informed Buckner that that decision was the purview of the War Department, essentially issuing what Buckner termed a "pocket veto" of the proposed command structure, Buckner decided the drop the matter until the operation began.[48] Then the Tenth Army would then be out of Richardson's administrative control and he could settle the secession issue directly with Nimitz.[49]

Spruance also shared Buckner's liking of Geiger, once referring to him as one of the few "born brave man." He admired Geiger's fighting spirit as exemplified by Geiger's accompaniment of the UDTs on their forays prior to the invasion of Guam, believing that a commander must conduct his own personal reconnaissance, and his habit of popping up on the front lines unannounced.[50] Their friendship was such that Spruance occasionally targeted him for practical jokes. While fighting on Okinawa, Geiger came down with the mumps and, embarrassed at contracting a childhood disease, wanted to hide the fact from his men. In a fit of puckishness, Spruance sent him a present of a diaper and safety pin. Geiger sent back word that he would treasure it as a battle trophy.[51]

Of course, not everyone shared his confidence in Geiger, particularly Turner who confided to Buckner that he "didn't consider Generals Geiger or Schmidt very intelligent."[52] However, in the end, Buckner got his way and, over many objections, designated Geiger the operation's alternate commander. As Buckner saw it, Geiger had already proved his ability to work with the army at Guam and had demonstrated "that at least one marine general knew how to lead a corps with competence."[53] His confidence in Geiger was echoed by many who had observed him in action: "one of the marines' most carefully educated officers"; "Vigorously intolerant of bungling . . . equally verbose in praising high achievement"; "a handy man to have around"; and "thickset, poker-face, chilly-eyed General Geiger is another marine's marine."[54]

1st Marine Division "The Old Breed"

It was fitting that the division that conducted the first landing in the first battle of the Pacific theater (Guadalcanal) would take part in the last battle of the war. The 1st Marine Division had been more or less in continuous combat and training since 1942 and had participated in three additional operations.[55] Three years of combat created a unit with few similarities to the division that stormed ashore at Guadalcanal. This was the marines' most experienced division and by the time training began for Okinawa, one-third of the division's men had fought in at least two actions, another third had fought in one, and the final third were new replacements.[56]

Fortunately for these replacements, the division had four months in which to conduct training, most of which was conducted on Pavuvu, a tiny island only about one mile wide. It was a nasty, fetid jungle, filled with piles of rotted coconuts so deep that they actually hampered movement.[57] Despite this, the division worked through small-unit tactical problems, as well as undergoing specialized training for jungle, chemical, and urban warfare. In addition, as the Okinawa operation would be the first time that the division landed as part of a much bigger force, training also emphasized large-scale field maneuvers. However, the lack of an adequate training area hampered such large training operations and forced artillery, regimental, and division exercises to be conducted on a rotational basis on Guadalcanal.[58] Pavuvu also did not offer much terrain variety that would have allowed the division to prepare for the beaches, jungles, open plains, and mountains it would face on the more sprawling Okinawa.[59] One of the regimental commanders later commented that despite the lack of time or space for true rehearsals, after four campaigns the division had enough veterans that it managed to solve the majority of its problems before loading up and heading out to Okinawa.[60]

Leading the division was General Pedro del Valle. Just as Geiger the aviator was anomalous among marine commanders, so was del Valle the artillery officer. In fact, artillery officers so rarely made senior rank that at the start of the war, he was the only artillery colonel in the entire Marine Corps.[61] Del Valle had attended Annapolis, only the second Puerto Rican to do so, and he was the first to enter the marines. He did well academically at the academy, but skirted the edge in discipline. In fact, he was nearly kicked out of the marines before his career could even start when one of his Annapolis moneymaking schemes—selling the translations of the Spanish textbooks—caught up with him as a second lieutenant.[62] He would also face court martial at the beginning of WWII for allegedly speaking contemptuously of President Roosevelt, but the charges were dropped during the pre-trial investigation.[63]

Soon after graduation, he found himself as the first man ashore when America seized Santo Domingo during World War I. Afterwards he was sent to Scapa Flow and the Firth of Forth, where he remained for the rest of World War I. By that time, he had begun his lifelong passion for the "black art of field artillery." Peacetime ammunition and budget shortfalls meant that most artillerymen had to learn their profession from books rather than practice. To compensate, del Valle picked the brains of every experienced artillery non-commissioned officer he could find, until he had mastered the "simple mathematical formulas that could solve almost any artillery problem."[64]

In the opening stages of the Pacific offensive del Valle commanded the 1st MARDIV artillery on Guadalcanal, where he shared a vision with Collins, the Americal Division commander, on innovative uses of artillery as close support.[65] However, he had little time to test his theories as at the end of operations, he took command of the marine forces in the Guadalcanal area before returning to the United States to head up the Marine Corps Equipment Board. In that capacity he was an observer of operations on Saipan, but had no direct combat role. In April 1944, del Valle returned to the Pacific Theater as commander of III Amphibious Corps artillery, arriving just in time to support the landing on Guam. Here he had the satisfaction of seeing that the artillery innovations, such as using artillery barrages directly in front of troop lines and the use of forward observers, which he and Collins had championed on Guadalcanal, were now standard practice.[66] In November 1944, he took command of the 1st Marine Division just as it began preparations for Okinawa.

Since the training areas on Pavuvu were inadequate, del Valle gave his subordinate commanders free rein to improvise their training schemes and sought their input into the final operations plan. This led to a number of small but crucial innovations to the invasion plan, such as the adoption of a corporal's suggestion to take along ladders for use in climbing the cliffs seen in reconnaissance photos. Del Valle's stance was that he was not "a stiff shirt general giving orders; [I] was a man working with a lot of other men and taking their ideas . . . so that everyone felt it was part of his plan."[67]

6th Marine Division "The Striking Sixth"

The 6th Marine Division had the singular honor of being the only marine division never to serve in the United States.[68] However, the division was anything but green. It consisted of the 4th Marines, reconstituted from the original regiment lost on Bataan by uniting the marines from the raider battalions into a single regiment. It also controlled the 22nd Marines, which had fought as the 1st Provisional Marine Brigade on Guam. These two regiments were soon joined by the 1st Battalion, 29th Marines, which had fought on Saipan. The final two battalions of the 29th Marines—the only part of the division to have any time in the United States—joined the 1st MARDIV on Guadalcanal for training. However, even these two battalions, while not battle-tested as a unit, contained a large proportion of veterans from other divisions. Shepherd said of the regiment, "The 29th was formed of some the finest non-commissioned officers . . . who had done a great deal of the training at Parris Island and San Diego (the two large marine training centers)."[69]

The division commander, General Lemuel Shepherd, another future Commandant of the Marine Corps, had led the 1st Provisional Marine Brigade (now the 22nd Marines) on Guam. Just 48 years old, Shepherd was one of the youngest division commanders in the theater. His reputation as a fearless warrior had begun in 1918, on the battlefields of France. He was twice wounded at Belleau Wood and then once more in the Meuse-Argonne offensive. He also received both the Army Distinguished Service Cross and the Navy Cross. Immediately after the war, Shepherd served as aide-de-camp to then-Commandant of the Marine Corps, General John Lejeune. Afterwards, he served overseas in Brazil and China before coming back in 1937 to work with Holland Smith on the development of amphibious doctrine. At the outbreak of World War II, he took command of the 9th Marine Regiment before being selected as brigadier general. Shepherd fought in Guadalcanal and Cape Gloucester with the 1st MARDIV and then took the 1st Marine Provisional Brigade into Guam.

Unlike many of the other divisions slated for the Okinawa operation, the 6th MARDIV had the luxury of almost six months' training time on Guadalcanal prior to boarding ship for Okinawa. Given this much time, the division could conduct the full range of training events, starting with individual and small unit tactics. Knowing that, as on Guam, the division would face the probability of urban combat, Shepherd ordered the construction of streets and buildings so as to practice house-to-house fighting, which would prove useful as the division had to capture the city of Naha, which had 60,000 residents.[70] The training culminated in an eight-day division exercise along the coast of Guadalcanal.[71] This proved a valuable experience, as the coast of Guadalcanal closely mirrored the conditions they would face on the shores of Okinawa. The division was also able to spend extra time focusing on combined operations such as tank-infantry and air-ground cooperation that had proved to be a continuing challenge throughout the war.[72] In fact, it was Buckner's observation of this training that convinced him to drop the requirement for monthly divisional training reports.[73]

Shepherd later said of the division, "I think when we left for Okinawa we had the most professionally trained division of the Marine Corps. We just concentrated on every phase of operations—tank, infantry, attacking towns, fortified towns and all types of warfare . . . I think they were the tops."[74] As the division embarked for the operation, it might have been the first battle for the division, but most of the men onboard understood what they would be facing as the first wave of the landing force.

RESERVE UNITS

2nd Marine Division "Follow Me"

The 2nd MARDIV had seen some of the toughest fighting and highest casualties of the war. On Saipan, it had taken the highest number of losses of any division in the battle. By the end of operations on Saipan and Tinian the division was down to 12,000 marines (from a high of over 22,000). The Marine Corps transferred a further 2,800 to provide the cadre for newly formed 6th Marine Division. Although it received over 8,000 replacements before the start of the Okinawa operation, over half the division's combat battalions consisted of green troops. If it was going to be ready for operations on Okinawa, the division required a thorough training regimen starting at the individual level and working up to a division-level exercise.[75]

Part of the division training included mopping-up operations on Saipan, which allowed it to season its new recruits in a combat environment.

Unfortunately, being on Saipan meant that the division had limited access to training facilities. On his visit in February 1945, Buckner observed, "Training facilities were meager, but the 2nd appears to be . . . the best of the MARDIVS."[76] He also had a chance to meet with the division's senior leaders and later commented to Oliver Smith that he had never seen such "an alert bunch of battalion commanders."[77] One thing that especially impressed him was the "Second Division Japanese Language School" run by two junior officers, which originated from the helplessness the marines had felt when they were unable to communicate with Saipan's civilian population and had watched whole families jump to their deaths rather than be taken prisoner by the Americans. This language school helped all of the division's marines gain at least a rudimentary knowledge of the language. Although the Okinawan civilians spoke their own dialect, most of them knew enough standard Japanese to understand the Americans.[78]

Tenth Army identified the division as the floating reserve, and as such it needed to be prepared to launch any of a myriad of on-call missions: act as the demonstration force and conduct a diversionary landing; land in support of the assault force; capture the island of Ie Shima; or capture any of the other small islands east of the big island, should there be significant enemy fire coming from them. Furthermore, the division had the alternate mission of providing artillery support and reinforcements to the assault forces as needed.[79] This meant that the division needed to carve out training time to cover all of the various missions it might have to perform. Fortunately, once Saipan was pacified, the division was able to focus the final two months of training on regimental and battalion-level training.

After having participated in so many harrowing landings with other units, the leadership understood the importance of landing rehearsals and devoted the entire month of February to loading and landing operations. When it came time to do a final rehearsal, Watson made the decision to focus on rehearsing regiment-level landings and conducting one large demonstration landing. However, the weather and other elements conspired to wreck these plans. High, rough seas made it impossible for the navy to launch landing craft, forcing the division to simulate the landings. Furthermore, this inability to conduct a full-scale rehearsal meant that the division never had a chance to test its communications equipment.[80] Immediately after this pseudo-rehearsal, the division loaded its equipment and embarked for Okinawa. En route the division learned that it would conduct diversionary landings on 1 and 2 April, followed by landings in support of the assault force.

27th Infantry Division "O'Ryan's Roughnecks"

By late August 1944, both the brutal combat with the Japanese and the vicious intramural political battle with the marines were over, and the 27th Division departed Saipan for the island of Espiritu Santo. There they expected to have several months to recuperate and prepare for its next operation. The 27th Division scarcely resembled the unit that had left Hawaii more than eighteen months earlier and could no longer be considered a "National Guard" unit, since fewer than half of its original members remained. Saipan alone had cost the division over 2,000 casualties. Moreover, the final outcome of the Smith versus Smith debate had led to a new division commander, a new assistant division commander, two new regimental commanders (although the 105th Commander, Colonel Leonard Bishop, was relieved more for his health than for his performance), and five new battalion commanders.[81] Worse, the army was not able to provide replacements to make up for what was lost on Saipan. As the division boarded ship for Okinawa, it remained dangerously shorthanded by almost 1,800 soldiers, mainly infantry. Each infantry company would, therefore, enter combat already lacking approximately 40 riflemen.[82]

Commanding the 27th ID was Griner, who had taken over from Jarman on 28 June. He was a World War I veteran who had previously commanded the 13th Airborne and 98th Infantry Divisions and had been the assistant division commander of the 77th ID, but had not seen combat with any of those units. From Spruance's and Turner's viewpoint, Griner had gotten the 27th ID moving again on Saipan and they considered him the division's best hope for redeeming its reputation and reviving its fighting spirit.

Griner took command of a unit reaching a low point in morale. Much of the division had been overseas with no break for over two-and-a-half years. A general disgruntlement over its long service without a rest was compounded when Robert Sherrod's articles accusing the division of cowardice appeared in *Time* magazine.[83] In an attempt to defend the unit's reputation and enhance the division's morale, Griner wrote a letter to *Time*'s editors defending his soldiers' performance. Marshall, however, viewed the letter as further "pot-stirring" and, in the name of interservice solidarity, refused to allow its publication.[84] When Buckner inspected the 27th in January 1945, he tersely noted, "They look good but are more concerned with furlough than with fighting."[85] Griner did what he could to raise spirits by bringing in entertainment and cycling soldiers on furlough, although the number allowed to go each month was so small that one soldier quipped that he expected to get home in 1949.[86]

Despite the fact that Espiritu Santo had been a training site since the beginning of the war, the 27th found itself assigned to a desolate, malarial coconut grove on the island. The area was so undeveloped that the division did not even have barracks and had to spend the first two months building everything they might need. Because of the time needed to build the camp, the division did not start serious training until the end of October, when it received word that it would become part of Tenth Army. Nevertheless, this gave the division more training time than all the other divisions, save the 1st MARDIV.[87] Using the voluminous lessons learned on Saipan, the staff embarked on a four-phase training plan that would not only bring the replacements up to speed, but also address the deficiencies identified amongst its more veteran units.

The first four-week block focused on basic individual combat training and weapons familiarization. Then the division moved through squad/platoon training, then to company and battalion-level tasks. The capstone event was two weeks of practicing battalion-sized amphibious assaults including three live-fire exercises.[88] Griner made it a special point to have the units focus on three areas of weakness identified in Saipan: night-fighting, jungle operations, and infantry-tank cooperation.[89]

Despite this, the division neglected to address one glaring weakness: the regimental staffs never once directed or participated in any of the exercises, except to set up and take down the command posts. This was a surprising omission given that two of the regimental commanders were relatively new and that the third had just returned after several months of convalescence.[90] It is hard to determine if the division's uneven performance was exacerbated by this, but it certainly did not help the soldiers who were already feeling let down by their leaders.

Part of this training oversight might have resulted from the fact that, as on Saipan, no one informed the division of its actual mission and the staff was busy with devising multiple operations plans. In total, the Tenth

Army had the 27th ID staff draw up plans for three different operations: landing on the eastern islands; landing on Ie Shima; and landing on the western coast of Okinawa. In reality, the Tenth Army initially planned to use the 27th as the garrison force, although their final role was not determined until after the operation began.

The division sailed for Okinawa at the end of March and finally arrived off the island's coast on 3 April. For several days, it was a floating reserve, still unsure of its mission. In the end, one regiment, the 106th, went to assist the 77th ID in the capture of the outer islands, while the remaining two began landing on 9 April in order to reinforce the XXIV Corps.

77th Infantry Division "Statue of Liberty"

The 77th Infantry Division had had little respite in the last year. In July 1944, the division, along with the 3rd Marine Division, assaulted Guam. From there, the soldiers sailed directly to the Philippines and participated in operations at Leyte. When these operations concluded in February 1945, Buckner tapped the division to conduct the landings on the Kerama Islands adjacent to Okinawa, scheduled for six days before the main landings.

Throughout these years of hard fighting, the division had had the same commander: General Andrew Bruce. Bruce was another intellectual heavyweight and had seen action in every major American battle in World War I, where he earned the Distinguished Service Cross. But he had served the majority of the interwar years either teaching or attending school. Not only had he attended both the Army and Navy War Colleges, but he devoted his time on the army staff revising doctrinal textbooks. During the early war years he organized a tank destroyer center at the newly opened Fort Hood, Texas, before taking command of the 77th Division.[91]

Bruce seemed immune from the army-marine rivalry that had marked interservice relations during other battles. His two campaigns fighting alongside marine units in Guam and Leyte were exemplars of harmonious interservice cooperation. He was especially friendly with Geiger, under whom he had fought on Guam.[92] He was also widely recognized as one of the army's best division commanders, with both Buckner and even the normally taciturn Stilwell singling him out for particular praise. After inspecting the Tenth Army in combat on Okinawa, Still-well wrote, "Bruce is the only man I've met who remembers his tactics."[93] Even the army-loathing Holland Smith wrote of Bruce on Guam, "I was very much impressed by Bruce and his men and felt they would give an excellent account of themselves . . . when the 77th did move, it moved fast."[94] In fact, Bruce may have been the only army officer to receive such praise from Smith.

The Kerama Island mission suited Bruce, as he was something of a loner as well as a maverick. Oliver Smith later remembered, "He wanted to operate alone. He was never happy when he had to be a part of the army or the corps [unit]."[95] However, because the division had to depart ahead of the main body, Bruce had had scant time to put his division through its paces in preparation for its new mission. Moreover, a substantial amount of the training time available had to be given over to rest and rehabilita-tion for the battle-weary combat battalions. The division did, however, manage to find time to conduct a week of practice landings in Leyte Gulf before sailing on 18 March.[96]

Given his lack of combat experience, Buckner could not have asked for a better group of leaders underneath him. Not only did their experi-ence balance out his lack thereof, but these men were all well-versed in joint operations. In many cases, they had fought together and forged a trust in one another. With the miasma of the Saipan controversy hanging over the operation, it was these leaders who would set the example for those below them and put service loyalties aside for the sake of the mis-sion. This could not have been easy, especially with the 27th Division— the epicenter of the controversy—in their midst. Furthermore, given the short amount of time available for planning and training, it is doubtful that this operation could have been accomplished if the divisions had been less experienced. For this reason, Okinawa could truly be seen as a capstone of all that had come before it.

OPERATIONS

Enemy Operations

After the disastrous blow suffered by the Japanese navy during the "Great Marianas Turkey Shoot," the commander of Japan's Combined Fleet introduced a new tactic of crash-diving loaded bombers into American ships. These *kamikaze* attacks had had limited effect to date, but that did not stop the Japanese planners from hatching *Ten Go* ("Heavenly Operation") to hinder the attack on Okinawa and, they hoped, cut the invasion force off from its supplies and reinforcements. The plan involved four thousand airplanes and hundreds of suicide boats, including Japan's remaining warships, which primarily targeted American transport ships and aircraft carriers. The planned attacks would come north from Formosa and south from Kyushu, the most southwest of the so-called "Home Islands" that constituted Japan proper.

These attacks began a week before the landings, as several hundred kamikaze planes came hurtling at the American carrier groups steaming towards Okinawa. When the first attacks were over, four carriers and several smaller ships were damaged, but the Japanese had lost 163 planes. While U.S. factories could replace that many planes in twelve hours, it took the Japanese more than two weeks to do the same while their experienced pilots were lost forever.[97] However, the Japanese naval command spun these minor injuries to the U.S. fleet into a great triumph over the Americans, even claiming to have stopped the fleet's progress.[98] This gave the Japanese new hope that a larger use of *kamikazes*, coupled with a renewed offensive spirit, might suffice to stop the Americans from ever setting foot on Japanese soil.

However, the *kamikaze* attacks were only one of many tactical changes that the Japanese had made. After suffering a long series of demoralizing defeats at American hands, the commanders on Okinawa decided to rethink their defensive strategy. In the past, the Japanese had fought according to a simple dictate: destroy the invaders at the water's edge. When that failed, they relied on suicidal night banzai attacks as their primary offensive tactic. Unfortunately for the defenders, these had produced little except piles of dead Japanese soldiers. In fact, one officer observed that the most efficient and least costly way to kill Japanese was to let them attack at night, since their inability to coordinate the attacks and their "blind fanatic frenzy" prevented them from learning from its errors.[99] On Okinawa, for the first time Japanese commanders acknowledged that the materiel advantage enjoyed by the Americans probably trumped the perceived spiritual superiority of the Japanese soldier.[100]

The revolutionary (to the Japanese army at least) idea of establishing a defense-in-depth would not have worked on some of the smaller islands, but it ideally suited the topography and size of Okinawa. The Japanese army first tested this idea on the island of Biak in New Guinea in May 1944 and followed up on subsequent operations. There the defenders allowed the Americans to land unopposed and then subjected them to a long, grinding battle of attrition. Although the Japanese eventually lost each island, they had exacted a stiff price in blood and materiel. The marine intelligence report on Okinawa noted, "Recent combat operations against the enemy have demonstrated that well trained Japanese will conduct a different defense than is seen in the past . . . the enemy, with a few exceptions, used the terrain well and coordinated his defense and attacks."[101]

The first part of the Japanese plan allowed the Americans to land unmolested. During that phase, the actual target of Japanese efforts was the ships arrayed around the island with attacks by the *kamikazes*. The Japanese commander on Okinawa also designated Shuri Castle as the centerpiece of his defense. The bulk of the Japanese defensive lines spread to the sea on either side, to the city of Naha in the west and to Yonabaru Airfield in the east, with Shuri Castle near the center. Other soldiers occupied the Oroku Peninsula and some were scattered throughout the northern part of the island. His troops—almost 100,000 strong—consisted of highly experienced units pulled back from China, combined with newly formed combat units and Okinawan conscripts. The motto of the defending force, composed by its commander, was "One plane for one warship; One boat for one ship; One man for ten of the enemy or one tank."[102] And so the defenders sat in their defensive positions and waited for the Americans to come.

The Japanese based their defenses in southern Okinawa around three major defensive strongholds, all designed to protect Shuri. The northernmost line ran along the Kakazu Ridge, a few miles north of Shuri. The second, and main, perimeter lay across the north side of Shuri Castle. The third ran across the southern tip of the island from the town of Itoman through to the town of Gusichan. A complex network of caves and tunnels crisscrossed and connected the various parts of island, allowing troops free movement, protected from indirect fire. These tunnels also allowed the Japanese units to fall back relatively intact ahead of an American advance.

Moreover, the east-west nature of the ridgelines would slow the American advance and allow the Japanese to exploit fully the relatively protected reverse slopes of each ridgeline with artillery and machine gun positions. The Japanese also made full use of the stone Okinawan tombs, which provided ready-made pillboxes. This turned almost every one of them into a weapons position. They also sited these positions so as to force the advancing Americans to walk into sheets of interlocking fire. However, the downside of these cave-based defenses was that while they protected the soldiers from indirect fire, they were vulnerable to a combination of infantry-tank attacks. Captured Japanese documents revealed just how much they feared the tank attacks and that the primary mission of the Japanese artillery was to destroy tanks.[103]

For five days after the invasion, the defenders allowed the Americans to move across the island, taking airfields, while they mounted little more than token resistance. The Japanese plan called for a three-pronged counterattack. The first prong, *Ten-Go*, began on 6 April. For the next ten weeks over 4,000 airplanes—both *kamikaze* and conventional—launched from bases in Formosa and Kyushu. Simultaneously, hundreds of suicide motorboats hurled themselves at the American fleet. To support these suicide attacks the Imperial Navy sent the *Yamato*, the largest battleship in the world, along with nine smaller warships, on a one-way voyage. This small fleet, a mere shadow of what the Imperial Navy could muster at the war's beginning, was supposed to fight its way through the American ships and deliberately beach its ships on Okinawa to allow the *Yamato* to hammer the Americans on the island with its mighty guns. When the ships were eventually destroyed, the crews were to join the ground forces in defense of the island. At the same time, the army would launch the third prong, a grand counterattack on the American forces already ashore. With the Americans deprived of naval, aerial, and logistical support, the Japanese hoped that it would be easy to roll up the U.S. army and marine divisions in one final ground battle.

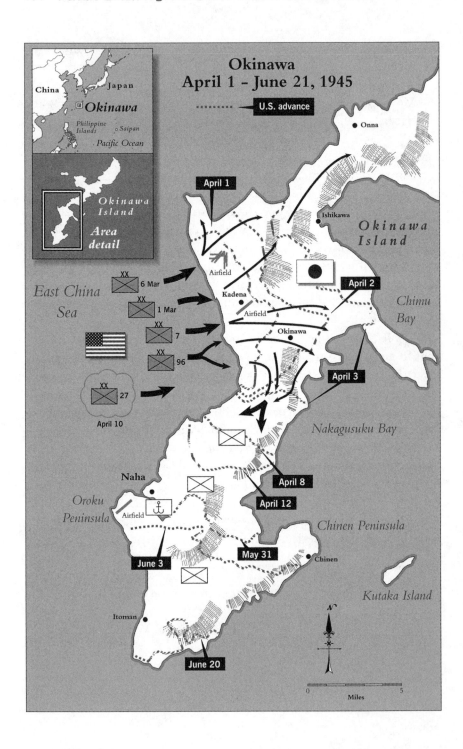

Okinawa
April 1 - June 21, 1945

U.S. advance

Landing Operations [104]

Phase I officially began on 25 March when the UDTs slipped into the water surrounding the Kerama Islands as a task force patrolled the area in case of Japanese naval or air attacks. The UDTs then turned their focus on clearing channels through the reefs off of the various landing beaches. Not only did they look for obstacles, but they also provided invaluable reconnaissance almost all the way to the beaches.[105] Fortunately, the only obstacles that they found were easily cleared wooden stakes intended to tear up the bottoms of the amtracs. Each division provided seven observers to accompany the UDTs so that they could take the final intelligence directly back to each of the staffs, from the battalion level up.[106]

For days, prior to the UDTs beginning their work, naval and aerial fire had bombarded the island, seeking to wipe out enemy emplacements that might impede the landings. As 1 April 1945 dawned, more than 1,400 ships lay off the coast of Okinawa. Looking at the landing through his binoculars, one Japanese soldier remarked the seas looked like 30 percent water and 70 percent ships.[107] The marines from the 1st and 6th Marine divisions, joined by the 7th and 96th Infantry divisions, boarded their landing craft and girded themselves for the hailstorm of enemy artillery and machine-gun fire so many of them had endured before. Instead, they encountered an eerie silence as wave after wave landed with little more than sporadic enemy fire that inflicted little damage. In fact, the worst casualties suffered that day were in the 2nd MARDIV, which was conducting a diversionary feint off the southeastern coast. A kamikaze raid struck the convoy, resulting in the destruction of one transport ship and one LST with fifty-three casualties.[108]

By the end of the day, more than 50,000 troops had landed and moved up to 5,000 yards inland along an eight-mile front at a cost of 28 killed, 104 wounded, and 27 missing.[109] Veterans who had suffered devastating losses in previous landings could scarcely believe the ease with which they had literally strolled onto the beaches and taken their first day objectives. Spruance noted in his after action report that, "naturally, all attack commands were highly elated with this unexpected situation. The fierce fighting and heavy casualties considered unavoidable in taking this area had not materialized due to the sudden withdrawal of the unpredictable [enemy]."[110] Of course, this was just a false lull. Three months of brutal combat lay ahead before the Americans could declare the island secure.

Battle Summary[111]

By the afternoon of 2 April, the 7th ID had reached the eastern coast of Okinawa and, joined by the 96th ID, it pivoted south. At that point, the operation was eleven days ahead of schedule. However, if the army thought the entire campaign would be as easy as the landing, the Japanese quickly disabused them of that notion. Along the fortified ridgelines north of the Shuri stronghold, the fighting soon dissolved into vicious hand-to-hand combat. When the soldiers finally cleared this ridgeline three days later, they had suffered 1,500 casualties, against 4,500 Japanese killed or captured. Ahead of them, though, lay Kakazu Ridge followed by Shuri Castle and the main body of the Japanese army.

It was a slow, bloody slog through fields of direct and indirect fire. Time and again the Japanese repelled the American advance on Kakazu Ridge. The Japanese might have been able to keep up this grinding attrition indefinitely if the senior commanders on the island had stuck to the original defense plan. However, the offensive impulse proved too strong and they ordered an assault for 12 April in conjunction with amphibious landings intended to ambush the Americans from the rear. The attack resulted in the loss of four battalions, as well as all of the amphibious troops, who were caught at sea and annihilated before they reached shore.[112]

The 27th Division, which landed on 7 April, joined the other two army divisions on 19 April to renew the forward drive. Even with this reinforcement, it took five more days before the three divisions finally pushed through and destroyed the first line of defenses around Shuri. The Japanese had fought hard for every yard and when the smoke cleared, the Japanese retreated back into their warren of caves and tunnels, as the weary Americans regrouped and prepared for further assaults.

As the stalemate in the south continued, the marines focused on clearing the north, where resistance was initially even lighter than what the soldiers faced in the south. The 1st MARDIV reached the eastern shore on 3 April and spent the better part of the month mopping up as the 6th MARDIV began its drive up the Motobu Peninsula. As tanks were virtually useless in the rugged northern terrain, it remained for the infantry to slog steadily north, rolling up the Japanese pillboxes and caves along the way. By 19 April, the 6th MARDIV had settled into mopping up operations, which would last for the next several weeks.

During this time, the Japanese ramped up Operation *Ten-Go* and were starting to inflict serious losses on the American fleet. Thankfully, the damage was not as extensive as it might have been, as the attacks were uncoordinated and the pilots progressively less skilled. Nonetheless, they managed to sink 26 American ships and damage a further 164. With their fleet and air force in a shambles, the Japanese ace-in-the-hole was supposed to be the *Yamato*, the Imperial Navy's sole remaining super-battleship, in a naval kamikaze attack. Unfortunately for its hapless crew, Americans detected the ship almost as soon as it left port on 6 April and hammered it and its accompanying fleet with hundreds of torpedo planes and dive bombers. The *Yamato*, along with all but four of its accompanying cruisers and destroyers, was sunk on 7 April without getting anywhere near Okinawa.[113]

On 16 April the 77th ID, which had been idle since its conquest of the Kerama Islands on 26–29 March, invaded Ie Shima. The small island not only had several airfields, but also offered a commanding overview of the Motobu Peninsula. The island proved to be better defended than anyone anticipated and it took almost a week for the division to clear out the last Japanese defenders. Bruce, the 77th ID commander, called the fighting there "the bitterest [he] had ever seen." It was also the site of a personal blow to all American servicemen as machine-gun fire killed Ernie Pyle, the beloved journalist who had spent the last four years telling the story of the war from the point of view of the average soldier. Eventually, the division was able to clear the island. After repairing the destroyed airfields, the Americans had a new base from which to launch air attacks on the main island.

In the meantime, the marines had completed the conquest of the northern part of the island and joined the army divisions for the assault on the Shuri stronghold. The 27th and the 96th had suffered such heavy casualties that they needed to pull back in order to repair equipment and integrate replacements. By this point the 77th had left Ie Shima and landed on Okinawa. They were immediately ordered forward to replace the 96th, while the 1st MARDIV replaced the 27th.

It made little difference. The stalemate continued. On 11 April, Buckner wryly noted in his journal, "As usual [Bruce] is rarin' to try a landing behind the Jap [*sic*] main position in southern Okinawa."[114] Bruce, whose 7th ID had conducted a similar successful operation in Leyte, had advocated the move for a while. In what turned out to be the most controversial decision of the campaign, Buckner rejected the idea for a variety of reasons. The first was that the G-4 (logistics) could not supply ammunition to such an operation. The second was that the dangerous reefs would slow down the landings and leave the division vulnerable to the Japanese artillery that overlooked the beaches. Moreover, intelligence suspected that the Japanese reserve lay in the area and it would be impossible to get any support to the division should it find itself trapped. Finally, Buckner recognized that by the time the 77th ID would be available after the Ie Shima operations, the other combat divisions would need relief after almost a month of continuous combat. At this point the 2nd MARDIV was back in Saipan preparing for a landing on Kakai, an island north of Okinawa, in July, thus leaving the 77th as the only available reserve.[115]

On 4 May, Japanese commitment to the "cult of the offensive" again came to the Americans' rescue. They abandoned their defensive plans and launched a banzai attack, this time in conjunction with kamikaze attacks at sea. As it had every other time, the banzai attack failed miserably, costing the Japanese over 5,000 soldiers—almost all of their reserves. The kamikazes had better luck, sinking or damaging 17 American ships. But this made no difference to the battle's outcome. It seems that at that point, the Japanese leadership concluded that only remaining hope for victory was to inflict as much damage on the invading force as possible.

By this time, the Tenth Army had regrouped and prepared for a new offensive, designed to envelop Shuri. The 96th ID had returned to the line, replacing the 7th ID and, along with the 77th ID, moved to storm the fortress from the east. The 1st and 6th MARDIVs planned to do the same from the west. The Americans launched the attack on 11 May and for the next two weeks the two corps measured their progress in yards. The casualties on both sides piled up—over 23,000 on the American side and 64,000 on the Japanese side. In desperation, the Japanese began a "tactical redeployment" to the southeast right under the Americans' eyes. By 29 May, when the divisions finally took Shuri, the tunnels and caves were largely empty. They had expected to end the campaign then and there, but now had to pivot and face the remnants of the Japanese force that had redeployed from the Shuri line.[116] This force was dug in along a large coral outcropping, the Yaeju-Dake Escarpment, and prepared for a last stand. It took another month for the Americans to pivot and destroy this final stronghold.

However, the Japanese did have one final triumph. On 18 June, while he was visiting the 1st Marine Division area of operation, a Japanese artillery shell struck the coral outcropping under which Buckner stood and a fragment of the coral tore through his chest. To the stunned amazement of the uninjured soldiers standing around him, Buckner bled to death in just a few minutes.

His staff had long fretted at Buckner's habit of visiting the front with only his aide and driver. His chief of staff, Major General Elwyn Post, and Oliver Smith had discussed this issue, with Post admitting that he knew that there was a chance Buckner would get "bumped off," but that he could not dissuade him from making the trips every morning. Smith agreed, noting that Geiger did more or less the same thing, but somehow managed to not take as many chances as Buckner did.[117]

In accordance with Buckner's wishes, Geiger took command of the Tenth Army, making him the first marine to command a full army. Although his command would be short-lived—just five days—during that time Geiger managed to declare the island secure and announce the end of major combat operations. Soldiers who served with him remembered that they had "no unforeseen problems and, unlike the fiasco on Saipan, things went easily . . . [Geiger] was a much smoother commander than Howling Mad Smith."[118] On 23 April, General Joseph Stilwell took command to oversee the final mopping-up operations.

ANALYSIS

Planning

Buckner realized early on that in order for the operation to succeed and to put the ghosts of Saipan behind them, it was crucial that his staff be a truly joint one. In past operations, while lip service was paid to joint planning, the nature of the operations meant that each division conducted individual planning without consulting the other services. Even at higher levels senior commanders had been reluctant to make much use of officers from the other services. For instance, in the Marianas Holland Smith was far too partisan, and too disillusioned with army capabilities, to allow much army input on his planning staff.

As mentioned earlier, Buckner may have gone overboard in his desire to ensure the navy and marines were well represented on his staff and as a result, his staff became bloated. In fact, even after O. P. Smith removed one-third of the marine and naval officers, the headquarters remained so large (approximately 340 officers) that he divided it into a forward echelon, a rear echelon, and a liaison detachment that remained at Pearl Harbor. During movement, the forward echelon was further divided into a command echelon, which consisted of all the senior officers and was on Buckner's command ship, and a working staff, scattered among three ships.[119] Despite his staff's haphazard and awkward organization, it functioned together well, something that could probably be attributed first and foremost to the congenial working relationship between Buckner and O. P. Smith. Smith also had a close relationship with his army counterpart, General Lawrence Schick, whom Smith called "the finest staff officer with whom I have had the pleasure of serving."[120]

The marine and navy officers did not form separate staff sections. Instead, they were integrated seamlessly into the existing staff structure. Unlike the army officers on Holland Smith's staff in earlier operations, the marines did not feel that their views were ignored, such as when Buckner took O. P. Smith's advice on training. Even the way in which Buckner referred to marines under his command as "my marines" was a direct contrast to Holland Smith, who never once referred to soldiers serving under him as "my soldiers." As one marine commander pointed out, "General Buckner was a very good army commander, and he had on his staff a deputy, O. P. Smith, who was a very brilliant marine."[121] These two—Buckner and O. P. Smith—managed to fuse together a truly joint team that was able to overcome interservice issues for the good of the mission.

Intelligence

Intelligence for the invasion of Okinawa was derived mainly from aerial photography. However, the first limiting factor of aerial photography was that the various photographs were not set to a standard scale, making it almost impossible to accurately compare photographs of the same terrain taken from different sorties. In order to mitigate this, the intelligence staff created and distributed accurate maps, which the divisions began receiving in February. More importantly, the staff updated the maps constantly, as reconnaissance revealed new details.[122] For the 1st MARDIV veterans in particular, the memory of hand-sketched maps at Guadalcanal was still fresh in their minds and they were grateful that that fiasco was not repeated.[123]

Secondly, these photographs gave an excellent overview view of the landing beaches and, when combined with accurate maps and terrain models, allowed leaders to become intimately familiar with the terrain before they landed. However, once they moved in from the beachhead, aerial photography was less useful due to the inability of analysts to pinpoint enemy emplacements in the black-and-white pictures.[124]

This was a recurring problem in large part due to the excellence of Japanese camouflage techniques.[125] Further complicating matters was the fact that the Okinawa defenses consisted mainly of caves and tunnels dug into the sides of the many hills scattered across the island. These tunnels were virtually impossible to spot by air. Indeed, if it were not for the eruptions of gunfire as they advanced on the caves, soldiers and marines would have been hard pressed to detect the entrances. The Americans also had to discover the hard way that the Japanese used the elaborate stone tombs as both weapons positions and ammunition caches.

Training

As detailed earlier, training was difficult, particularly for the XXIV Corps divisions, which found themselves engaged in combat until less than a month before embarkation. It is a testament to the organization and discipline of the staffs that they managed to pack in as much training as they did in the short time allocated.[126] However, every one of these divisions had already been through at least one landing. During these past operations, the ground forces and the navy had learned each other's language and developed enough common doctrinal practices that any of these army or marine divisions could land with any naval unit with a minimum of rehearsals. And so, even though rehearsals had been unsatisfactory, the landings themselves were nearly flawless. In fact, the only criticism—and it was slight indeed—was that one wave was eight minutes late in landing.[127]

Some of the army shortcuts such as training a small number of soldiers on a piece of equipment and then sending them back to their units to train the other soldiers, worked well.[128] Others, such as the 77th ID's "specialist system" of weapons training, fell short. In that case, each man trained on only one or two weapons. But as casualties and the general melee of battle separated teams, the 77th ID found itself short on personnel qualified to use crucial weapons, especially the flamethrowers and demolition material. As a result, there were times when soldiers had to learn how to use a certain weapon in the midst of a firefight.[129]

For the marine divisions, which had almost five months to train, the major hindrance to training was inadequate facilities. For example, the 1st Division did not even have a small arms range on Pavuvu; the 2nd Division on Saipan had to construct its own facilities. Only the 6th Division on Guadalcanal had access to well-developed training and living facilities.[130] Despite this, the marine divisions judged their training and rehearsals as adequate, mainly because of the number of experienced soldiers in each unit.

A common training shortfall in earlier operations had been the inability of the Americans to conduct night operations. This had been a recurring issue since Guadalcanal, and every division focused on improving their night capabilities in training. The Japanese had grown used to controlling the night. When the Japanese staged small night raids (as opposed to the large-scale banzai attacks), they often won back the ground that they had lost during the day. The introduction of the new sniperscopes and snooperscopes, which used infrared radiation to help see in the dark, gave the Americans a new advantage at night. Each division received 110 carbine-mounted sniperscopes for night firing and 140 hand-held snooperscopes for observation and signaling.[131] To their enemy's surprise, the Americans began launching their own night attacks, at times pinning the Japanese in their caves and overrunning objectives where they had found themselves stalemated during the daytime.[132]

The Japanese commander on Okinawa wrote during the campaign, "The enemy's power lies in its tanks. It has become obvious that our general battle against the American forces is a battle against their M1 and M4 tanks." Unlike in the Gilberts, the Americans now brought medium tanks to island battles and these were most effective, especially when assaulting enemy caves and pillboxes as well as attacking artillery emplacements. Due to the terrain there was no way to mass the tanks against enemy formations or strongholds, so they were used to form small tank-infantry groups. However, the lack of training facilities and shortage of time meant that the two were unable to conduct combined arms training. As a result, it took some time during actual combat operations before the tanks and infantry became proficient in working as a team.[133] Although, by this point of the war, infantry commanders generally understood the capabilities of tanks and vice versa, it did not mean that they used one another to the fullest extent. In fact, even late in the campaign, tanks continued to be used improperly, such as when they were used as artillery or sent through unsuitable terrain. The infantry also had to learn that they needed to allocate sufficient maintenance time for the tanks in their plans. This had often frustrated commanders when they were in the attack because they felt that the tanks slowed them down when they had to stop when a tank needed some repair. One tank commander later commented that although they had operated successfully together, the tankers often felt like "a bastard child at a family picnic" because the infantry never understood their logistics or maintenance needs.[134]

After taking casualties from the caves for too long, the Americans finally found a way to combat the Japanese camouflage techniques. Troops used flamethrowers, phosphorous grenades, or even rockets and bazookas to start fires and expose the positions.[135] The tank-mounted flamethrowers proved to be especially adept at this task, with the added benefit that they could get closer to the Japanese positions than the infantry.

Casualties[136]

If Saipan had been a test of marine tactics, then Okinawa was a test of army methods. This was army-type warfare, slow and deliberate, far removed from the marines' emphasis on quick and explosive operations. This frustrated many of the marines, who longed for a chance to move more quickly. One marine commander later mused, "I'm not too sure that sometimes when they whittle you away, 10 or 12 men a day, then maybe it would be better to take 100 [casualties] a day if you can get out within 10 days."[137] However, the statistics show that casualty rates for the two operations were virtually identical. In the end, the army suffered 4,644 killed/ missing in action and 18,010 wounded; the marines had 2, 877 killed/ MIA and 13,388 wounded. There were approximately 183,000 servicemen in combat, making this a 21 percent casualty rate—the exact same as the non-landing battle casualty rate on Saipan. In comparison, the Japanese had 107,359 killed and a further 7,131 wounded/captured. The ratio of 14.3 Japanese killed to each American killed was one of the highest in the war. This high ratio is explained by the fact that the largest number of American casualties generally came during landing operations and this landing was unopposed.

Given the length of the operation and the presence of such diseases as malaria, dengue, and typhus, non-battle casualties were surprisingly low when compared to other long-range operations such as Guadalcanal or Saipan. These low rates were due to the fact that, unlike Guadalcanal, the medical staff conducted preventive measures such as immunizations, prophylactic medicine, and the spraying of DDT to minimize the effects of disease as much as possible. In addition, the medical sanitation units established plentiful water points to reduce the number of water-borne illnesses. In the end, there were no outbreaks of communicable disease. While 26,221 soldiers were non-battle casualties, the majority were able to continue duty or required just a few days to recuperate, so daily duty rates were surprisingly high.[138]

In fact, the biggest cause of non-battle casualties was battle-fatigue and neuropsychiatric casualties were larger than in any other operation. This was a result of a combination of the exhaustion of troops who had had little time between combat operations, the effective and large-scale use of enemy artillery, and the prolonged close-in combat. To counter this problem, the Tenth Army set up a convalescent camp where medics could bring neurological casualties for up to seven days, well away from the combat area. Anyone who could not return to duty after that time was sent off of the island.[139] Because of the effectiveness of these camps, 90 percent of the milder cases and 80 percent of the more severe cases returned to duty, although not all could go back to combat duty.[140]

Commanders

Spruance and his staff had been in continuous combat since Iwo Jima in February 1945. Recognizing the limits of his commanders, on 26 May Nimitz made the unprecedented call to replace the three main naval commanders, Spruance, Turner, and Mitscher, with Halsey, Hill, and Admiral John McCain. This was no reflection on their abilities, but rather an acknowledgment of the constant stress they had endured and a desire for them to rest before launching the planning for the attack on Japan.[141]

Buckner had many detractors who pushed for his removal—if not during this operation, then prior to the Tenth Army's commitment to the invasion of Japan. Foremost among these was MacArthur, who told General Robert Eichelberger, Eighth Army Commander, that, should the Tenth Army ever come under him, he would relieve Buckner for "selling us out to our sister services."[142] Buckner admitted to his wife, "With MacArthur now taking over the army forces it is difficult to predict my future assignments since he has his own group of generals."[143]

Stillwell, commander of the Army Ground Forces, had been lobbying Marshall and MacArthur to give him command of the Tenth Army after Okinawa. In early June, Marshall gave Stilwell permission to conduct an inspection tour of the units on Okinawa, if he made his own arrangements to get out there. He arrived unannounced at the Tenth Army Headquarters on 3 June and commenced to visit the various command posts, particularly the 7th ID, which he had once commanded.[144] If Buckner was annoyed at this unexpected visit, he did not betray his feelings and dispassionately recorded Stilwell's movements around the battlefield in his diary.

Stilwell, on the other hand, was not known as "Vinegar Joe" for nothing and had no problem criticizing Buckner and other commanders in his own diary. He considered Buckner a sellout of the army for his attempts to work harmoniously with the naval services and viewed his choice of Geiger as his backup as no more than "playing" the navy. He sarcastically recorded Buckner's attitude as so much playacting:

[In Buckner's opinion] Nimitz is perfect. His [Nimitz's] staff is perfectly balanced. Cooperation is magnificent. The marine divisions are wonderful. In fact everything is just dinky. His own staff is perfect—he picked them himself. It is all rather nauseating.[145]

Stilwell then went to meet with MacArthur, the presumptive commander of the invasion of Japan, to ensure that he would either get the Tenth Army or, if the navy would not release it, get command of another army for the invasion. He recorded that MacArthur "had no high opinion of Buckner. Agreed he [is] facetious . . . He will welcome Buckner's relief and my transfer."[146] It is only speculation as to whether Stillwell arrived on Okinawa intent on relieving Buckner and assuming command himself. Moreover, it is uncertain if Stillwell could have made any changes to the operational plans that would have accelerated the pace of the attack. Of course, that became a moot point as within a week Buckner was dead and the operation ended just days later. Stilwell finally had Buckner's command but by that time the operation was over.

Around the time of Stilwell's visit, a journalist for the *New York Herald Tribune* attempted to stir up interservice ill-will by running articles about the progress on Okinawa and laying the blame on the army's conservative tactics and Buckner's lack of combat experience.[147] Another columnist called the operation a "fiasco" and Buckner incompetent.[148] Buckner would not bite, writing to his wife just four days before his death that cooperation between the services was "splendid . . . in spite of unpatriotic attempts on the part of certain publicity agents who are trying to stir up a controversy between the army and marines."[149] Nimitz also jumped to his defense, releasing a statement to the press defending Buckner's tactics, particularly the lack of a second landing, and stating, "During the operation each service took losses and each service inflicted great damage on the enemy. Comparisons between the services are out of place and ill-advised."[150] Unfortunately, Buckner did not live to see that statement, which was released the day before he was killed.

O. P. Smith later also defended Buckner's refusal to conduct a second landing, pointing out that the idea had come from Bruce, who preferred to operate alone and was miserable when his command was dropped in the middle of the battle and he was forced to coordinate and cooperate with adjacent units. Buckner and his staff were concerned that the Japanese reserve might be hidden near the southeastern landing site and that an American division could easily be trapped there. Moreover, if he had to send a relief or reinforcing force to support a second landing it would severely weaken the original front and the main effort.[151]

Of course, given what had happened on Saipan, everyone was intensely interested in the performance of the 27th Division. When Buckner had the 1st Marine Division relieve the division, the press tried to read something in the action. In actuality, the simple fact was that the 27th Division was designated as island garrison and Buckner wanted them to leave the front line in order to take over those duties.

However, there were some signs that, despite the massive change of leadership at the regimental and division level, the 27th still had lingering leadership problems. The commander of the 6th MARDIV complained that the 27th had not buried their dead and that the army had to send a team back to take care of that, although this cannot be verified.[152] Furthermore, General Louis Jones, the 1st Division assistant division commander, was also critical of some of the 27th leadership, although he had been friends with Griner and his assistant division commander, General William Bradford, before the war. During the 1st MARDIV relief of the 27th, he had temporarily had command of the 165th Regiment. He was especially dismissive of the 165th regimental commander (Kelley, who was relieved from command on 27 April for the regiment's slow progress and the disorganized way he had dispersed his units) and complained that the regiment could not handle their 800-yard front and that one-half a marine regiment had to take an extra 200 yards, giving them a 4,600-yard front to the army's 600 yards.[153] Oddly, Jones had respect for the soldiers of the 165th Regiment, calling them the "69th Marines."[154] He said of the soldiers, "Their men were good . . . Under our command they would do fine."[155]

Apparently the army did not have a monopoly on poor leadership as the marines relieved three regimental commanders on Okinawa: 29th Marines commander Colonel Victor Bleasdale on 15 April, 1st Marines commander Colonel Kenneth Chappell on 5 May, and 22nd Marines commander Colonel Merlin Schneider on 16 May. Bleasdale had won the Distinguished Service Cross and the Navy Cross in the World War I and a second Navy Cross in Nicaragua. However, Shepherd relieved him after he recklessly pushed his regiment forward into an ambush on the Motobu Peninsula.[156] One of the marines assigned to 29th Reconnaissance Company recalled, "We led the division up . . . moving with some care to avoid an ambush . . . Bleasdale kept pushing us, urging us to go faster . . . we had pulled off to the right and let the 29th go by. They continued on [and] ran into a major ambush."[157] None of the soldiers serving under him could find anything positive to say about his hard, authoritative leadership style or the way he trained his men until exhaustion.[158] Del Valle relieved Chappell for failure to make significant gains on a key Japanese position on the east coast.[159] The only commander not relieved for incompetence was Schneider. Shepherd later said that the commander was "fatigued physically and mentally, combat fatigue . . . it was time for him to go home. No disgrace. He was a nice fellow, so I pinned a Bronze Star on him and sent him back to the states."[160]

LESSONS LEARNED

Okinawa was supposed to be the "practice run" for invasion of the Japanese home islands that was obviated by the atomic bombs dropped on Hiroshima and Nagasaki. As the last operation of the Pacific theater, there was no chance, or need, to implement the lessons learned. Instead, Okinawa was studied as the capstone of everything that the services had learned in the 3-plus years of war. However, with no future operations, there was no way to gauge the effect of these studies.

In retrospect, the most interesting thing about the after-action reports is the fact that there were no major operational issues arising from this campaign. There were no requests for new equipment, no need to develop new tactics, no new recommended unit capabilities. The services finally understood how to conduct island warfare and all that remained was tinkering around the edges.

— CONCLUSION —

In August 1942, all that stood between the Japanese and total domination of the Western Pacific was a near-starving, pitifully small band of marines, lining a few miserable ridges on Guadalcanal. Supporting them was a naval force that was nearly wrecked at Pearl Harbor and further depleted by a disastrous engagement off Savo Island. From this inauspicious beginning, the United States in the span of three years built a fighting force more powerful than anything the world had ever seen. In that time, the United States military went from an underfunded skeleton force, numbering less than 400,000, to a dominant war machine of more than 12,000,000. Just as impressive was the sheer volume of materiel churned out by a pitiless American industrial base mobilized to equip and supply this massive force.

By the conclusion of the war the scorecard of Allied victories won by the Central Pacific force was impressive, as the Japanese advance was first stopped, and then rolled back. What became a massive allied counterattack uncoiled slowly, but gained momentum with each passing month. Still, Japan never yielded an inch without forcing American soldiers and marines to engage in grinding battles of attrition. But as the Americans fought they also learned. It was knowledge bought only at great cost. All along the 5,000-mile route from Hawaii to Okinawa, the blood of tens of thousands of Americans soaked the reefs, beaches, and jungles of dozens of islands. There had been no playbook for the kind of war fought on these islands, just some general principles and a determination to master the deadly practice of amphibious warfare. Along the way, the American military built and refined the concepts of modern joint operations. It would have been difficult for a homogenous force to educate and prepare itself for the challenges faced by the U.S. military in the Central Pacific. It was doubly difficult when it became necessary to merge army and marine units into a single fighting force. Their respective leaders not only had to build a professional force out of a mob of untrained civilians, but simultaneously assimilate diverse—and distinct—service cultures into a cohesive force.

Very little of the required adaptation would have been possible without the institution of a rigorous program for the organized collection of post-engagement lessons learned. For, although the basic principles of amphibious landings remained unchanged, their actual implementation was a matter of continuous improvement and refinement. As technology changed and materiel became more abundant the American approach in the Pacific changed. Such change started at the strategic level, as commanders adjusted their attitudes from a desperate defense to strategic offensives along multiple lines of advance. Executing these plans was never as simple as drawing arrows on a map and ordering one's forces forward. Troops had to be trained, supplies stockpiled, new equipment integrated, and doctrine updated. All of this had to be accomplished before the advance began for it is this pre-engagement preparation that often decides the outcome of any battle.

In combat the devil is truly in the details, and it is in such detailed preparation that the U.S. military in World War II excelled. Of course, such preparations, on a previously unimaginable scale, were rarely accomplished without overcoming profound difficulties, which often frayed tempers and sometimes threatened to halt all forward progress. In fact, one does not have to peel back many layers before revealing a degree of ugliness that has been neglected in other histories of the war. But, it was here where American leadership, even at the bleakest moments of the war, demonstrated a genius for pragmatism that was to drive their forces to victory. Through a formal process, the lessons of each engagement were promulgated throughout the force. What worked was reinforced. What failed was ruthlessly discarded.

How this came about was not an accident. From the beginning of the war the American command system and the nation's military forces were designed on the assumption that rapid adaption was not only desirable, but necessary. The entire American way of war was premised on the military system's ability to take millions of raw recruits and mold them into an effective military machine. With few preconceptions on how wars should be fought, these recruits, including tens of thousands of officers with no previous military experience, were constantly on the lookout for better ways to do things. Moreover, with a responsive industrial base churning out massive quantities of whatever materiel was needed, ideas could be translated into reality with unprecedented rapidity.

As we have seen, the overwhelming military force that stormed ashore on Okinawa was not created out of whole cloth. Rather, it was built through a painstaking process of trial-and-error, where mistakes were paid for in lives. This process was birthed in the run-up to the battle for Guadalcanal and reached full stride in the wake of the invasion of Tarawa. It had not yet reached its culmination before the dropping of the atomic bomb brought down the curtain on the Pacific War.

For current and future commanders looking for that one crucial ingredient that made everything else possible it can be summed up in one word: leadership. If one was to single out one factor to explain how well the marines and army integrated their operations on Guadalcanal, they had to look no further than generals Vandergrift and Patch, who both made strenuous efforts to keep themselves and their subordinates focused on the mission rather than struggling for service preeminence. As a result, despite their dissimilar tactical approaches and service cultures, the army and marines gave their full attention to fighting the Japanese. This fell apart when Holland Smith came into the picture. When in a command role his hyperpartisan nature and inability to consider alternative viewpoints exaggerated underlying army-marine tensions, to the tremendous detriment of ongoing operations. Once Smith was replaced by the Buckner-Geiger team, harmony reigned once again. Maintaining interservice peace was never easy, and it sometime seemed that for every senior leader trying to work closely with other services there were two trying to thwart them. But in the end just enough leaders, who realized success depended on teamwork, came to the fore.

In just three years these leaders took the U.S. military from a small, disorganized, and inefficient force to a huge, thoroughly professional, and integrated joint force. They did so by merging unique marine and army cultures into a cohesive single joint force that crushed the Japanese Empire far faster than anyone believed possible in 1942.

However, despite the undeniable joint success against Japan, the postwar historical writing continued to perpetuate the myth of the army and marine corps at constant loggerheads. As the primary record shows, Holland Smith's relief of Ralph Smith caused a brief ripple of conflict between the two services that, even with the media's escalation of the event, soon faded in the general consciousness. Indeed, even the soldiers and marines directly affected soon forgot the dispute as they focused on the common enemy. After all, the relief of a general officer was not as uncommon as one might think. During the course of the war, five corps commanders and fifteen other division commanders were relieved for cause (not to mention the dozen or so division commanders relieved for health reasons or the 33 National Guard division commanders released at the beginning of the war).[1] In fact, the Smith versus Smith controversy might, and should, have gone down as a mere footnote in the campaign. Instead it became a dominant narrative that not only affected the historical view of joint operations, but contributed to the shape of army-marine relations until after Vietnam.

As shown earlier, it was Holland Smith himself who brought the issue back to the national consciousness in the midst of the defense unification battle. This stirred up latent resentment on the part of army leaders, who had viewed the marines as "glory hounds" since World War I. Since European theater veterans dominated the postwar army leadership, few had had direct operational contact with marines, which made it more difficult to let go of innate prejudices (J. Lawton Collins was a notable exception and he had left the Pacific theater before Holland Smith arrived). Therefore, these leaders were more willing to believe the worst of their marine counterparts, and Holland Smith's self-serving memoir reinforced this antipathy.

The Marine Corps, on the other hand, constantly existed under the threat of extinction and was treated as a minor member of the services. This was reinforced in 1947, when the Air Force received recognition as a separate service and received full membership in the Joint Chiefs of Staff, something that the marines would not receive until the 1970s. For this reason, Marine Corps leadership understood that they needed to continually self-promote and viewed the Pacific campaign as a golden opportunity. Even there, they had to compete with the Navy and MacArthur, a master of self-promotion.

The Korean War did little to alleviate this resentment; indeed it probably did more damage to the relationship. Again, the vast majority of army leaders in the war were European veterans, who were dismissive of marine tactics and fighting prowess. Even harder for the marines was the fact that overall command rested with MacArthur, a man who still rankled over having to share command of "his" theater in the Pacific Campaign with other services. This tension is best illustrated by the high-profile conflict between the X Corps Commander General Edward "Ned" Almond and the 1st MARDIV Commander General Oliver P. Smith during operations at Chosin. Again, these issues resided mainly at the senior officer level, not in the foxholes.

Thus, the army and marine corps, while not in open clash, circled one another at the highest levels with a measure of distrust and suspicion through the Vietnam War. However, as senior leaders without World War II experience moved up through the ranks, the ghost of Holland Smith receded further behind. In 1986, the Goldwater-Nichols Reorganization Act mandated joint training and doctrine, the wisdom of which was shown during the wars in Iraq and Afghanistan under commanders who had spent their entire careers looking at operational problems through a joint prism. As command moved seamlessly between the various services with nary a complaint, the army and marine corps had finally seen the fruits of the small vine planted on the shores of Guadalcanal seventy years ago.

— NOTES —

INTRODUCTION

1. Robert Coakley, *American Military History*, "Chapter 23: World War II: The War Against Japan" (Washington, DC: Department of the Army, 1988), 503.

2. According to Edward M. Coffman, 87.2 percent of the army and 74.3 percent of the marines had served for less than a year. In fact, the marine brigade was three times the size of the entire Marine Corps a little more than a decade before. See: Edward Coffman, *The War to End All Wars: The American Military Experience in World War I* (Lexington: University Press of Kentucky, 1998), 151–52.

3. Edgar Raines, "The Army-Marine Corps Relationship," Center of Military History Information Paper, 8 September 2009.

4. Robert Mitchler, "Heroes—Drafted or Volunteer—Are Made, Not Born," *Leatherneck*, 30 January 2009.

5. Tinian and Guam are not covered because these were merely follow-on operation to Saipan; Leyte is not covered because this operation was not in the Central Pacific and was under MacArthur as opposed to Nimitz and thus had a different planning staff.

CHAPTER 1 Guadalcanal: The Ad Hoc Operation

1. Russel Reeder, "Notes on Jungle Warfare from the U.S .Marines and U.S. Infantry on Guadalcanal Island," 2 December 1942, Guadalcanal Collection, Marine Corps Archives, Quantico, VA. Hereafter Guadalcanal Collection USMC.

2. Grace Person Hayes, *The History of the Joint Chiefs of Staff in World War II: The War Against Japan* (Annapolis, MD: Naval Institute Press, 1982), 99.

3. Louis Morton, *United States Army in World War II: War in the Pacific: Strategy and Command: The First Two Years* (Washington, DC: Department of the Army, 1962), 289–95. Hereafter *Strategy and Command*.

4. Rabaul housed Japanese army and navy command, had an airfield and good port system. Memorandum, George Marshall to POTUS, "The Pacific Theater versus 'Bolero,'" 6 May 1942, George Marshall Papers, G. C. Marshall Research Library, Lexington, VA. This topic is also covered in Morton, *Strategy and Command*, 289–95, and Maurice Matloff and Edwin Snell, *United States Army in World War II: Strategic Planning for Coalition Warfare, 1941–1942* (Washington, DC: Department of the Army, 1952), 240–63.

5. Morton, *Strategy and Command*, 294.

6. Memorandum, Ernest King to Franklin Delano Roosevelt, 5 March 1942, National Archives, RG 38.

7. Richard Sutherland and DeWitt Peck, "Guadalcanal Combat Observations," [undated]. Guadalcanal Collection USMC.

8. John Miller, Jr., *United States Army in World War II: War in the Pacific: Guadalcanal: The First Offensive* (Washington, DC: Department of the Army, 1949), 14–17, and Frank Hough, Verge E. Ludwig and Henry I. Shaw, *History of Marine Corps Operations in World War II, Volume I: Pearl Harbor to Guadalcanal* (Washington, DC: U.S. Marine Corps, 1958), 239–42. Hereafter *Pearl Harbor to Guadalcanal*.

9. Memorandum, Ernest King to George Marshall, "Offensive Operations in the South and Southwest Pacific Area," 25 June 1942, National Archives, RG 38.

10. Richard B. Frank, *Guadalcanal: The Definitive Account of the Landmark Battle* (New York: Penguin, 1992), 33.

11. Morton, *Strategy and Command*, 300–1. No evidence has ever come to light of the larger conspiracy MacArthur alleged.

12. Memorandum, George Marshall to Ernest King, "Offensive Operations in the South and Southwest Pacific Areas," 26 June 1942, Marshall Papers.

13. Memorandum, Ernest King to George Marshall, "Offensive Operations in the South and Southwest Pacific Areas, 26 June 1942," National Archives, RG 38.

14. Memorandum, George Marshall to Ernest King, 29 June 1942, Marshall Papers. Notes by Sutherland and Peck indicate that MacArthur might have threatened to withhold air support and that in regards to "flight assistance, etc. no help up to Guadal[canal] save to fly Twining and McKean." However, this is not been corroborated anywhere else.

15. Memorandum, George Marshall, "Memorandum for Higher Commanders," 11 September 1942, Marshall Papers. This memorandum, which also covered conduct with Allies and government officials, was sent to the War Department assistant chiefs of staff, commanding generals of the Army Air Forces Army, Army Ground Forces, and Services of Supply as well as all commanders down to the division level.

16. Sutherland and Peck observations.

17. William L. McGee, *The Solomons Campaigns 1942–1943 from Guadalcanal to Bougainville—Pacific War Turning Point, Volume 2 (Amphibious Operations in the South Pacific World War II)* (Santa Barbara, CA: BMC Publications, 2002), XLIII. See also Morton, *Strategy and Command*; and Hayes manuscript.

18. Hayes, *Joint Chiefs*, 99.

19. "Young" was a relative term as Ghormley was in his late fifties at the time. Edwin Hoyt, *How They Won the War in the Pacific: Nimitz and His Admirals* (New York: The Lyons Press, 2000), 58.

20. Kenneth Friedman, *Morning of the Rising Sun: The Heroic Story of the Battles for Guadalcanal* (Charleston, SC: BookSurge Publishing, 2007), 23.

21. Frank, *Guadalcanal*, 56.

22. Message, Chester Nimitz, 18 October 1942, National Archives RG 38.

23. Gerald Thomas interview transcript, 1967, page 256, Marine Corps Archives, Quantico, VA.

24. Morton, *Strategy and Command*, 257.

25. Ibid., 260.

26. Richard Leighton and Robert Coakley, *United States Army in World War II: Global Logistics and Strategy: 1940–1943* (Washington, DC: Department of the Army, 1955), 18.

27. Memorandum, George Marshall to Millard Harmon, "Instructions to CG USAF-ISPA," 7 July 1942, Guadalcanal Collection USMC.

28. Millard Harmon to Henry Arnold, 5 August 1942, Harmon Papers, Air Force Historical Research Agency, Andrews AFB, MD.

29. Sutherland and Peck observations.

30. A. A. Vandegrift and Robert Asprey, *Once a Marine: The Memoirs of General A. A. Vandegrift, USMC* (New York: Ballantine Books, 1966), 164.

31. Thomas transcript, 394.

32. Hoyt, *How They Won*, 119.

33. In keeping with naming conventions, Marine divisions are always referred to as such (e.g. 1st Marine Division or 1st MARDIV), while Marine regiments do not use the descriptor (e.g. 5th Marines). Army divisions are referred to by their combat capability and/or level (e.g. 1st Infantry Division or 1st ID) while regiments only use the combat capability or just their number (e.g. 25th Infantry or the 25th). Battalions are designated by a number and the regimental designation (e.g. 2/5 Marines or 1/25 Infantry).

34. 1st Marine Division, "Division Commander's Final Report," 1 July 1943, Guadalcanal Collection USMC.

35. U.S. Army Forces in the South Pacific Area, "Commander's Report on the Army in the South Pacific, 6 June 1944," page 19, Guadalcanal Collection, Military History Institute, Carlisle, PA. Hereafter Guadalcanal Collection USA.

36. Memorandum, Chester Nimitz, 10 July 1942, Chester Nimitz Papers, Naval Historical Center, Washington, D.C. Also referenced by Sutherland and Peck.

37. COMSOPAC War Diary, 9 May 1942, National Archives, RG 38.

38. Frank, *Guadalcanal*, 54.

39. Vandegrift and Asprey, *Once a Marine*, 120.

40. Sutherland and Peck observations.

41. Thomas transcript, 262.

42. Vandegrift and Asprey, *Once a Marine*, 120.

43. In the 1985 book *And I Was There: Pearl Harbor and Midway*, Edwin T. Layton, Chief Intelligence Officer to Admiral Husband E. Kimmel, Commander of the Pacific Fleet, makes a persuasive case that Turner was in fact the main person culpable in the Pearl Harbor disaster due to his poor analysis and monopolization of intelligence.

44. Frank, *Guadalcanal*, 16–17.

45. Vandegrift and Asprey, *Once a Marine*, 118.

46. John Zimmerman, "Interview Notes," undated, Guadalcanal Collection USMC.

47. Thomas transcript, p. 258.

48. Hough, et al., *Pearl Harbor to Guadalcanal*, 240–41.

49. "Landing Operations Doctrine," U.S. Navy, 1938, and "Landing Operations on Hostile Shores," U.S. Army, 1941.

50. William H. Russell, "Genesis of FMF Doctrine," *Marine Corps Gazette*, Nov. 1955, 14–19.

51. "Joint Action of the Army and Navy," FTP-155, 1935, 6.

52. "Landing Operations Doctrine," 29–31.

53. Hough et al., *Pearl Harbor to Guadalcanal*, 15.

54. Thomas transcript, 310.

55. Ibid., 397.

56. Ibid., 441.

57. Ibid., 251–52.

58. Clifton Cates interview transcript, 1967, Marine Corps Archives, Quantico, VA, p. 131.

59. Vandegrift and Asprey, *Once a Marine*, 113.

60. Thomas transcript, 262–63.

61. The grave situation on Guadalcanal forced the cancellation of the Ndeni landing.

62. While the development of the amphibious landing craft, the refinement of naval gunfire and combat loading, and the maturation of close air support are all interesting and important stories, they are beyond the scope of this work and will not be addressed.

63. Interview by the author with George Tosi, 2002.

64. The East Coast Marines referred to themselves as "Raggedy Ass Marines" and derisively referred to the West Coast Marines as "Hollywood Marines."

65. Allan Millett, *Semper Fidelis: The History of the Marine Corps* (New York: Simon & Schuster, 1980), 349.

66. Samuel Eliot Morison, *History of United States Naval Operations in World War II, Volume 5: The Struggle for Guadalcanal, August 1942–February 1943* (Boston, MA: Little, Brown & Co., 1951), 15.

67. Vandegrift and Asprey, *Once a Marine*, 63.

68. David Ulbrich, *Preparing for Victory: Thomas Holcomb and the Making of the Modern Marine Corps 1936–1943* (Annapolis, MD: Naval Institute Press, 2011), 28–29.

69. 1st MARDIV, "Final Report." It is a curious coincidence that the training area and the operational area had the same name.

70. Thomas transcript, 228.

71. Interview by author with Maj. Gen. H. Lloyd Wilkerson, 24 March 2008.

72. 1st Marine Division, "Final Report."

73. Ibid.

74. Vincent Kramer interview transcript, 21 February 1995, Rutgers Oral History Archives of World War II, New Brunswick, NJ.

75. 1st Marine Division, "Final Report."

76. "History of the First Marine Regiment," National Archives, RG 127.

77. Cates transcript, 131.

78. Radio message, CINCPAC to COMSOPAC, 7 July 1942, CINCPAC Grey Book, Book One, 7 December 1941–31 August 1942, Naval Historical Center, Washington, DC.

79. Zimmerman, "Interview Notes."

80. 1st MARDIV, "Final Report," 3.

81. Thomas transcript, 261.

82. William Bartsch, "Operation Dovetail: Bungled Guadalcanal Rehearsal, July 1942," *The Journal of Military History* (April 2002): 471.

83. Lincoln Stoddard, "Narrative History of Task Force 6814 and Americal Division: January 23, 1942 to June 30, 1943," page 1, Americal Division Association Archives, Greensboro, NC. Hereafter Americal Archives.

84. Francis D. Cronin, *Under the Southern Cross: The Saga of the Americal Division.* 3rd ed. (Washington, DC: Combat Forces Press, 1981), 4.

85. Sebree was a member of the Class of 1921 that graduated early to meet the needs of World War I. "West Point Breaks Graduation Record," *The New York Times*, 2 November 1918. He participated in the D-Day Landings as Assistant Division Commander of the 35th Infantry.

86. Stoddard, "Americal Division," 2.

87. Morton, *Strategy and Command*, 208.

88. Only a single gun guarded the harbor. Not only had the gun not been fired for twenty years, but there were only 96 rounds of ammunition in the world for it. Stoddard, "Americal Division," 3.

89. Thomas Strobridge and Bernard Nalty. "From the South Pacific to the Brenner Pass: General Alexander M. Patch," *Military Review* (June 1981), 42.

90. William Wyant, *Sandy Patch: A Biography of Lt. Gen. Alexander M. Patch* (New York: Praeger Publishers, 1991), 58–59.

91. Ibid., 2–3.

92. Ibid., 12–14.

93. United Forces in New Caledonia Headquarters, "General Orders No. 10," 27 May 1942, Carleton Elliot Simensen Military Heritage Collection, 164th Infantry Association Records, University of North Dakota, Grand Forks, ND.

94. The other was the Philippine Division. Americal was a contraction of American forces at New Caledonia, a name suggested by PFC David Fonesca.

95. Morton, *Strategy and Command*, 209–10.

96. The law allowed the president to revoke the commissions of reserve officers at his discretion. Mark Watson, *Chief of Staff: Prewar Plans and Preparations* (Washington, DC: Department of the Army, 1950), 241.

97. Robert C. Muehrcke, ed., *Orchids in the Mud: Personal Accounts of Soldiers of the 132nd Infantry Regiment* (Chicago, IL: 132nd Infantry Division Association, 1985), 23–25.

98. Paul Gavan, "Personal Observations," 19 May 43, National Archives RG 407.

99. The third, Colonel LeRoy Nelson, commanding the 132nd Infantry, was replaced on the eve of the battle of Mount Austen by Colonel Alexander George, yet another West Pointer.

100. Charles Walker, *Combat Officer: Memoirs of War in the South Pacific* (New York: Presidio Press, 2004), 3.

101. Interview with Charles Walker by Les Groshang, 23 December 2005. A transcript of this interview was given to the author by Mr. Groshang.

102. Cronin, *Under the Southern Cross*, 33.

103. Terry L. Shoptaugh, "I Am Ready: The 164th Infantry in World War II," unpublished history, pages 5–7, Americal Archives.

104. Muehrcke, *Orchids in the Mud*, 44.

105. Walker, *Combat Officer*, 3.

106. E. J. Kahn, Jr. and Henry McLemore, "Fighting Divisions," Army Ground Forces Study (Washington, DC: Department of the Army, 1945), 31.

107. General Order 53, Headquarters Hawaiian Department, 26 September 1941. J. Lawton Collins Papers, Eisenhower Presidential Library, Abilene, KS. Hereafter Collins papers KS.

108. Donna Everett. *World War II Division Chronicles: 25th Infantry Division* (Washington, DC: US Government Printing Office, 1995), 1–2.

109. "Operations of the 25th Infantry Division: Guadalcanal," undated, Collins papers KS.

110. William McCulloch to the Men and Officers of the 27th Infantry Regiment, 12 February 1943, 27th Infantry Regiment Archives, Schofield Barracks, HI.

111. Melvin Walthall, "Lighting Forward: A History of the 25th Infantry Division," unpublished manuscript, 1973, Collins papers KS.

112. Gary Wade, "Conversations with General J. Lawton Collins," Combat Studies Institute Study No. 5 (Fort Leavenworth, KS: 1983), 1.

113. Ibid., 2.

114. J. Lawton Collins, *Lightning Joe: An Autobiography* (Baton Rouge: Louisiana State University Press, 1979) and unpublished annotated manuscript, page 137, U.S. Army Military History Institute, Carlisle, PA. Hereafter Collins papers PA.

115. Stanley Larsen interview transcript, 18 August 1976, page 41, U.S. Army Military History Institute, Carlisle, PA.

116. Collins, *Lightning Joe*, 131–32.

117. The VII Corps staff boasted no fewer than three future four-star generals: Collins, John Hodge, and John Hull.

118. *General Headquarters Study No.1*, 1946, U.S. Army Military History Institute, Carlisle, PA. These maneuvers are also covered in Kent Roberts Greenfield, Robert Palmer, and Bell Wiley, *The Organization of Ground Combat Troops* (Washington, DC: Department of the Army, 1947) and Christopher Gabel, *U.S. Army GHQ Maneuvers of 1941* (Washington, DC: Center of Military History, 1991).

119. As a result of these maneuvers, 11 of 15 army and corps commanders and 20 of 27 division commanders were replaced with younger men.

120. Collins transcript, 85.

121. Collins, *Lightning Joe*, 137.

122. Larsen transcript, 1–2.

123. 27th Infantry Regiment Association Archives.

124. Elson Lowell Matson, "The Story of the 161st Regiment," unpublished manuscript, 1944, U.S. Army Military History Institute, Carlisle, PA.

125. Collins transcript, 100–1, 118–20.

126. William McCulloch to the Men and Officers of the 27th Infantry Regiment, 12 February 1943.

127. "25th Infantry Division on Guadalcanal," 23.

128. Chester Nimitz to J. Lawton Collins, 25 November 1942, Collins papers KS.

129. Danny Crawford, et al., *History of the Second Marines* (Washington, DC: Marine History and Museums Division, 2001), 2.

130. James Donovan, *Out Post in the North Atlantic: Marines in the Defense of Iceland* (Washington, DC: Marine Corps Historical Branch, 1995).

131. 6th Marine Regiment, "Report of Activities 25 May 41 to 30 Nov 41," 13 Dec 1941, Guadalcanal Collection, Marine Corps Archives, Quantico, VA.

132. William Jones, *A Brief History of the Sixth Marines* (Washington, DC: Marine History and Museums Division, 1987), 49.

133. James Santelli, *History of the Eighth Marines* (Washington, DC: Marine History and Museums Division, 1976), 12.

134. Crawford, *The Second Marine Division*, 18.

135. 8th Marine Regiment, "Report on Operations of Eighth Marines Reinforced, October 22, 1942 to February 9, 1943: Guadalcanal Campaign," 16 April 1943, Guadalcanal Collection USMC.

136. While the CAM proved successful, the lack of time and suitable training areas, not to mention the issues of command, meant that the CAM would be a one-time conglomeration based on circumstances on the ground.

137. Clayton Vogel to John Marston, "2nd Division Command," 28 November 1942, Guadalcanal Collection USMC.

138. Thomas Holcomb to Clifton Cates, "2nd Division Command," 30 December 1948, Thomas Holcomb Papers, Marine Corps Archives, Quantico, VA.

139. Frank, *Guadalcanal*, 135.

140. Larsen transcript, 25.

141. Jeter Isely and Philip Crowl, *The U.S. Marines and Amphibious War: Its Theory and Its Practice in the Pacific* (Princeton, NJ: Princeton University Press, 1951), 131.

142. "Notes on the Japanese—from their Documents," Intelligence Bulletin, Volume II, No. 2: October 1943.

143. "Some Defense Techniques Used by the Japanese," Intelligence Bulletin, Volume II, No. 3: November 1943.

144. Parliament.

145. "Japanese Explanation of S.W. Pacific Reverses," Intelligence Bulletin, Volume I, No. 8: April 1943.

146. Unless otherwise noted landing summary taken from Miller, *Guadalcanal: the First Offensive*, 82–167, 59–81, and Hough et al., *Pearl Harbor to Guadalcanal*, 254–62.

147. C. H. Metcalf, "Narrative: Marine Corps Units in Guadalcanal Campaign, 6 Sep 1943," Guadalcanal Collection USMC.

148. Frank, *Guadalcanal*, 61.

149. Ibid., 72.

150. Frank Jack Fletcher to Hanson Baldwin, 8 July 1947, Frank Jack Fletcher Collection, University of Wyoming, Laramie, WY. Most of Fletcher's papers were lost

in combat and he consistently refused to submit to an interview with Samuel Eliot Morison, the navy historian.

151. Two recent books attempt to rehabilitate this image of him: Stephen Regan, *In Bitter Tempest: The Biography of Admiral Frank Jack Fletcher* (Ames: Iowa State Press, 1994) and John Lundstrom, *Black Shoe Carrier Admiral: Frank Jack Fletcher at Coral Sea, Midway and Guadalcanal* (Annapolis, MD: Naval Institute Press, 2006).

152. Vandegrift, "Final Report."

153. Frank Jack Fletcher to Hanson Baldwin, 8 July 1947, Fletcher papers.

154. Miller, *Guadalcanal*, 81.

155. Jerry McConnell, "Our Survival Was Open to the Gravest Doubts: A Marine Private's Personal Account of the Battle for Guadalcanal," Unpublished manuscript, 2002, page 42. Guadalcanal Collection USMC.

156. Vandegrift, "Final Report."

157. Ibid.

158. Ibid.

159. Unless otherwise noted battle summary is taken from Miller, *Guadalcanal: the First Offensive*, 82–167, 190–350 and Hough et al., *Pearl Harbor to Guadalcanal*, 263–374.

160. It was also referred to as "Edson's Ridge."

161. Puller was the most decorated marine in history and is a symbol for marine *esprit de corps*. Even today, new recruits end each day with the declaration, "Good night Chesty Puller, wherever you are!"

162. Burke Davis, *Marine! The Life of Lt. Gen. Lewis B. (Chesty) Puller* (Boston: Little, Brown & Co, 1962), 158.

163. Ibid., 160.

164. The 147th was an independent infantry regiment attached for the operation.

165. Millard Harmon, "Commander's Report," page 19, Harmon Papers.

166. Vandegrift, "Final Report."

167. Sutherland and Peck observations.

168. Walker interview transcript, 23 December 2005.

169. Merrill Twining, *No Bended Knee: The Battle for Guadalcanal* (New York: Presidio Press, 1994), 41–51.

170. Vandegrift, "Final Report."

171. Hough et al., *Pearl Harbor to Guadalcanal*, 247.

172. Vandegrift, "Final Report."

173. Miller, *Guadalcanal*, 44.

174. "Transcript of Plans and Policies conference with Major General A. A. Vandegrift," 1 February 1943, Guadalcanal collection USMC.

175. Frank, *Guadalcanal*, 78–79, 613–14. These numbers are regarded as the most accurate count of KIA/MIA during the campaign.

176. A further 863 Japanese and 122 Americans were killed during the battles on Florida, Tulagi, and Gavutu.

177. John Boyd Coates, ed., *United States Army in World War II: Preventive Medicine in World War II, Volume VI: Communicable Diseases* (Washington, DC: Office of the Surgeon General, 1963), 427. Hereafter *Preventive Medicine*.

178. Vandegrift, "Final Report," Annex T (medical).

179. Coates, *Preventive Medicine*, 427.

180. Author interview with Les Groshang, 25 March 2008.

181. "1st Marine Amphibious Corps: Comment: Medical 7 May 1943," Guadalcanal collection USMC.

182. Later Hunt became the assistant division commander for the 2nd Marine Division during the Marianas and Okinawa campaigns before taking over the division. He later retired as a four-star general.

183. Vandegrift and Asprey, *Once a Marine*, 160–61.

184. Vandegrift, "Final Report," 20–21.

185. Ulbrich, *Preparing for Victory*, 146–47.

186. Thomas transcript, 771.

187. Larsen transcript, 12.

188. Reeder, "Operations on Guadalcanal."

189. William Hopkins, *The Pacific War: The Strategy, Politics and Players that Won the War* (Minneapolis, MN: Zenith Press, 2008), 134.

190. Vandegrift, "Final Report," 2

191. Ibid., 9.

192. Frank Halsey, "Operations of the 132nd Infantry (Americal Division) at Mount Austen, 15 December 1942–9 January 1943," page 16, Manouevre Center of Excellence Library, Ft Benning, GA. Hereafter MCEL.

193. U.S. Army G3, Combat Lessons No. 1, 40–41.

194. Ibid., 38–39.

195. Louis Trezza interview transcript, 2004, Rutgers Oral History Project, Rutgers University, New Brunswick, NJ.

196. Larsen transcript, 10.

197. Guadalcanal would particularly dominate the Marines for more than twenty years. Starting on 1 January 1944, the next five commandants were Guadalcanal veterans: Vandegrift, Cates, Shepard, Pate and Shoup. This ended with the appointment of General Wallace Green on 1 January 1964.

CHAPTER 2   The Gilberts: Parallel Operations

1. Philip A. Crowl and Edmund G. Love, *United States Army in World War II: The War in the Pacific: Seizure of the Gilberts and Marshalls* (Washington, DC: Department of the Army, 1955), 8.

2. Meeting minutes Anfa Camp, 14 January 1943. Joint Chiefs of Staff History Office, Pentagon, Alexandria, VA.

3. Ibid. Despite his assurances, King really wanted to double the resources being sent into the Pacific theater and specifically asked for 30 percent of the total war effort, after first claiming that the Pacific was only getting 15 percent.

4. Combined Chiefs of Staff, "Situation to be Created in the Eastern Theater (Pacific and Burma) in 1943," 17 January 1943. National Archives, RG 218.

5. Hayes, 307–8. Also covered in Henry I. Shaw, Jr.,Bernard C. Nalty, and Edwin T. Turnbladh, *History of Marine Corps Operations in World War II, Volume III: Central Pacific Drive* (Washington, DC: U.S. Marine Corps, 1966), 10–11.

6. Hayes, *Joint Chiefs*, 330–34.

7. As pointed out in Hayes' *Joint Chiefs* and Crowl and Love's *Seizure of the Gilberts and Marshalls*, despite its name, this document was nothing more than a broad strategy paper and lacked any of the operational details normally seen in a military plan.

8. At the time there were 4 amphibious and 14 infantry divisions. This estimate missed the final total by 3 divisions.

9. Combined Chiefs of Staff, "Operations in the Pacific and Far East in 1943–44," May 20, 1943. National Archives, RG 218. The last objective was added at the insistence of Admiral King, who felt that it allowed the naval commander greater scope of operations. He also strenuously objected to the addition of Burma in the Pacific plan.

10. Minutes of the Combined Chiefs of Staff 92nd Meeting, 21 May 1943, Joint Chiefs of Staff History Office.

11. Crowl and Love, *Seizure of the Gilberts and Marshalls*, 20.

12. Isely and Crowl, *Amphibious War*, 196.

13. Minutes of Casablanca Conference, Joint Chiefs of Staff History Office, Pentagon, Alexandria, VA.

14. Memorandum, William Halsey to Ernest King, 9 February 1943, National Archives, RG 38.

15. Hayes, *Joint Chiefs*, 416.

16. Matlof, *Strategic Planning*, 187.

17. While the actual islands attacked were Betio (Tarawa) and Butaritari (Makin), for simplicity's sake we will refer to them by the names of the atolls.

18. Minutes of the 97th Meeting of the Joint Chiefs of Staff, 29 June 1943, Joint Chiefs of Staff History Office.

19. Raymond Spruance to Jeter Isely, 14 January 1949, Raymond Spruance Papers, Hoover Institute, Stanford, CA.

20. Isely and Crowl, *Amphibious War*, 192.

21. Matlof, *Strategic Planning*, 190–91.

22. Crowl and Love, *Seizure of the Gilberts and Marshalls*, 25.

23. Hayes, *Joint Chiefs*, 417.

24. Memorandum, George Marshall to Ernest King, "Release of the 1st or 3rd Marine Divisions for Operations in the Central Pacific," 29 July 1943, Marshall Papers.

25. Memorandum, Richard Edwards to George Marshall, 31 July 1942, Marshall Papers.

26. Thomas Buell, *The Quiet Warrior: A Biography of Admiral Raymond A. Spruance* (Annapolis, MD: Naval Institute Press, 1987), 47.

27. Ibid., 199.

28. Ibid., 171.

29. Ibid., 185.

30. William Tuohy, *America's Fighting Admirals: Winning the War at Sea in World War II* (Minneapolis, MN: Zenith Press, 2007), 36.

31. George Dyer, *The Amphibians Came to Conquer: The Story of Admiral Richmond Kelly Turner* (Washington, DC: Government Printing Office, 1972), 599–600.

32. Tuohy, *America's Fighting Admirals*, 100.

33. Raymond Spruance, "Report of Amphibious Operations for the Capture of the Gilbert Islands," 4 December 1943, Spruance Papers.

34. Charles J. Moore interview transcript, 1970, pages 651–52.

35. Holcomb to Vandegrift, 29 September 1942.

36. Norman Cooper, *A Fighting General: The Biography of Gen Holland M. "Howlin' Mad" Smith* (Quantico, VA: Marine Corps Association, 1987), 68–69.

37. Holland Smith papers.

38. Emmett Forrestel, *Raymond Spruance: A Study in Command* (Washington, DC: Government Printing Office, 1966), 69.

39. Holland M. Smith and Percy Finch, *Coral and Brass* (New York: Charles Scribner's Sons, 1949), 111; and Raymond Spruance to Jeter Isely, 14 January 1949, Spruance Papers. This letter outlines a meeting between Nimitz and a group of his commanders, including Smith, whom they recommended going into the Gilberts before the Marshalls.

40. Julian Smith interview transcript, 1973, page 164, Marine Corps Archives, Quantico, VA.

41. Edmund Love to Ralph Smith, 22 August 1949, Ralph Smith Papers, Hoover Institute, Stanford, CA.

42. In particular, I will comment on Smith's autobiography, *Coral and Brass* and Dr. Norman Cooper's biography, *A Fighting General*. Much of this was covered in Harry Gailey, *Howlin' Mad vs. the Army: Conflict in Command, Saipan 1944* (Novato, CA: Presidio Press, 1986); however I only use his arguments when I can independently verify them through primary source material.

43. S. L. A. Marshall, *Bringing Up the Rear* (Novato, CA: Presidio Press, 1979), 69.

44. Cooper, *A Fighting General*, 92–94.

45. Ibid., 94.

46. Rather than picking a hotshot young lieutenant, Spruance chose an older former enlisted man, Lieutenant E. H. McKissick, who was an expert in the lost art of flag communications.

47. Buell, *The Quiet Warrior*, 189.

48. Ibid., 193.

49. These Marines were picked up by Japanese forces from a nearby island and beheaded on Kwajalein about a month later. After the war, the Japanese commander, Vice Admiral Koso Abe, was hanged for war crimes for this act. The story of the Makin Raid, its results and aftereffects have been well covered in a variety of books such as Benis Frank and Henry I. Shaw, *History of Marine Corps Operations in World War II, Volume V: Isolation of Victory and Occupation* (Washington, DC: U.S. Marine Corps, 1968), 744; and George Smith, *Carlson's Raid: The Daring Marine Assault on Makin* (Novato, CA: Presidio Press, 2001).

50. Intelligence Center Pacific Ocean Areas (ICPOA), "Bulletin # 30-43," 5 May 1943, 206.

51. John Baker, George Howe and S. L. A. Marshall, *The Capture of Makin* (Washington, DC: Department of the Army, 1946), 8.

52. Shaw et al., *Central Pacific Drive*, 29. Japanese officers and enlisted men had markedly different latrines, which made it relatively easy to extrapolate the number of troops on an island.

53. Ralph Smith, "Notes on Preparation for Makin," Ralph Smith Papers.

54. Smith and Finch, *Coral and Brass*, 111. This is contradicted by virtually every other book on the topic.

55. Samuel Eliot Morison, *History of United States Naval Operations in World War II, Volume 7: Aleutians, Gilberts and Marshalls, June 1942–April 1944* (Boston, MA: Little, Brown & Co., 1961), 85.

56. Raymond Spruance to C. A. Youngdale, 24 July 1962, Spruance Papers.

57. Also included in the operation the occupation of Apemama. Since this island was essentially unoccupied and taken without incident after the end of major combat operations, it has no bearing on the battle.

58. Raymond Spruance to Jeter Isely, 14 January 1949, Spruance Papers.

59. Japanese codebreakers thought that three generals named Smith were codenames to conceal the real names of the commanders.

60. Crowl and Love, *Seizure of the Gilberts and Marshalls*, 25.

61.Memorandum, Robert Richardson to Chester Nimitz, 27 December 1943, Robert Richardson Papers, Hoover Institute, Stanford, CA. In this conviction he was supported by General George Marshall. See Memorandum, George Marshall to Robert Richardson, 19 January 1944, Marshall Papers.

62. Buell, *The Quiet Warrior*, 195.

63. Ralph Smith command diary, 9–19 October 1943, Ralph Smith Papers.

64. Central Pacific Force, "OPLAN 1-43," 11–12, Gilbert Islands Collection, Marine Corps Archives, Quantico, VA. Hereafter Gilbert Islands Collection, USMC.

65. Ibid., 12.

66. Task Force 54, "Operation Plan No. A2-43," 23 October 1943, page 9, Gilbert Islands Collection, USMC.

67. Smith and Finch, *Coral and Brass*, 113.

68. 2nd Marine Division, "Estimate of the Situation—Gilberts," 5 October 1943, pages 2–3, Gilbert Islands Collection, USMC.

69. Ibid., 13–14.

70. Julian Smith transcript, 308.

71. Ibid., 289.

72. Graves Erskine interview transcript, Marine Corps Archives, Quantico, VA, 200–1.

73. Julian Smith transcript, 283–84.

74. V Amphibious Corps, "G-2 Study of the Theater of Operations, Gilbert, Nauru and Ocean," 20 September 1943, pages 61–68, Gilbert Islands Collection, USMC.

75. Smith and Finch, *Coral and Brass*, 115, and Cooper, *A Fighting General*, 114.

76. Ralph Smith command diary, 9 October 1943, Ralph Smith Papers.

77. V Amphibious Force, "Report of GALVANIC Operation," 4 December 1943, page 3, Gilbert Islands Collection, USMC.

78. The other two were Illinois' 33rd Division and Pennsylvania's 28th Division.

79. Edmund G. Love, *The 27th Infantry Division in World War II* (Washington, DC: Government Printing Office, 1949), 8–11.

80. The 69th traces its lineage to 1775 and claims over 50 battle rings, more than any other American regiment. In 1947 the 165th Infantry was formally redesignated the 69th Infantry Regiment.

81. Love, *The 27th Infantry Division*, 13.

82. Gabel, *The U.S. Army GHQ Maneuvers of 1941*, 172.

83. Ibid., 185.

84. Charles Kaune, "The National Guard in War: An Historical Analysis of the 27th Infantry Division (New York National Guard) in World War II," unpublished thesis, Command and General Staff College, 1990, pages 43–44, Combined Arms Research Library, Fort Leavenworth, KS. Hereafter CARL.

85. "Army: Discipline Wanted," *Time*, 13 October 1942.

86. Hilton Railey, "Morale of the United States Army: An Appraisal for the *New York Times*, Report, Washington, DC, 29 September 1941, Gilbert Islands Collection, USA.

87. Memorandum, George Marshall to Omar Bradley, 30 March 1940, Marshall Papers.

88. Omar Bradley and Clay Blair, *A General's Life* (New York: Simon & Schuster, 1983), 483.

89. Kaune, "The National Guard in World War II," 22–23.

90. Mark Watson, *United States Army in World War II: Chief of Staff: Prewar Plans and Preparations* (Washington, DC: Department of the Army, 1950), 258–60.

91. William Schnorr interview transcript, 28 August 2003, page 12, Rutgers Oral History Archives of World War II, New Brunswick, NJ.

92. Joseph Sykes, Army Service Questionnaire, Military History Institute, Carlisle, PA.

93. Vincent W. Walsh, Army Service Questionnaire, Military History Institute, Carlisle, PA.

94. In 1941, there were only 5 officers in the 27th Division who had attended CGSS.

95. Kaune, "The National Guard in World War II," 38.

96. One of the aftermaths of the GHQ maneuvers was a general weeding out of officers due to new regulations governing the age of commanders.

97. Love, *The 27th Infantry Division*, 14.

98. William Howard, "Citizen Soldiers," *New York Archives*, Winter 2004, 11.

99. Love, *The 27th Infantry Division*, 14–15.

100. Howard, "Citizen Soldiers," 12.

101. See Chapter 2 for further discussion of triangularization.

102. Kaune, "The National Guard in World War II," 53.

103. Ibid., 53.

104. He also led a long life. When he died in 1998 at the age of 104, General Smith was the oldest surviving general officer.

105. Eric Pace, "Gen Ralph C. Smith, Honored for War Bravery Dies at 104," *New York Times*, 26 January 1998.

106. Geoffrey Perret, *There's a War to Be Won: The United States Army in World War II* (New York: Random House, 1991), 273–74.

107. Gailey, *Howlin' Mad vs. the Army*, 43.

108. Leonard Lerwill, *The Personnel Replacement System in the U.S. Army* (Washington, DC: Department of the Army, 1954), 248–49.

109. Smith and Finch, *Coral and Brass*, 118; and Cooper, *A Fighting General*, 114.

110. United States Army Forces, Central Pacific Area (USAFCPA), "Participation of United States Army Forces in the Central Pacific Area in GALVANIC Operation," 17 June 1944, 129–30. CARL.

111. Kaune, "The National Guard in World War II," 55.

112. Love, *The 27th Infantry Division*, 25.

113. Bill Glisson, "Reflections of a 27th Division Artilleryman," *The Orion Gallivanter*, December 1994, page 8, Gilbert Islands Collection USA.

114. Baker, et al., *The Capture of Makin*, 25.

115. V Amphibious Corps, "Report of GALVANIC Operation," 5.

116. Merritt Edson to Gerald Thomas, 25 January 1944, Julian Smith Papers, Marine Corps Archives, Quantico, VA.

117. Richard Johnston, *Follow Me! The Story of the Second Marine Division in World War II* (New York: Random House, 1948).

118. Dispatch from Staff Sergeant Fred Feldkamp, Marine Corps Combat Correspondent, "The Man Who Took Tarawa," 23 January 1944, Julian Smith Papers.

119. Raymond Murray interview transcript, 1988, page 147, Marine Corps Archives, Quantico, VA.

120. Dispatch, "The Man Who Took Tarawa," 23 January 1944.

121. Tropical sprue is an absorption problem that leads to painful and debilitating vitamin deficiencies, particularly of B12.

122. See Chapter 2 "Guadalcanal" for a detailed discussion of the 2nd MARDIV and its regiments.

123. Julian Smith transcript, 266.

124. Julian Smith to Alexander Vandegrift, 22 July 1943, Julian Smith Papers.

125. Memorandum, Maurice Holmes to Alexander Vandegrift, "Unsatisfactory fitness report for 1 May—21 December 1943," 20 January 1944, Julian Smith Papers.

126. Julian Smith to Thomas Holcomb, 1 September 1943, Julian Smith Papers.

127. Shaw et al., *Central Pacific Drive*, 46.

128. Julian Smith to Thomas Holcomb, 1 September 1943, Julian Smith Papers.

129. Joseph Alexander, *Across the Reef: The Marine Assault on Tarawa* (Washington, DC: Marine Corps Historical Branch, 1992), 6.

130. Robert Sherrod, *Tarawa: The Story of a Battle* (New York: Duell, Sloan and Pearce, 1944), 181.

131. Rear Admiral H. B. Knowles, Commander Transport Group. Sherrod, *Tarawa*, 155.

132. Shaw et al., *Central Pacific Drive*, 48–49.

133. "Japanese Defense Notes," *Intelligence Bulletin* 2, no. 4, December 1943.

134. Joseph Alexander, *Utmost Savagery: The Three Days of Tarawa* (Annapolis, MD: Naval Institute Press, 1995), 157–59. It appears that he gave up his blockhouse so that wounded soldiers might shelter there.

135. Unless otherwise noted, this landing summary is taken from *Central Pacific Drive*, 51–74, and *Across the Reef: The Marine Seizure of Tarawa* and *Seizure of the Gilberts and Marshalls*, 127–42.

136. 2nd Marine Division, "Estimate of the Situation—Gilberts," 7.

137. Julian Smith transcript, 306, and Raymond Murray interview transcript, 141.

138. The time of the bombardment had been changed two weeks earlier, but no one has ever been able to discover why Hill and his staff were not aware of the new time.

139. Because Smith and his staff mistook an artillery unit for Hall's unit and assumed that they had just landed on the wrong beach, no one was looking for them.

140. Unless otherwise noted, this landing summary is taken from *Seizure of the Gilberts and Marshalls*, 76–126, and *The Capture of Makin*, 29–132.

141. 2/165th Infantry, "Report on the Actions of BLT 165- on the Makin Atoll from November 20th to 24th 1943," 9 December 1943, Ralph Smith Papers.

142. Unless otherwise noted, this landing summary is drawn from *Central Pacific Drive*, 72–102, and *Across the Reef: The Marine Seizure of Tarawa* and *Seizure of the Gilberts and Marshalls*, 143–55.

143. Unless otherwise noted, this battle summary is taken from *Seizure of the Gilberts and Marshalls*, 76–126, and *The Capture of Makin*, 29–132.

144. USAFCPA "Participation in GALVANIC Operation," 129.

145. Alexander, *Across the Reef*, 50.

146. Julian Smith transcript, 287, 308.

147. Interview, Raymond Spruance with George Dyer, Spruance Papers.

148. V Amphibious Corps, "Report of GALVANIC Operation," Intelligence section, pages 2–3, Gilbert Islands Collection, USMC.

149. Smith and Finch, *Coral and Brass*, 118.

150. V Amphibious Corps, "G-2 Study of the Theater of Operations," 20 September 1943, page 68, Gilbert Islands Collection, USMC.

151. Commander, 2/165, "Report on the Actions of BLT 165," 9 December 1943, Gilbert Islands Collection, USA.

152. 2nd Marine Division, "Report on Gilbert Islands—Tarawa Operation," 23 December 1943, page 57, Gilbert Islands Collection, USMC.

153. Ibid., 66, Gilbert Islands Collection, USMC.

154. V Amphibious Corps, "Report of GALVANIC Operation," 4.

155. Dispatch, "The Man Who Took Tarawa," 23 January 1944.

156. As always, it is difficult to determine the actual number of enemy killed because so many were killed by shells or buried in the pillboxes. All casualty numbers are taken from *The Seizure of the Gilberts and Marshalls* and *Central Pacific Drive*, which are derived directly from the combat reports and are regarded as the most accurate.

157. Alexander Vandegrift to Senator David Walsh, 15 December 1943. Reprinted in full in the *Army-Navy Journal* 81, no 17 (25 December 1943): 1, Vandegrift papers.

158. The Navy had protested this design, but was overruled by its civilian leadership.

159. Dyer, *Amphibians Came to Conquer*, 679.

160. Perret, *There's a War to Be Won*, 275.

161. 27th Infantry Division, "Observations and Recommendations—the Makin Operations," 27 February 1944, page 4, Gilbert Islands Collection USA; and 2nd Marine Division, "Observations on Galvanic Operation," 15 December 1943, pages 74–75, Gilbert Islands Collection, USMC.

162. The other three were: 1LT Alexander Bonnyman, SSG William Bordelon and 1LT William Dean Hawkins.

163. Leo Hermle interview transcript, 1973, page 79, Marine Corps Archives, Quantico, VA.

164. Elmer Hall to Julian Smith, 10 March 1944, Julian Smith Papers.

165. Julian Smith to Alexander Vandegrift, 3 March 1944, Julian Smith Papers.

166. Marshall, *Bringing Up the Rear*, 62.

167. Smith and Finch, *Coral and Brass*, 126

168. 165th Infantry Regiment Command Journal, 21 November 1943, Ralph Smith Papers.

169. Gerard Kelley to Mrs. Gardiner Conroy, 14 February 1949; Father Yarbrough to Ralph Smith, 17 February 1949, Ralph Smith Papers.

170. Shaw et al., *Central Pacific Drive*, 46.

171. 2/165th Infantry, "Report on the Actions of BLT 165."

172. Bernard Ryan interview with Harry Gailey, 27 February 1984, Ralph Smith Papers.

173. U.S. Army G-3, "Combat Lessons No. 3," 3 July 1944, CARL.

174. Interview, Ralph Smith with Harry Gailey, 7 October 1983, Ralph Smith Papers.

175. "Combat Lessons No. 3," 78, CARL.

176. Ibid.

177. James Mahoney interview with Harry Gailey, 28 January 1984, Ralph Smith Papers.

178. Shaw et al., *Central Pacific Drive*, 104.

179. Memorandum, David Shoup to Julian Smith, "Report of Operations: GAL-VANIC," 17 December 1943, Gilbert Islands Collection, USMC; 6th Marines, "Report of Operations, Galvanic, 19 December 1943," page 16, Gilbert Islands Collection, USMC; and 27th Infantry Division, "Observations and Recommendations—the Makin Operations," 1.

180. USAFCPA, "Participation in GALVANIC Operation," pages 43–44; and V Amphibious Corps "Report of Operations, Galvanic," 17–18.

181. 27th Infantry Division, "Observations and Recommendations—the Makin Operations," 2.

182. 2nd Marine Division, "Observations on Galvanic Operation," 5.

183. USAFCPA, "Participation in GALVANIC Operation," pages 23, 99; and V Amphibious Corps "Report of Operations, Galvanic," 17.

184. Shoup, "Report of Operations, GALVANIC," and USAFCPA, "Participation in GALVANIC Operation," 30.

185. Isely and Crowl, *Amphibious War*, 204

186. V Amphibious Corps, "Report of GALVANIC Operation," Enclosure G, 7.

187. Ibid., Enclosure K.

CHAPTER 3 The Marshalls: The Perfect Operation

1. Ernest Holmes, "Observer's Report of Flintlock Operations," 22 February 1944, Marshall Islands Collection USMC.

2.Shaw, et al., *Central Pacific Drive*, 10–12.

3. Hayes, *Joint Chiefs*, 370.

4. In addition to the Marshalls, Japan also gained the Marianas, the Palaus and the Carolines.

5. Crowl and Love, *Seizure of the Gilberts and Marshalls*, 168.

6. Hayes, *Joint Chiefs*, 479.

7. Memorandum, William Halsey, 14 December 1943, National Archives, RG 38.

8. Morison, *Aleutians, Gilberts and Marshalls*, 206.

9. Crowl and Love, *Seizure of the Gilberts and Marshalls*, 169–70.

10. Smith and Finch, *Coral and Brass*, 141.

11. Richmond Kelly Turner to Harry Hill, 28 November 1948. Harry Hill Papers, Hoover Institute, Stanford, CA; Raymond Spruance to CA Youngdale, 24 July 1962, Spruance Papers; Buell, *The Quiet Warrior*, 231–232; Forrestel, *Raymond Spruance*, 99.

12. Richmond Kelly Turner to Harry Hill, 28 November 1948, Hill Papers.

13. Raymond Spruance to Jeter Isely, 3 July 1949, Spruance Papers.

14. Heinl and Crown, *The Marshalls*, 14–15.

15. Memorandum, Charles Corlett to William Halsey, 23 December 1943, Charles Corlett Papers, Military History Institute, Carlisle, PA.

16. Ibid.

17. Stephen Taaffe, *Marshall and his Generals: U.S. Army Commanders in World War II* (Lawrence, KS: University of Kansas Press, 2011), 174.

18. Shaw et al., *Central Pacific Drive*, 123.

19. V Amphibious Corps, "Operation Plan No. 1-44: Marshall Islands Operation," 5 January 1944, page 4, Marshall Islands Collection, Marine Corps Archives, Quantico, VA. Hereafter Marshall Islands Collection USMC.

20. Charles Corlett to Lemuel Shepard, 29 November 1952, Corlett Papers.

21. Richmond Kelly Turner to Harry Schmidt, 29 March 1949, Harry Schmidt Papers, Hoover Institute, Stanford, CA.

22. Smith and Finch, *Coral and Brass*,147.

23. Marshall, *Bringing Up the Rear*, 62; and Morison, *Aleutians, Gilberts and Marshalls*, 257. Although this exchange has not been verified, Smith did not go ashore until invited and when Vandegrift asked about it in a "personal and secret" letter, Smith told him he would not put it in writing, but would send a personal messenger to give him the true picture. Holland Smith to Alexander Vandegrift, 4 February 1944.

24. Holland Smith to Alexander Vandegrift, 4 February 1944.

25. Unnamed, undated speech, Corlett Papers.

26. Charles Corlett to the Historical Division, Department of the Army, "Specific Comments on the Manuscript *The Gilbert-Marshalls Campaign*," 13 January 1948, Corlett Papers.

27. 7th Infantry Division, "Flintlock Operation Field Orders and Report of Operations,"1944, pages 1–2, 90–92, 114–17, 118–19, Marshall Islands Collection, Military History Institute, Carlisle, PA. Hereafter Marshall Islands Collection USA.

28. Shaw, et al., *Central Pacific Drive*, 175–76.

29. Ibid., 189.

30. Heinl and Crown, *The Marshalls*, 21.

31. 4th Marine Division, "Operations Plan No. 3-43 Marshall Islands Operation," 31 December 1943, page i, Marshall Islands Collection USMC.

32. Love, *The Hourglass*, 5.

33. George MacGarrigle, *The U.S. Army Campaigns of World War II: Aleutian Islands* (Washington, DC: 1992), 12.

34. Smith and Finch, *Coral and Brass*, 105–6.

35. Venzon, *From Whaleboats to Amphibious Warfare*, 78–79.

36. Corlett, "Specific Comments on the Manuscript *The Gilbert-Marshalls Campaign*," Corlett papers.

37. Ibid.

38. Cole Kingseed, *Old Glory Stories: American Combat Leadership in World War II* (Annapolis, MD: 2006), 108.

39. Unnamed, undated speech, Corlett papers.

40. 767th Tank Battalion, "Report of Tank Operations FLINTLOCK," 28 February 1944, page 35, Marshall Islands Collection USMC.

41. Corlett, "Specific Comments on the Manuscript *The Gilbert-Marshalls Campaign*," Corlett papers.

42. Carl Proehl, *The Fourth Marine Division in World War II* (Washington, DC: U.S. Marine Corps, 1947), 9.

43. John Chapin, *The 4th Marine Division in World War II* (Washington, DC: U.S. Marine Corps, 1976), 1.

44. 4th Marine Division, "Report of Marshall Islands Operation," 17 March 1944, page 3, Marshall Islands Collection USMC.

45. James Underhill interview transcript, page 131, Marine Corps Archives, Quantico, VA.

46. Robert D. Heinl and John A. Crown, *Marines in World War II Historical Monograph: The Marshalls: Increasing the Tempo* (Washington, DC: U.S. Marine Corps, 1954), 20. Hereafter *The Marshalls*.

47. In fact, one of the observers was killed during the landing and another assumed command of the 2nd BN, 2nd Marines when its commander was killed.

48. 4th Marine Division, "Report of Marshall Islands Operation," 4.

49. Evans Carlson, "Report of Observations on GALVANIC Operation," 27 November 1943, page 8, Marshall Islands Collection USMC.

50. 4th Marine Division, "Final Report of Marshall Islands Operations," 28 March 1944, page 88, Marshall Islands Collection USMC.

51. 4th Marine Division, "Report of Marshall Islands Operation," 6.

52. Louis Metzger to Lemuel Shepherd, 13 November 1952.

53. Heinl and Crown, *The Marshalls*, 3.

54. Crowl and Love, *Seizure of the Gilberts and Marshalls*, 211–13.

55. Heinl and Crown, *The Marshalls*, 5.

56. CG Central Pacific Area, "Marshall Islands Japanese Defenses and Battle Damage," 1 March 1944, 2.

57. Heinl and Crown, *The Marshalls*, 31.

58. Ibid.

59. United States Fleet, "Amphibious Operations in the Marshall Islands," 26 May 1944, sec. 4, p. 3, Marshall Islands Collection USMC.

60. Smith and Finch, *Coral and Brass*, 138.

61. Chet Cunningham, *The Frogmen of World War II: An Oral History of the U.S. Navy's Underwater Demolition Units* (New York: Pocket Star, 2005), 233.

62. Unless otherwise noted, landing summary is taken from *Seizure of the Gilberts and Marshalls*, 219–40 and Edmund Love, *The Hourglass: A History of the 7th Infantry Division in World War II* (Washington, DC: Government Printing Office, 1950), 121–28.

63. "Extracts from Observer's Comments on FLINTLOCK Operation," 12 April 1944, page 8, Marshall Islands Collection USMC.

64. Unless otherwise noted, landing summary is taken from *Central Pacific Drive*, 142–65 and *The Marshalls: Increasing the Tempo*, 37–53.

65. Message, Louis Jones to Harry Schmidt, 1311 and 1326, 1 February 1944, Marshall Islands Collection USMC.

66. Unless otherwise noted, this landing summary is taken from *Seizure of the Gilberts and Marshalls*, 219–300 and *The History of the 7th Infantry Division in World War II*, 128–73.

67. 7th Infantry Division, "184th Infantry Regiment Report," 1–2 February 1944, Marshall Islands Collection USA.

68. Unless otherwise noted, this battle summary is taken from *Central Pacific Drive*, 163–75 and *The Marshalls: Increasing the Tempo*, 64–99.

69. Ibid., sec. 1, p. 1.

70. Raymond Spruance to Lemuel Shepherd, 12 January 1953, Spruance Papers.

71. U.S. Army Forces Pacific Ocean Area (USAFPOA), "Lessons Learned Kwajalein-Eniwetok," 30 November 1944, page 7, Marshall Islands Collection USA.

72. 2nd Marine Division, "Training Memorandum No. 54-44," 18 March 1944, page 4, Marshall Islands Collection USMC.

73. Task Force 53, "Report on Flintlock Operations," 23 February 1944, page 5, Marshall Islands Collection USMC.

74. V Amphibious Corps, "Report on Flintlock," 6 March 1944, page 16, Marshall Islands Collection USMC.

75. 4th Division, "Final Report of Marshall Islands Operations," 77.

76. V Amphibious Corps, "Report on Flintlock," 253.

77. 4th Marine Division, "Final Report of Marshall Islands Operations," 78.

78. V Amphibious Corps, "Report on Flintlock," 17.

79. Ibid., 16.

80. United States Fleet, "Amphibious Operations in the Marshall Islands," 4–5.

81. Fifth Amphibious Force, "Report of FLINTLOCK Operation," 17 March 1944, page 18, Marshall Islands Collection USMC.

82. USAFPOA, "Lessons Learned Kwajalein-Eniwetok," 13.

83. Ibid., 9.

84. Charles Corlett to Lemuel Shepard, 29 November 1952, Corlett Papers.

85. USAFPOA, "Lessons Learned Kwajalein-Eniwetok," 2.

86. 4th Marine Division, "Final Report of Marshall Islands Operations," 110.

87. 7th Infantry Division, "Report of the 7th Division Participation in FLINTLOCK Operations," 8 February 1944, page 16, Marshall Islands Collection USA.

88. Ibid., 17.

89. 4th Marine Division, "Final Report of Marshall Islands Operations," 4.

90. As always, it is difficult to determine the actual number of enemy killed because so many were killed by shells or buried in the pillboxes. These casualty numbers are taken from the battle report and reflect the best estimates on the ground. See USAF-POA, "Marshall Islands Japanese Defenses and Battle Damage," 1 March 1944, pages 7–8, Marshall Islands Collection USA.

91. V Amphibious Corps, "Report on Flintlock," 13.

92. Smith and Finch, *Coral and Brass*, 146.

93. Cooper, *A Fighting General*, 67.

94. Marshall, *Bringing Up the Rear*, 62.

95. Charles Corlett to Lemuel Shepard, 29 November 1952.

96. 7th Infantry Division, "Report of the 7th Division Participation in FLINTLOCK Operations," page 3.

97. Ibid.

98. Ibid.

99. Despite this distinction, Corlett's legacy is mixed, as General Omar Bradley relieved him of command of XIX Corps in 1944.

100. V Amphibious Corps, "Report on Flintlock," 19–20.

101. USAFPOA, "Lessons Learned Kwajalein-Eniwetok," 15.

102. USAFPOA, "Marshall Islands Japanese Defenses and Battle Damage," 53.

103. United States Fleet, "Amphibious Operations in the Marshall Islands," sec. 3, p. 5.

104. Ibid., sec. 3, p. 10.

105. V Amphibious Corps, "Report on Flintlock," 11.

106. United States Fleet, "Amphibious Operations in the Marshall Islands," sec. 8, p. 2

107. Ibid., sec. 3, p. 17.

108. Ibid., sec. 8, p. 1.

109. Ibid., sec. 3, p. 31.

110. 2nd Marine Division, "Training Memorandum No. 54-44," 18 March 1944, page 3, Marshall Islands Collection USMC.

111. USAFPOA, "Lessons Learned Kwajalein-Eniwetok," 2.

112. V Amphibious Corps, "Report on Flintlock," 14.

113. 7th Infantry Division, "Report of the 7th Division Participation in FLINTLOCK Operations," 144.

114. USAFPOA, "Lessons Learned Kwajalein-Eniwetok," 5.

115. 2nd Marine Division, "Training Memorandum No. 54-44," 7.

116. USAFPOA, "Lessons Learned Kwajalein-Eniwetok," 10.

117. 7th Infantry Division, "Report of the 7th Division Participation in FLINTLOCK Operations," 14.

CHAPTER 4   Saipan: Smith Versus Smith

1. Hayes, *Joint Chiefs*, 542.

2. Minutes of Casablanca Conference, Joint Chiefs of Staff History Office, Pentagon, Alexandria, VA.

3. Dyer, *Amphibians Came to Conquer*, 856.

4. Shaw, et al., *Central Pacific Drive*, 232.

5. Philip A. Crowl, *United States Army in World War II: The War in the Pacific: Campaign in the Marianas* (Washington, DC: Department of the Army, 1959), 16–17.

6. George Marshall to Ernest King, 10 February 1944, National Archives, RG 38.

7. Hayes, *Joint Chiefs*, 18.

8. E. B. Potter, *Bull Halsey* (Annapolis, MD: Naval Institute Press, 2003), 276.

9. Warner McCabe, "Personal Experiences of the Aide to the Division Commander," Infantry Officer Advanced Course 1948–49, page 6, MCEL.

10. Committee 8, "Armor in Operation Forager," Armored School Officers Advanced Course, May 1949, pages 9–10, CARL.

11. Northern Troops and Landing Forces Command and Staff Assignments, 20 July 1944. Marianas Collection, Marine Corps Archives, Quantico, VA. Hereafter Marianas Collection USMC.

12. Smith and Finch, *Coral and Brass*, 153.

13. Donald Nahrgang, "The Operations of the 6th Marine Regiment (Personal Experience of a Regimental S-2)," Infantry Officer Advanced Course, 1946, page 5, MSEL.

14. Ibid., 241–42.

15. Ibid., 240–41.

16. V Amphibious Corps, "G-3 Report, Phase I (Saipan)," 25 May 1944, page 7, Marianas Collection USMC.

17. Ibid., 7–8.

18. Shaw, et al., *Central Pacific Drive*, 240.

19. John Chapin, *Breaking the Outer Ring: Marine Landings in the Marshall Islands* (Quantico, VA: Marine Corps Historical Branch, 1994), 4.

20. Task Force 56, "Report by G-3 on Forager," 4 September 1944, pages 4–6, Marianas Collection USMC.

21. Shaw et al., *Central Pacific Drive*, 252–53.

22. Although a marine division had over 22,000 soldiers, only about 6,000 were combat troops, so this loss represented a much higher loss that would initially indicate.

23. Carl Hoffman, *Saipan: The Beginning of the End* (Quantico, VA: U.S. Marine Corps, 1950), 34.

24. 4th Marine Division, "Operations Report—Saipan," 18 September 1944, page 6, Marianas Collection USMC.

25. Ibid., 1–2.

26. 24th Marine Regiment, "Operations Report," 28 August 1944, pages 4–5, Marianas Collection USMC.

27. 4th Tank Battalion, "Report of Operations," 28 August 1944, pages 1–2, Marianas Collection USMC.

28. 24th Marine Regiment, "Operations Report," 6–7.

29. Kaune, 93–94.

30. Ibid., 94.

31. See a detailed discussion of this in Chapter 2.

32. Kaune, 98.

33. USAFCPA, "United States Army Forces Participation in the Central Pacific Area: Marianas Operation," 1 April 1945, pages 23–24. Marianas Collection, Military History Institute, Carlisle, PA. Hereafter Marianas Collection USA.

34. Holman Hamilton, "Report of Canadian Officers Attached to the 27th Infantry Division," 24 October 1944, Marianas Collection USA.

35. John Lemp, "Observer Report on the Mariana Operation (Forager)," 11 July 1944, pages 12–13, Marianas Collection USA.

36. McCabe, "Personal Experiences of the Aide," 9.

37. Lemp, "Observer Report on the Mariana Operation (Forager)," 5.

38. Smith and Finch, *Coral and Brass*, 168.

39. Memorandum, George Griner to Robert Richardson, "Combat service under the command of Lieutenant General H. M. Smith, USMC," 11 October 1944, Buckner Report, Center for Military History, Fort McNair, VA.

40. Sanderford Jarman, Memorandum for Record, 6 September 1944, Buckner Report.

41. McCabe, "Personal Experiences of the Aide," 4.

42. 4th Marine Division G-3, "Operations Report—Saipan Annex E Special Comments," 11 July 1944, page 28, Marianas Collection USMC.

43. V Amphibious Corps Assistant Chief of Staff G-2, "Special Interrogation of Major Kiyoshi Yoshida," 11 July 1944, Marianas Collection USMC.

44. 4th Marine Division G-3, "Saipan Annex E Special Comments," 29–30.

45. 23rd Marine Regimental Combat Team, "Operations Report," 28 August 1944, page 5, Marianas Collection USMC.

46. 106th Infantry, "Forager Comments: Unit Comments," 6 August 1944, pages 4–5, Marianas Collection USA.

47. USAFPOA G-2, "Intelligence Bulletin No. 14," 20 April 1945, page 9, Marianas Collection USA.

48. 4th Marine Division, "Operations Report—Saipan," 37.

49. Unless otherwise noted, landing summaries are taken from Crowl, *Campaign in the Marianas*, 71–95; Shaw et al., *Central Pacific Drive*, 263–79;

50. Dyer, *Amphibians Came to Conquer*, 901–2.

51. Hoffman, *Saipan*, 248.

52. V Amphibious Corps, "Special Interrogation of Major Kiyoshi Yoshida."

53. USAFPOA G-2, "Intelligence Bulletin No. 14," 20 April 1945, 9.

54. V Amphibious Corps, "Special Interrogation of Major Kiyoshi Yoshida."

55. Hoffman, *Saipan*, 47.

56. Unless otherwise noted, battle summaries are taken from Crowl, *Campaign in the Marianas*, 95–266; Shaw et al., *Central Pacific Drive*, 280–352; and Hoffman, *Saipan*, 77–246.

57. Charles Hallden, "Personal Experiences of a Company Commander: Company L, 3rd Battalion, 106th Infantry," Infantry Officer Advanced Course 1947–48, page 16, MSEL.

58. 165th RCT Unit Journal, FORAGER Operation, Saipan, 29 June 1944, National Archives RG 407.

59. Max LaGrone, "Personal Experiences of a Regimental S-4: 2nd Marine Regiment, Infantry Officer Advanced Course 1947–48, page 14, MSEL.

60. V Amphibious Corps Assistant Chief of Staff G-3, "G-3 Report Phase I (Saipan)," 11 July 1944, page 742, Marianas Collection USMC.

61. V Amphibious Corps, "G-3 Report Phase I (Saipan)," 11 July 1944, page 743, Marianas Collection USMC.

62. USAFCPA, "Participation in the Marianas Operation," 37.

63. 4th Marine Division, "Final Report on Saipan Operation," 1.

64. Northern Troops and Landing Force, "Staff Memorandum 13–44," 7 June 1944, page 2, Marianas Collection USMC.

65. Hamilton, "Report of Canadian Officers," 2.

66. Lemp, "Observations of Saipan Operations," 11 July 1944, 2.

67. 106th Infantry, "Forager Comments: Unit Comments," 4.

68. 4th Marine Division, "Operations Report—Saipan," 34.

69. 106th Infantry, "Forager Comments: Unit Comments," 8.

70. George Griner to Harry Schmidt, 16 July 1944, Schmidt Papers.

71. James Bartholomees, "Personal Experiences of a Battalion Executive Officer: 773rd Tractor Battalion," Infantry Officer Advanced Course 1947–48, page 14, MSEL.

72. V Amphibious Corps "G-3 Report Phase I (Saipan)."

73. 24th Marine Regimental Combat Team, "Operations Report," 28 August 1944, 2.

74. Second Command Class, CGSC, FORAGER, Annex C, page 4, MSEL.

75. Hallden, "Personal Experiences of a Company Commander," 37.

76. 4th Marine Division "G-3 Operations Report—Saipan Annex C," 18 September 1944, page 13, Marianas Collection USMC.

77. Ibid., 9.

78. Task Force 56, "Report on Marianas Operations," 327.

79. V Amphibious Corps, "G-3 Report Phase I (Saipan)."

80. 4th Marine Division G-3, "Operations Report—Saipan Annex E Special Comments," 22.

81. As always, it is difficult to determine the actual number of enemy killed because so many were killed by shells or buried in the pillboxes. These casualty numbers are taken from the G-1 battle report and reflect the best estimates on the ground. Numbers take from Headquarters Expeditionary Force 56, "Report by G-1 on Forager," 1 September 1944, pages 3–5.

82. This number only reflects divisional troops, not 152 V Corps troops.

83. Smith and Finch, *Coral and Brass.*

84. Memorandum, Edgar Colladay to George Griner, 3 September 1944, Buckner Report.

85. Memorandum, George Griner to Holland Smith, 16 July 1944, Buckner Report.

86. USAFCPA, "Participation in the Marianas Operations," 29 July 1945, pages 154–55, CARL.

87. 106th Infantry, "Forager Comments: Unit Comments," 3.

88. Hill transcript, 447.

89. Gailey, *Howlin' Mad vs. the Army*, 100.

90. Mccabe, "Personal Experiences of the Aide," 24.

91. Crowl, *Campaign in the Marianas*, 230.

92. Brown 7th ID at Attu; Hardin 32nd ID at Buna and Hester 43rd ID at New Georgia.

93. Collins, *Lightning Joe*, 106.

94. George Marshall to Lesley McNair, 6 October 1942.

95. Buckner Report, 1944.

96. Buell, *The Quiet Warrior*, 319–20.

97. Gailey, *Howlin" Mad vs. the Army*, 232.

98. Memorandum, Thomas Handy to the Buckner Board, 16 August 1944, Buckner Report.

99. Crowl, *Campaign in the Marianas*, 196.

100. V Amphibious Corps, "G-3 Report Phase I (Saipan)."

101. Ibid., 113–14.

102. Holland Smith to Alexander Vandegrift, 18 July 1944, Holland Smith Papers, Auburn University, Auburn, AL. Hereafter Holland Smith Papers AL.

103. "The Generals Smith," *Time*, 18 September 1944.

104. Richmond Kelly Turner to Harry Schmidt, 29 March 1949; Chester Nimitz to Harry Schmidt.

105. Harry Hill to Richmond Kelly Turner, Hill Papers.

106. Crowl, *Campaign in the Marianas*, 85.

107. V Amphibious Corps Assistant Chief of Staff G-3, "G-3 Report Phase I (Saipan)."

108. Ibid. and 4th Marine Division G-3, "Operations Report—Saipan Annex C," 39.

109. Ibid., 27–28.

110. Task Force 56, "Report on Marianas Operations," pages 1393, 1535.

111. 4th Marine Division G-3, "Operations Report—Saipan Annex C," pages 15–16.

112. 4th Tank Battalion, "Report of Operations," 7.

113. 23rd Marine Regiment, "Operations Report," 5.

114. 24th Marine Regiment, "Operations Report, 30.

115. McCabe, "Personal Experiences of the Aide," 17.

116. Nahrgang, "Personal Experiences of a Regimental S-2," 17.

117. George Feifer, *The Battle of Okinawa: The Blood and the Bomb* (Guilford, CT: The Lyons Press,1992), 308.

118. 4th Marine Division G-3, "Operations Report—Saipan Annex E Special Comments," 11; 24th Marine Regimental Combat Team, "Operations Report," 28 August 1944, 34.

119. 23rd Marine Regiment, "Operations Report," 4.

CHAPTER 5   Okinawa: The Final Victory

1. Roy Appleman, James Burns, Russell Gugeler, and Jon Stevens, *Okinawa: The Last Battle* (Washington, DC: Department of the Army, 1948), 19.

2. Simon Bolivar Buckner, Jr. Diary, 2 September 1944, Simon Bolivar Buckner Papers, Eisenhower Library, Lawrence, KS.

3. CINCPOA, "Operations Plan 14-44, Annex F: Command Relationships in Ryukus Operation," 31 December 1944, Okinawa Collection, Marine Corps Archives, Quantico, VA. Hereafter Okinawa Collection USMC.

4. Memorandum, Raymond Spruance to Chester Nimitz, "Command Relationships in the Ryukus Operation," 27 October 1944, National Archives, RG 38.

5. Memorandum, Chester Nimitz to Raymond Spruance "Command Relationships," 21 November 1944, National Archives, RG 38.

6. Robert Leckie, *Okinawa: The Last Battle of World War II* (New York: Penguin Books, 1995), 6–7.

7. On 12 October 1944, Third Fleet launched attacks against the Japanese bases on Taiwan, destroying over 500 Japanese aircraft—almost the entire Japanese airpower in the area. As a result, there was almost no Japanese air support for either Leyte or Okinawa.

8. Isely and Crowl, *Amphibious War*, 534.

9. Chester Nimitz to Ernest King, 27 October 1944, National Archives, RG 38.

10. Buckner diary, 18 July 1944.

11. Ibid., 13 September 1944.

12. Ibid., 7 October 1944.

13. Feifer, *The Battle of Okinawa*, 181.

14. Ibid., 181.

15. Oliver Smith interview transcript, page 152, Marine Corps Archives, Quantico, VA.

16. Taaffe, *Marshall and His Generals*, 296.

17. Buckner diary, 10 August 1944.

18. Oliver Smith transcript, 152.

19. Ibid., 25.

20. Ibid., 153.

21. Buckner diary 1943–45.

22. Richmond Kelly Turner to Richard Conolly, 28 December 1944, Richmond Kelly Turner Papers, Naval Historical Center, Washington, DC.

23. Oliver P. Smith, "Tenth Army and Okinawa," unpublished manuscript, page 25, Oliver Smith Papers, Marine Corps Archives, Quantico, VA.

24. Oliver Smith Personal Narrative, undated, page 43, Oliver Smith Papers.

25. Oliver Smith transcript, 155.

26. Army Ground Forces, "Report on Okinawa Operation," 1 May 1945, page 7, CARL.

27. Oliver Smith transcript, 159–60.

28. Frank and Shaw, *Victory and Occupation*, 85.

29. Appleman, et al., *Okinawa*, 40.

30. 7th Infantry Division Artillery, "Report of Ryukus Campaign" 26 July 1945, Okinawa Collection, Military History Institute, Carlisle, PA. Hereafter Okinawa Collection USA.

31. Marshall, *Bringing Up the Rear*, 80.

32. Gerald Astor, *Operation Iceberg: The Invasion and Conquest of Okinawa in World War II* (New York: Dutton Adult Publishers, 1995), 149.

33. Edwin Emerson, "Personal Experience of a Rifle Platoon Leader," Infantry Officer Advanced Course 1948–49, page 9, MCEL.

34. Dennis Neill, "A Tank Company on Okinawa," Infantry Officer Advanced Course 1947–48, pages 1–2, MCEL.

35. James Hewette, "Personal Experiences of a Company Commander and Battalion S-3," Infantry Officer Advanced Course 1946–47, page 5, MCEL.

36. Claudius Easley, Jr., "The Operations of the 96th Infantry Division in the Amphibious Landing and Initial Action on Leyte," Infantry Officer Advanced Course 1949–50, pages 8–9, MCEL.

37. Arsene Bonifas, "Personal Experiences of a Battalion S-3 3rd Battalion, 381st Infantry," Infantry Officer Advanced Course 1948–49, page 8, MCEL.

38. Frank and Shaw, *Victory and Occupation*, 85.

39. Appleman, et al., *Okinawa*, 40.

40. J. H. Howe, "Observer's Report—96th Infantry Division," 26 May 1945, page 5, Okinawa Collection USA.

41. 96th Infantry Division, "Action Report Ryukus Campaign," 28 July 1945, sec. V, p. 1, Okinawa Collection USA.

42. Ibid., 5–6.

43. Roger Willock, *Unaccustomed to Fear: A Biography of the Late General Roy S. Geiger* (Quantico, VA: Marine Corps Association, 1983), 207–30.

44. Ibid., 285.

45. Merwin Silverthorn interview transcript, 1973, 339, Marine Corps Archives, Quantico, VA.

46. Willock, *Unaccustomed to Fear*, 287–88.

47. Buckner diary, 7 February 1945.

48. Ibid., 4 March 1945.

49. Oliver Smith transcript, 154.

50. Willock, *Unaccustomed to Fear*, 261–62.

51. Buell, *The Quiet Warrior*, 390.

52. Buckner diary, 12 March 1945.

53. Williamson Murray and Allen Millett, *A War to Be Won* (Cambridge, MA: Harvard University Press, 2000), 361.

54. Willock, *Unaccustomed to Fear*, 242.

55. Cape Glouchester December 1943; New Britain February 1944; and Peleliu February 1944.

56. 1st Marine Division, "Special Action Report 1 April–30 June 1945," 10 July 1945, pages 41–42, Okinawa Collection USMC.

57. Louis Jones transcript, 1973, page 128, Marine Corps Archives, Quantico, VA.

58. 1st Marine Division, "Special Action Report," 41.

59. Buckner diary, 24 January 1945.

60. Edward Snedeker interview transcript, 1968, page 71, Marine Corps Archives, Quantico, VA.

61. Pedro del Valle interview transcript, 1966, page 185, Marine Corps Archives, Quantico, VA.

62. Pedro del Valle, *Semper Fidelis: An Autobiography* (Hawthorne, CA: Christian Book Club of America, 1976), 18.

63. del Valle transcript, 129–31.

64. del Valle, *Semper Fidelis*, 17.

65. del Valle transcript, 135–36.

66. Ibid., 176.

67. Ibid., 178.

68. The division was only in existence for 19 months, September 1944–March 1946.

69. Lemuel Shepherd interview transcript, 1978, page 9, Perry Library Archives, Old Dominion University Library, Norfolk, VA.

70. Raymond Gillespie, "The K-Company Marines,"1966, page 83, Okinawa Collection USMC.

71. Alan Shapley interview transcript, 1971, page 90, Marine Corps Archives, Quantico, VA.

72. 6th Marine Division, "Special Action Report on Okinawa Operations Phases I and II," 30 April 1945, page 17, Okinawa Collection USMC.

73. Oliver Smith transcript, 158.

74. Shepherd transcript, 9.

75. 2nd Marine Division, "Action Report, Phase I Nansei Shoto, 21 May 1945," page 23, Okinawa Collection USMC.

76. Buckner diary, 2 February 1945.

77. Oliver Smith transcript, 161.

78. Johnston, *Follow Me!*, 257..

79. 2nd Marine Division "Action Report," 7–8.

80. "Ibid., 25-26.

81. Love, *The 27th Infantry Division*, 520–21.

82. Kaune, "The National Guard in World War II," 131.

83. Ibid., 135.

84. Love, *The 27th Infantry Division*, 523.

85. Buckner diary, 20 January 1945.

86. Love, *The 27th Infantry Division*, 522.

87. Appleman, et al., *Okinawa*, 40.

88. 27th Division, "Operation Report Nansei Shoto Phase I," 16 July 1945, page 18, Okinawa Collection USA.

89. Love, *The 27th Infantry Division*, 523.

90. 27th Division, "Operation Report Nansei Shoto Phase I," 21.

91. Cyril O'Brien, *Marines in World War II Commemorative Series: Liberation: Marines in the Recapture of Guam* (Washington, DC: Marine Corps Historical Branch,1994)

92. Buckner diary, 11 August 1944.

93. Joseph Stilwell diary, 6 June 1945, Joseph Stillwell Papers, Hoover Institute, Stanford, CA.

94. Smith and Finch, *Coral and Brass*, 217–18.

95. Oliver Smith transcript, 164.

96. Appleman, et al., *Okinawa: The Last Battle*, 40.

97. Stewart Wilson, *Aircraft of World War II* (Sydney: Australian Aviation, 1999), 103.

98. Robert Gandt, *The Twilight Warriors* (New York: Broadway, 2010), 81.

99. Army Ground Forces, "Report on the Okinawa Operation," 27.

100. Leckie, *Okinawa*, 152.

101. 6th Marine Division, "D-2 Estimate of the Enemy Situation," 7 February 1945, page 3, Okinawa Collection USMC.

102. Appleman, et al., *Okinawa*, 49.

103. Neill, "A Tank Company on Okinawa," 15.

104. Unless otfherwise noted, landing summary is taken from Crowl, *Campaign in the Marianas*, 71–95; Shaw et al., *Central Pacific Drive*, 263–79.

105. Army Ground Forces, "Report on the Okinawa Operation," 16.

106. Howe, "Observer's Report," 6.

107. Laura Homan Lacey, *Stay Off the Skyline: The Sixth Marine Division on Okinawa* (Dulles, VA: Potomac Books, 2005), 44.

108. Isely and Crowl, *Amphibious War*, 536.

109. Joseph Alexander, *Storm Landings* (Annapolis, MD: Naval Institute Press, 1997), 158.

110. Task Force 51, "Okinawa Gunto Report Volume I," page 2, CARL.

111. Unless otherwise noted, this battle summary is taken from Crowl, *Campaign in the Marianas*, 95–266; Shaw et al., *Central Pacific Drive*, 280–352; and Hoffman, *Saipan*, 77–246.

112. Hiromichi Yahara, *The Battle for Okinawa: A Japanese Officer's Eyewitness Account of the Last Great Campaign of World War II* (New York: John Wiley and Sons, 1995), 36.

113. Ibid., 33.

114. Buckner diary, 11 April 1945.

115. Appleman, et al., *Okinawa*, 258–60.

116. Yahara, *The Battle for Okinawa*, 108.

117. Oliver Smith transcript, 162.

118. Astor, *Operation Iceberg*, 419.

119. Oliver Smith transcript, 163.

120. Oliver P. Smith, "The Tenth Army and Okinawa," undated, page 3, Oliver Smith Papers, Marine Corps Archives, Quantico, VA.

121. Shapely transcript, 91.

122. 1st Marine Division, "Special Action Report," sec. X, p. 30.

123. Ibid., sec. VIII, p. 9.

124. 77th Infantry Division, "Operation Report: Iceberg," 1 October 1945, page 9, CARL.

125. USAFPOA, "Participation in the Okinawa Operation," 15 March 1946, page 707, CARL.

126. Army Ground Forces, "Observer's Report," 17.

127. Ibid., 19.

128. 96th Infantry Division, "Action Report Ryukus Campaign" 28 July 1945, sec. V, p. 2, CARL.

129. USAFPOA, "Participation in the Okinawa Operation," 706.

130. Tenth Army, "Action Report: Ryukus," 25 September 1945, 4-0-3, CARL.

131. Appleman, et al., *Okinawa*, 38.

132.1st Marine Division, "Special Action Report: Okinawa," 499.

133. 96th ID, "Operations Report," sec. XI, p. 6.

134. 711th Tank Battalion, "Operations with the 7th Infantry Division," July 1945, CARL.

135. War Department, "Combat Lessons No. 8," 26 September 1945, page 14, Military History Institute, Carlisle, PA.

136. As always, it is difficult to determine the actual number of enemy killed because so many were killed by shells or buried in caves and tunnels. These casualty numbers are taken from the Tenth Army battle report and reflect the best estimates on the ground. Numbers take from Tenth Army, "Action Report: Ryukus," 25 September 1945, 9-IV-1.

137. Shapely transcript, 91.

138. Tenth Army, "Action Report," 9-IV-1 and 11-XV-17.

139. 77th Infantry Division, "Operation Report: Iceberg Phase I," 12 October 1945, pages 75–76, CARL.

140. Tenth Army, "Operations Report," 11-XV-20.

141. Dyer, *Amphibians Came to Conquer*, 116.

142. Robert Eichelberger and Jay Luvaas, *Dear Miss Em* (San Francisco, CA: Greenwood Press, 1972), 230.

143. Simon Bolivar Buckner to Adele Buckner, 13 May 1945, Buckner Papers.

144. Buckner diary, 3 June 1945.

145. Stilwell diary, 6 June 1945.

146. Ibid., 18 June 1945.

147. Nicholas Evan Sarantakes, *Seven Stars: The Okinawa Battle Diaries of Simon Bolivar Buckner, Jr. and Joseph Stilwell* (College Station: Texas A&M University Press, 2004), 78.

148. Samuel Eliot Morison, *History of United States Naval Operations in World War II, Volume 14: Victory in the Pacific, 1945* (Boston: Little, Brown & Co., 1960), 273.

149. Simon Bolivar Buckner to Adele Buckner, 17 June 1945, Buckner papers.

150. Sarantakes, *Seven Stars*, 81.

151. Oliver Smith transcript, 168–70.

152. Ibid., 168.

153. Louis Jones transcript, 136.

154. In World War I, the 165th Regiment had been the famed "Fighting 69th" and this nickname was the marine way of commending the fighting spirit of the regiment.

155. Louis Jones transcript, 135.

156. In his book *Goodbye Darkness*, William Manchester claims to have been present when Shepard fired Bleasdale, supposedly for not being able to pinpoint the location of his battalions, but this has not been corroborated anywhere.

157. Astor, *Operation Iceberg*, 243.

158. Lacey, *Stay Off the Skyline*, 144. Interestingly, these same men claim that the 29th Marines received the highest marks in training and that is why they were held back as the division reserve during the landing.

159. Nichols and Shaw, *Okinawa: Victory in the Pacific* (Quantico: U.S. Marine Corps, 1955), 139.

160. Due to his previously stellar combat record, Schneider suffered no repercussions from his relief and retired as a brigadier general. Hallas, *Killing Ground on Okinawa*, 161–62.

CONCLUSION

1. Robert Bateman, "Cause for Relief," *Armed Forces Journal*, June 2008. Accessed at *http://www.armedforcesjournal.com/2008/06/3468975 18 October 2012.*

ー BIBLIOGRAPHY ー

PRIMARY SOURCES

164th Infantry Association Records, Carleton Elliot Simensen Military Heritage Collection, University of North Dakota, Grand Forks, ND

27th Infantry Regiment Association Archives, Apache Junction, AZ

Americal Division Archives, Greensboro, NC

Shoptaugh, Terry L., "I Am Ready: The 164th Infantry in World War II," unpublished history.

Stoddard, Lincoln, "Narrative History of Task Force 6814 and Americal Division: Jan. 23, 1942 to June 30, 1943," unpublished history.

Center for Military History, Washington, DC

"The Buckner Report"

"Operations of the 25th Infantry Division on Guadalcanal"

Unit records 27th Infantry Division

Raines, Edgar, "The Army-Marine Corps Relationship." Information Paper, 8 September 2009.

"Report on Canton, Kwajalein, Tarawa, Fiji, Guadalcanal, New Caledonia, Saipan, Tinian, Guam, Okinawa."

Combined Arms Research Library, Fort Leavenworth, KS

77th Infantry Division, "Operation Report: Iceberg," 1 October 1945.

96th Infantry Division, "Action Report Ryukus Campaign," 28 July 1945.

711th Tank Battalion, "Operations with the 7th Infantry Division," July 1945.

Army Ground Forces, "Report on Okinawa Operation," 1 May 1945

"Combat Lessons: Rank and file in combat: What They're Doing. How They Do It," Numbers 1–9, 1943–45.

Donahue, James, unpublished journal, 1942–1945.

Kaune, Charles, "The National Guard in War: An Historical Analysis of the 27th Infantry Division (New York National Guard) in World War II," CGSC thesis, 1990.

Task Force 51, "Okinawa Gunto Report Volume I," September 1945.

Tenth Army, "Action Report: Ryukus," 25 September 1945.

Wade, Gary, Combat Studies Institute Study No. 5, "Conversations with General J. Lawton Collins," 1983.

Donovan Research Library, Ft. Benning, GA

Adams, Richard E., "The Operations of Company 'B,' 715th Amphibian Tractor Battalion during the Assault Landing on Saipan Island, 15 June 1944 (Marianas Campaign): Personal Experience of Company Commander," Infantry Officers Advanced Course, Class No. 2, 1949–50.

Bartholomees, James B., "Operations of 773rd Amphibian Tractor Battalion (attached to 27th Division) in the Operation on Tanapag Plains, Saipan, 7–8 July 1944 (Western Pacific Campaign): Personal Experience of Battalion Executive Officer," Infantry Officers Advanced Course, Class No. 2, 1947–48.

Bereuter, Robert L., "The Operations of the 27th Infantry (25th Infantry Division) on Guadalcanal, Solomon Islands 10 January 1943–26 January 1943 (Guadalcanal Campaign): Personal Experiences of a Regimental S-2," Infantry Officers Advanced Course, Class No. 2, 1947–48.

Bonifas, Arsene, "Personal Experiences of a Battalion S-3 3rd Battalion, 381st Infantry," Infantry Officer Advanced Course 1948–49.

Callahan, Donald M., "Aggressive Action Where Opposing Forces Are Exhausted Will Often Meet with Success." Infantry Officers Advanced Course No. 1, 1949–50.

Campbell, Clark G., "The Operations of the First Battalion (Reinforced), 184th Infantry, 7th Infantry Division, in the Capture of Kwajalein Atoll, 31 January–6 February 1944 (Eastern Mandates Campaign): Personal Experience of a Battalion Operations Officer," Infantry Officers Advanced Course, Class No. 1, 1947–48.

Chenault, Theodore L., "The Operations of the 7th Infantry Division in the Capture of Kwajalein Atoll, 31 January–5 February 1944 (Eastern Mandates Campaign)." Infantry Officers Advanced Course, Class No. 2, 1947–48.

Committee 8, "Armor in Operation Forager," Armored School Officers Advanced Course, May 1949.

Easley, Claudius, Jr., "The Operations of the 96th Infantry Division in the Amphibious Landing and Initial Action on Leyte," Infantry Officer Advanced Course 1949–50.

Emerson, Edwin, "Personal Experience of a Rifle Platoon Leader," Infantry Officer Advanced Course, 1948–49.

Hallden, Charles H., "The Operations of Company L, 3rd Battalion, 106th Infantry (27th Infantry Division) in the Battle of Death Valley, Saipan, 23 June–28 June 1944 (Western Pacific Campaign): Personal Experience of Company Commander," Infantry Officers Advanced Course, Class No. 1, 1947–48.

Halsey, Frank J., Jr., "The Operations of the 132nd Infantry (Americal Division) at Mount Austen, Guadalcanal, Solomon Islands 15 December 1942–9 January 1943: Personal Experiences of an Anti-Tank Platoon Leader," Infantry Officers Advanced Course, Class No. 1, 1947–48.

Hewette, James, "Personal Experiences of a Company Commander and Battalion S-3," Infantry Officer Advanced Course, 1946–47.

Kalina, Edwin, "The Operation of Company M, 105th Infantry (27th Infantry Division) Battle of Makin Island, 30 Oct–25 Nov 1943: Personal Experiences of a Company Executive Officer," Infantry Officers Advanced Course, 1946–47.

LaGrone, Max H., "The Operations of the Second Regiment (Second Marine Division) on Saipan-Tinian, 15 June–1 August 1944: Personal Experiences of a Regimental S-4," Infantry Officers Advanced Course, 1946–47.

Mabry, Clarence James, "Operations of the 2nd Battalion, 7th Marines, 1st Marine Division at the Malimbiu River and the Metapona River on Guadalcanal Island, 1 November 1942–8 November 1942: Personal Experience of a Platoon Commander," Infantry Officers Advanced Course, Class No. 1, 1947–48.

McCabe, E. R. Warner, Jr., "The Operations of the 27th Infantry Division on Saipan Island, Marianas Group, Central Pacific, 16–24 June 1944: Personal Experiences of the Aide to the Division Commander," Infantry Officers Advanced Course, Class No. 2, 1948–49.

Nahrgang, Donald, "The Operations of the 6th Marine Regiment (Personal Experience of a Regimental S-2)," Infantry Officers Advanced Course, 1946.

Neill, Dennis, "A Tank Company on Okinawa," Infantry Officer Advanced Course, 1947–48.

Olson, Winston L., "The Operations of the 27th Infantry (25th Infantry Division) on Guadalcanal, Solomon Islands 10 January 1943–13 January 1943 (Guadalcanal Campaign): Personal Experiences of a Rifle Platoon Leader," Infantry Officers Advanced Course, Class No. 1, 1947–48.

Shellum, Alford C., "The Operations of the 1st Platoon, Company F, 164th Infantry (Americal Division) East of Henderson Field, 4-12 November 1942 (Offensive at Koli Point): Personal Experience of a Platoon Leader," Infantry Officers Advanced Course, 1946–47.

Shomion, Arthur M., "Operations of the 77th Infantry Division on Guam, 21 July–10 August 1944 (Western Pacific Campaign)," Infantry Officers Advanced Course No. 2, 1949–50.

Eisenhower Presidential Library, Abilene, KS

25th Infantry Division Unit Papers

Grice, Robert, Unpublished Diary, 1942–1943.

Kern, Frank, "Depression Kids," unpublished manuscript, 2001.

Knight, Raymond, "My Experiences 1941–1945," unpublished manuscript, 1985.

Walthall, Melvin, "Lighting Forward: A History of the 25th Infantry Division," unpublished manuscript, 1973.

Joint Chief of Staff History Office, Washington, DC

Minutes of Meetings of the Combined Chiefs of Staff

Minutes of Meetings of the Joint Chiefs of Staff

Minutes of Casablanca Conference

Minutes of Arcadia Conference

Minutes of Trident Conference

Minutes of Quadrant Conference

Minutes of Sextant Conference

Minutes of Octagon Conference

Marine Corps Archives, Quantico, VA

Tarawa Collection

Roi-Namur Collection

Saipan Collection

Okinawa Collection

Dispatch, "The Men Who Took Tarawa," 23 January 1944.

Gillespie, Raymond, "The K-Company Marines,"1966.

McConnell, Jerry, "Our Survival Was Open to the Gravest Doubts: A Marine Private's Personal Account of the Battle for Guadalcanal," unpublished manuscript, 2002.

Reeder, Russel P. "Notes on Jungle Warfare from the US Marines and US Infantry on Guadalcanal Island," Operations Division, 12 December 1942.

Military History Institute, Carlisle Barracks, PA

Guadalcanal Collection

Gilbert Islands Collection

Marshall Islands Collection

Marianas Collection

Ryukus Collection

Duncan, Basil D., "My Life as a Marine in World War II," unpublished autobiography, undated.

Hamilton, Holman, "Report of Canadian Officers Attached to the 27th Infantry Division," 24 October 1944.

Hayes, Taylor C. T., "Jungle Warfare Schools," Armored Officer Advanced Course Monograph, Ft Knox, KY, 5 May 1948.

Matson, Elson Lowell, "The Story of the 161st Regiment," unpublished manuscript, 1944.

"Objective Data on Tarawa Island, Gilbert Islands" Supplement No. 1–2, APO 958: G-2, USAFICPA, 1943

OPD Bulletins, 1944–1945

Rathgeber, David G., "The United States Marine Corps and the Operational Level of War," School of Advanced Military Studies, U.S. Army Command and General Staff College, 1994.

"The Story of the 161st Infantry"

U.S. War Department General Staff, "Summary of Pacific Operations." Compiled summaries, 1945.

U.S. War Department Military Intelligence Division, "Survey of the Central Pacific Islands," November 1943.

Walthall, Melvin, "Lighting Forward: A History of the 25th Infantry Division," unpublished manuscript, 1973.

Naval Historical Center, Washington, DC

CINCPAC Gray Book

National Archives, College Park, MD

RG 38 Records of the Office of Chief of Naval Operations
RG 107 Records of the Office of the Secretary of War
RG 127 Records of the United States Marine Corps
RG 218 Records of the Joint and Combined Chiefs of Staff
RG 407 Records of the Adjutant General (including unit records)

PERSONAL PAPERS

Air Force Historical Research Agency, Bolling Air Force Base, Washington, DC

Millard Harmon

Auburn University, Auburn, AL

Holland M. "Howling Mad" Smith

Eisenhower Presidential Library, Abilene, KS

Simon Bolivar Buckner
J. Lawton Collins

George C. Marshall Research Library, Lexington, VA

George C. Marshall

Hoover Institute, Stanford University, Palo Alto, CA

Harry Hill
Gerard Kelley
Charles Pownall
Robert Richardson
Harry Schmidt
Ralph Smith
Raymond Spruance
Joseph Stilwell

Marine Corps Archives, Quantico, VA

Graves Erskine
Fred E. Harris
Thomas Holcomb
Robert Kriendler
Lewis B. "Chesty" Puller
Holland M. "Howling Mad" Smith
Julian Smith
Alexander Archer Vandegrift

Military History Institute, Carlisle, PA

J. Lawton Collins
Charles H. Corlett

Naval Historical Center, Washington, D.C

Samuel Eliot Morison
Chester W. Nimitz
Richmond Kelly Turner

Syracuse University, Syracuse, NY
Robert Sherrod

University of Wyoming, Laramie, WY
Frank Jack Fletcher

INTERVIEWS
Marine Corps Archives, Quantico, VA

Clifton Cates	Alfred Noble
Edward Craig	Alan Shapely
Pedro de Valle	David Shoup
Merritt Edson	Merwin Silverthorn
Graves Erskine	Julian Smith
Leo Hermle	Oliver Smith
Louis Jones	Edward Snedeker
Robert B. Luckey	Gerald C. Thomas
Charles J. Moore	James Underhill
Raymond Murray	Cecil Whitcomb

Military History Institute, Carlisle, PA
J. Lawton Collins
Stanley Larsen

Perry Library Archives, Old Dominion University Library, Norfolk, VA
Lemuel Shepherd

Personal Interviews
Les Groshang
George Tosi
Charles H. Walker
H. Lloyd Wilkerson

Rutgers Oral History Archives of World War II, New Brunswick, NJ
Alden F. Jacobs
Vincent Kramer
William C. Schnorr
Floyd Sykes
Louis Trezza
Roland Winter

SECONDARY SOURCES

Government Publications

Alexander, Joseph H. *Marines in World War II Commemorative Series: Across the Reef: The Marine Assault of Tarawa.* Washington, DC: Marine Corps Historical Branch, 1993.

———. *Marines in World War II Commemorative Series: The Final Campaign: Marines in the Victory on Okinawa.* Washington, DC: Marine Corps Historical Branch, 1996.

Anderson, Charles. *U.S. Army Campaigns of World War II: Guadalcanal.* Washington, DC: Army Center of Military History, 1994.

———. *U.S. Army Campaigns of World War II: Western Pacific.* Washington, DC: Army Center of Military History, 1993.

Appleman, Roy E., James M. Burns, Russell A. Gugeler, and John Stevens. *United States Army in World War II: The War in the Pacific: Okinawa: The Last Battle.* Washington, DC: Office of the Chief of Military History, Department of the Army, 1947.

Baker, John, George Howe, and S. L. A. Marshall. *The Capture of Makin (20–24 November 1943).* Washington, DC: Office of the Chief of Military History, Department of the Army, 1946.

Chapin, John C. *Marines in World War II Commemorative Series: Breaking the Outer Ring: Marine Landings in the Marshall Islands.* Washington, DC: Marine Corps Historical Branch, 1994.

———. *Marines in World War II Commemorative Series: Breaching the Marianas: The Battle for Saipan.* Washington, DC: Marine Corps Historical Branch, 1994.

Coates, John Boyd, ed. *United States Army in World War II: Preventive Medicine in World War II, Volume VI: Communicable Diseases.* Washington, DC: Office of the Surgeon General, 1963.

Conn, Stetson. *Historical Work in the United States Army 1862–1954.* Washington, DC: Office of the Chief of Military History, Department of the Army, 1980.

Condon-Rall, Mary Ellen, and Albert Cowdrey. *United States Army in World War II: Medical Services in the War Against Japan.* Washington, DC: Office of the Chief of Military History, Department of the Army, 1998.

Crowl, Philip A. *United States Army in World War II: The War in the Pacific: Campaign in the Marianas.* Washington, DC: Office of the Chief of Military History, Department of the Army, 1959.

Crowl, Philip A. and Edmund G. Love. *United States Army in World War II: The War in the Pacific: Seizure of the Gilberts and the Marshalls.* Washington, DC: Office of the Chief of Military History, Department of the Army, 1955.

Donovan, James A. *Marines in World War II Commemorative Series: Outpost in the North Atlantic: Marines in the Defense of Iceland.* Washington, DC: Marine Corps Historical Branch, 1991.

Fisch, Arnold G., Jr. *U.S. Army Campaigns of World War II: Ryukus.* Washington, DC: Army Center of Military History, 1994.

Frank, Benis, and Henry I. Shaw, Jr. *History of Marine Corps Operations in World War II, Volume V: Isolation of Victory and Occupation.* Washington, DC: Historical Branch, G-3 Division, Headquarters, U.S. Marine Corps, 1968.

Gabel, Christopher. *U.S. Army GHQ Maneuvers of 1941.* Washington, DC: Center of Military History, 1991.

Greenfield, Kent R., and Robert R. Palmer. *Origins of the Army Ground Forces: General Headquarters U.S. Army, 1940–1942, Study No. 1.* Washington, DC: Historical Section, Army Ground Forces, 1946.

Greenfield, Kent R., Robert R. Palmer, and Bell I. Wiley. *The Organization of Ground Combat Troops.* Washington, DC: Department of the Army, 1947.

Harwood, Richard. *Marines in World War II Commemorative Series: A Close Encounter: The Marine Landing on Tinian.* Washington, DC: Marine Corps Historical Branch, 1994.

Heinl, Robert D., and John A. Crown. *Marines in World War II Historical Monograph: The Marshalls: Increasing the Tempo.* Washington, DC: Marine Corps Historical Branch, 1954.

Hoffman, Carl W. *Marines in World War II Historical Monograph: Saipan: The Beginning of the End.* Washington, DC: Marine Corps Historical Branch, 1950.

———. *Marines in World War II Historical Monograph: The Seizure of Tinian.* Washington, DC: Marine Corps Historical Branch, 1951.

Hoffman, Jon T. *Marines in World War II Commemorative Series: From Makin to Bougainville: Marine Raiders in the Pacific War.* Washington, DC: Marine Corps Historical Branch, 1995.

Hough, Frank O., Verle E. Ludwig, and Henry I. Shaw, Jr. *History of Marine Corps Operations in World War II, Volume I: Pearl Harbor to Guadalcanal.* Washington, DC: Historical Branch, 1958.

Kahn, E. J., Jr., and Henry McLemore. *Fighting Divisions.* Army Ground Forces Study, 1945.

Joint Action of the Army and Navy, Pamphlet, FTP-155, 1935

Landing Operations Doctrine, Pamphlet, U.S. Navy, 1938.

Landing Operations on Hostile Shores, Pamphlet, U.S. Army, 1941.

Leighton, Richard, and Robert Coakley, *United States Army in World War II: Global Logistics and Strategy: 1940–1943.* Washington, DC: Office of the Chief of Military History, Department of the Army, 1955.

————. *United States Army in World War II: Global Logistics and Strategy: 1943–1945.* Washington, DC: Office of the Chief of Military History, Department of the Army, 1968.

Lerwill, Leonard. *The Personnel Replacement System in the U.S. Army.* Washington, DC: Office of the Chief of Military History, Department of the Army, 1954.

Lodge, O. R. *Marines in World War II Historical Monograph: Recapture of Guam.* Historical Branch, G-3 Division of Public Information, Headquarters, U.S. Marine Corps, 1954.

Marshall, S. L. A. *Island Victory: The Battle of Kwajalein Atoll.* Washington, DC: Office of the Chief of Military History, Department of the Army, 1944.

Matloff, Maurice. *United States Army in World War II: Strategic Planning for Coalition Warfare 1943–1944.* Washington, DC: Office of the Chief of Military History, Department of the Army, 1958.

Matloff, Maurice, and Edwin M. Snell. *United States Army in World War II: Strategic Planning for Coalition Warfare 1941–1942.* Washington, DC: Office of the Chief of Military History, Department of the Army, 1953.

Miller, John, Jr. *United States Army in World War II: War in the Pacific: Guadalcanal: The First Offensive.* Washington, DC: Office of the Chief of Military History, Department of the Army, 1949.

Mitchell, Robert, Sewell Tyng, and Nelson Drummond. *The Capture of Attu.* Washington, DC: Office of the Chief of Military History, Department of the Army, 1944.

Morison, Samuel Eliot. *History of United States Naval Operations in World War II, Volume 5: The Struggle for Guadalcanal, August 1942–February 1943.* Boston, MA: Little, Brown & Co., 1951.

————. *History of United States Naval Operations in World War II, Volume 7: Aleutians, Gilberts and Marshalls, June 1942–April 1944.* Boston, MA: Little, Brown & Co., 1961.

————. *History of United States Naval Operations in World War II, Volume 8: New Guinea and the Marianas, March 1944–August 1944.* Boston, MA: Little, Brown & Co., 1953.

————. *History of United States Naval Operations in World War II, Volume 14: Victory in the Pacific, 1945.* Boston, MA: Little, Brown & Co., 1960.

Morton, Louis. *United States Army in World War II: War in the Pacific: Strategy and Command: The First Two Years.* Washington, DC: Office of the Chief of Military History, Department of the Army, 1962.

Newell, Clayton. *The U.S. Army Campaigns of World War II: Central Pacific.* Washington, DC: US Army Center of Military History, nd.

Nichols, Charles S., Jr., and Henry I. Shaw, Jr. *Marines in World War II Historical Monograph: Okinawa, Victory in the Pacific.* Quantico, VA: U.S. Marine Corps, 1955.

O'Brien, Cyril J. *Marines in World War II Commemorative Series: Liberation: Marines in the Recapture of Guam.* Washington, DC: Marine Corps Historical Branch, 1994.

Plamer, Robert, Bell Wiley, and William Keast. *United States Army in World War II: The Procurement and Training of Ground Combat Troops.* Washington, DC: Office of the Chief of Military History, Department of the Army, 1948.

Sauffer, Alvin. *United States Army in World War II: The Quartermaster Department: Operations in the War Against Japan.* Washington, DC: Office of the Chief of Military History, Department of the Army, 1956.

Scott, Worall. *Beans, Bullets and Black Oil: The Story of Fleet Logistics Afloat in the Pacific During World War II.* Washington, DC: Naval History Branch, 1952.

Shaw, Henry I. Jr. *Marines in World War II Commemorative Series: First Offensive: The Marine Campaign for Guadalcanal.* Washington, DC: Marine Corps Historical Branch, 1992.

Shaw, Henry I. Jr., Bernard C. Nalty, and Edwin T. Turnbladh. *History of Marine Corps Operations in World War II, Volume III: Central Pacific Drive.* Washington, DC: U.S. Marine Corps Historical Branch, 1966.

Stewart, Richard W. *American Military History Volume II: The United States in a Global Era, 1917–2003.* Washington, DC: Department of the Army, 2005.

Stockman, James R. *Marines in World War II Historical Monograph: The Battle for Tarawa.* Washington, DC: Marine Corps Historical Branch, 1947.

Ulbrich, David J. *Preparing for Victory: Thomas Holcomb and the Making of the Modern Marine Corps 1936–1943.* Annapolis, MD: Naval Institute Press, 2011.

Watson, Mark. *United States Army in World War II: Chief of Staff: Prewar Plans and Preparations.* Washington, DC: Office of the Chief of Military History, Department of the Army, 1950.

Wright, Burton III. *U.S. Army Campaigns of World War II: Eastern Mandates.* Washington, DC: Army Center of Military History, 1994.

Zimmerman, John L. *Marines in World War II Historical Monograph: The Guadalcanal Campaign.* USMCR Historical Section, Division of Public Information, Headquarters, U.S. Marine Corps, 1949.

Biographies/Autobiographies

Bradley, Omar, and Clay Blair. *A General's Life.* New York: Simon & Schuster, 1983.

Buell, Thomas. *The Quiet Warrior: A Biography of Admiral Raymond A. Spruance.* Annapolis, MD: Naval Institute Press, 1987.

Collins, J. Lawton. *Lightning Joe: An Autobiography.* Baton Rouge: Louisiana State University Press, 1979.

Cooper, Norman. *A Fighting General: The Biography of Gen. Holland M. "Howlin' Mad" Smith.* Quantico, VA: Marine Corps Association, 1987.

Corlett, Charles. *Cowboy Pete: The Autobiography of Major General Charles H. Corlett.* New Mexico: Sleeping Fox Press, 1974.

Davis, Burke. *Marine! The Life of Lt. Gen. Lewis B. (Chesty) Puller.* Boston: Little, Brown & Co., 1962.

del Valle, Pedro. *Semper Fidelis: An Autobiography.* Hawthorne, CA: Christian Book Club of America, 1976.

Dyer, George C. *The Amphibians Came to Conquer: The Story of Admiral Richmond Kelly Turner.* Washington, DC: Government Printing Office, 1972.

Forrestel, Emmet Peter. *Raymond Spruance: A Study in Command.* Washington, DC: Government Printing Office, 1966.

Halsey, William, and Joseph Bryan. *Admiral Halsey's Story.* New York: Whittlesey House, 1947.

Hoffman, Jon T. *Once a Legend: Red Mike Edson of the Marine Raiders.* New York: Presidio Press, 2001.

Hoffman, Jon T. *Chesty: The Story of Lieutenant General Lewis B. Puller, USMC.* New York: Random House, 2002.

Layton, Edwin T., Roger Pineau, and John Costello. *And I Was There: Pearl Harbor and Midway.* New York: William Morrow & Co., 1985.

Leckie, Robert. *Helmet for My Pillow: From Parris Island to the Pacific.* New York: Simon & Schuster, 1957.

Lundstrom, John B. *Black Shoe Carrier Admiral: Frank Jack Fletcher at Coral Sea, Midway and Guadalcanal.* Annapolis, MD: US Naval Institute Press, 2006.

Manchester, William. *Goodbye, Darkness: A Memoir of the Pacific War.* New York: Little, Brown and Company, 1980.

Marshall, S. L. A. *Bringing Up the Rear.* Novato, CA: Presidio Press, 1979.

Potter, E. B. *Bull Halsey.* Annapolis, MD: Naval Institute Press, 2003.

———. *Nimitz.* Annapolis, MD: Naval Institute Press, 2008.

Regan, Stephen D. *In Bitter Tempest: The Biography of Admiral Frank Jack Fletcher.* Ames: Iowa State University Press, 1994.

Sledge, E. B. *With the Old Breed at Peleliu and Okinawa.* Oxford, UK: Oxford University Press, 1990.

Smith, Holland M., and Percy Finch. *Coral and Brass.* New York: Charles Scribner's Sons, 1949.

Vandegrift, Alexander Archer, and Robert B. Asprey. *Once a Marine: The Memoirs of General A. A. Vandegrift, USMC.* New York: Ballantine Books, 1966.

Venzon, Anne Cipriano. *From Whaleboats to Amphibious Warfare: Lt. Gen. Howling Mad Smith and the U.S. Marine Corps,* New York: Praeger Publishers, 2003.

Willock, Roger. *Unaccustomed to Fear: A Biography of the Late General Roy S. Geiger.* Quantico, VA: Marine Corps Association, 1983.

Wyant, William K. *Sandy Patch: A Biography of Lt. Gen. Alexander M. Patch.* New York: Praeger Publishers, 1991.

Unit Histories

Crawford, Danny, et al. *History of the Second Marines.* Washington, DC: Marine History and Museums Division, 2001.

———. *The Second Marine Division and Its Regiments.* Washington, DC: Marine History and Museums Division, 2001.

Cronin, Francis. *Under the Southern Cross: The Saga of the Americal Division.* Washington, DC: Combat Forces Press, 1981.

Everett, Donna. *World War II Division Chronicles: 25th Infantry Division.* Washington, DC: US Government Printing Office, 1995.

Johnston, Richard W. *Follow Me! The Story of the Second Marine Division in World War II.* New York: Random House, 1948.

Jones, William. *A Brief History of the Sixth Marines.* Washington, DC: Marine History and Museums Division, 1987.

Karolevitz, Robert F., ed. *25th Division and World War 2.* Baton Rouge: Army and Navy Publishing Company, 1946.

Lacey, Laura Homan. *Stay Off the Skyline: The Sixth Marine Division on Okinawa.* Dulles, VA: Potomac Books, 2005.

Love, Edmund G. *27th Infantry Division in World War II.* Washington, DC: Government Printing Office, 1949.

———. *The Hourglass: The 7th Infantry Division in World War II.* Washington, DC: Government Printing Office, 1950.

Muehrcke, Robert C., ed. *Orchids in the Mud: Personal Accounts of Soldiers of the 132nd Infantry Regiment.* Chicago: 132nd Infantry Division Association, 1985.

Santelli, James. *A Brief History of the Seventh Marines.* Washington, DC: Marine History and Museums Division, 1980.

———. *History of the Eighth Marines.* Washington, DC: Marine History and Museums Division, 1976.

Books

Alexander, Joseph. *Storm Landings: Epic Amphibious Landings in the Central Pacific.* Annapolis, MD: Naval Institute Press, 1997.

———. *Utmost Savagery: The Three Days at Tarawa.* New York: Ballantine Books, 1995.

Astor, Gerald. *Operation Iceberg: The Invasion and Conquest of Okinawa in World War II.* New York: Dutton Adult Publishers, 1995.

Beaumont, Roger A. *Joint Military Operations: A Short History.* Westport, CT: Greenwood Press, 1993.

Belote, James H., and William M. Belote. *Typhoon of Steel: The Battle for Okinawa.* New York: Bantam Books, 1984.

Bergerud, Eric M. *Touched with Fire: The Land War in the South Pacific.* New York: Penguin Books, 1996.

Brooks, Victor. *Hell Is Upon Us: D-Day in the Pacific—Saipan to Guam, June–August 1944.* Cambridge, MA: Da Capo Press, 2005.

Coffman, Edward M. *The War to End All Wars: The American Military Experience in World War I.* Lexington: University Press of Kentucky, 1998.

Cole, Henry. *The Road to Rainbow: Army Planning for Global War, 1934–1940.* Annapolis, MD: Naval Institute Press, 2002.

Corrigan, Gordon. *The Second World War: A Military History.* New York: Thomas Dunne Books, 2011.

Costello, John. *The Pacific War 1941–1945.* New York: Atlantic Communications, Inc., 1981.

Cunningham, Chet. *The Frogmen of World War II: An Oral History of the U.S. Navy's Underwater Demolition Units.* New York: Pocket Star, 2005.

Eichelberger, Robert, and Jay Luvaas. *Dear Miss Em: General Eichelberger's War in the Pacific, 1942–1945.* San Francisco, CA: Greenwood Press, 1972.

Fane, Francis Douglas, and Don Moore. *Naked Warriors.* Annapolis, MD: Naval Institute Press, 1956.

Feifer, George. *The Battle of Okinawa: The Blood and the Bomb.* Guilford, CT: The Lyons Press, 1992.

Frank, Benis. *Okinawa: The Great Island Battle.* New York: Elsevier-Dutton, 1978.

Frank, Richard B. *Guadalcanal: The Definitive Account of the Landmark Battle.* New York: Penguin Books, 1992.

Friedman, Kenneth. *Morning of the Rising Sun: The Heroic Story of the Battles for Guadalcanal.* Charleston, SC: BookSurge Publishing, 2007.

Gailey, Harry A. *"Howlin' Mad" vs. the Army: Conflict in Command, Saipan 1944.* Novato, CA: Presidio Press, 1986.

———. *The Liberation of Guam.* Novato, CA: Presidio Press, 1988.

———. *War in the Pacific: From Pearl Harbor to Tokyo Bay,* Novato, CA: Presidio Press, 1995.

Gandt, Robert. *The Twilight Warriors.* New York: Broadway, 2010.

Goldberg, Harold. *D-Day in the Pacific: The Battle of Saipan.* Bloomington: Indiana University Press, 2007.

Graham, Michael B. *Mantle of Heroism: Tarawa and the Struggle for the Gilberts, November 1943.* Novato, CA: Presidio Press, 1993.

Greenfield, Kent Roberts. *The Historian and The Army: The 1953 Brown and Haley Lectures.* Port Washington, NY: Kennikat Press, 1954.

Gregg, Charles. *Tarawa*. New York: Stein & Day, 1984.

Griffith, Samuel B. *The Battle for Guadalcanal*. Champaign: University of Illinois Press, 2000.

Hallas, James. *Killing Ground on Okinawa: The Battle for Sugar Loaf Hill*. Westport, CT: Praeger, 1996.

Hammel, Eric, and John E. Lane. *Bloody Tarawa: The 2nd Marine Division, November 20–23, 1943*. St. Paul, MN: Zenith Press, 2006.

Hammel, Eric. *76 Hours: The Invasion of Tarawa*. Pacific, CA: Pacifica, 1985.

Hart, B. H. Liddell. *History of the Second World War*. New York: G. P. Putnam, 1970.

Hastings, Max. *Inferno: The World at War 1939–1945*. New York: Knopf, 2011.

Hayes, Grace Person. *The History of the Joint Chiefs of Staff in World War II: The War Against Japan*. Annapolis, MD: Naval Institute Press, 1982.

Hersey, John. *Into the Valley: Marines at Guadalcanal*. New York: Alfred A. Knopf, Inc., 1943.

Hopkins, William. *The Pacific War: The Strategy, Politics and Players that Won the War*. Minneapolis, MN: Zenith Press, 2008.

Hoyt, Edwin P. *Guadalcanal*. New York: Stein and Day, 1982.

———. *How They Won the War in the Pacific: Nimitz and His Admirals*. New York: The Lyons Press, 2000.

———. *Storm Over the Gilberts*. New York: Mason, Charter Publishers, Inc., 1978.

———. *To the Marianas: War in the Central Pacific 1944*. New York: Van Nostrand Reinhold, 1980.

Isely, Jeter A., and Philip A. Crowl. *The U.S. Marines and Amphibious War: Its Theory and Its Practice in the Pacific*. Princeton, NJ: Princeton University Press, 1951.

Jersey, Stanley Coleman. *Hell's Island: The Untold Story of Guadalcanal*. College Station: Texas A&M University Press, 2008.

Keegan, John. *The Second World War*. New York: Penguin Books, 1990.

Kingseed, Cole. *Old Glory Stories: American Combat Leadership in World War II*. Annapolis, MD: Naval Institute Press, 2006.

Leckie, Robert. *Challenge for the Pacific: The Bloody Six Month Battle of Guadalcanal*. New York: Simon & Schuster, 1965.

———. *Okinawa: The Last Battle of World War II*. New York: Penguin Books, 1995.

———. *Strong Men Armed: The United States Marines Against Japan*. New York: Random House, 1962.

MacCloskey, Monro. *Planning for Victory World War II*. New York: Richard Rosen Press Inc., 1970.

Marshall, S. L. A. *Men Against Fire: The Problem of Battle Command*. New York: William Morrow, 1947.

McGee, William L. *The Solomons Campaigns 1942–1943 from Guadalcanal to Bougainville—Pacific War Turning Point, Volume 2 (Amphibious Operations in the South Pacific World War II)*. Santa Barbara, CA: BMC Publications, 2002.

Merillat, Herbert. *The Island: A History of the 1st Marine Division on Guadalcanal*. Boston: Zenger, 1944.

———. *Guadalcanal Remembered*. New York: Dodd, Mead & Co., 1982.

Miller, Edward S. *War Plan Orange: The U.S. Strategy to Defeat Japan, 1897–1945*. Annapolis, MD: Naval Institute Press, 2007.

Millett, Allan. *Semper Fidelis: The History of the Marine Corps*. New York: Simon & Schuster, 1980.

Murray, Williamson, and Allan R. Millett. *A War to Be Won: Fighting the Second World War*. Cambridge, MA: Harvard Press, 2000.

O'Brien, Francis A. *Battling for Saipan*. Novato, CA: Presidio Press, 2003.

Overy, Richard. *Why the Allies Won*. New York: W.W. Norton, 1996.

Perret, Geoffrey. *There's a War to Be Won: The United States Army in World War II*. New York: Random House, 1991.

Radike, Floyd. *Across the Dark Islands: The War in the Pacific*. Novato, CA: Presidio Press, 2003.

Roberts, Andrew. *The Storm of War: A New History of World War II*. New York: Harper, 2009.

Rottman, Gordon, and Peter Dennis. *World War II Armored Infantry Tactics*. Oxford, UK: Osprey Publishing, 2009.

Russ, Martin. *Line of Departure: Tarawa*. Garden City, NY: Doubleday, 1975.

Sarantakes, Nicholas Evan. *Seven Stars: The Okinawa Battle Diaries of Simon Bolivar Buckner, Jr. and Joseph Stilwell*. College Station, TX: Texas A&M University Press, 2004.

Shapiro, Milton. *Assault on Tarawa: The U.S. Marines in Combat*. New York: D. McKay Co., 1981.

Sherrod, Robert. *Tarawa: The Story of a Battle*. New York: Duell, Sloan and Pearce, 1944.

Sloan, Bill. *The Ultimate Battle: Okinawa 1945—The Last Epic Struggle of World War II*. New York: Simon & Schuster, 2007.

Smith, George. *Carlson's Raid: The Daring Marine Assault on Makin*. Novato, CA: Presidio Press, 2001.

———. *The Do-or-Die Men: The 1st Marine Raider Battalion at Guadalcanal*. New York: Pocket Books, 2003.

Smith, S. E., ed. *United States Marine Corps in World War II*. New York: Random House, 1969.

Spector, Ronald. *Eagle Against the Sun: The American War with Japan*. New York: Random House, 1985.

Taaffe, Stephen. *Marshall and His Generals: U.S. Army Commanders in World War II.* Lawrence: University of Kansas Press, 2011.

Tregakis, Richard. *Guadalcanal Diary.* New York: Random House, 2000.

Tuohy, William. *America's Fighting Admirals: Winning the War at Sea in World War II.* Minneapolis, MN: Zenith Press, 2007.

Twining, Merrill B. *No Bended Knee: The Battle for Guadalcanal.* New York: Presidio Press, 2004.

Van der Vat, Dan. *The Pacific Campaign: The U.S.-Japanese Naval War 1941–1945.* New York: Simon and Shuster: 1992.

Walker, Charles H. *Combat Officer: Memoirs of War in the South Pacific.* New York: Presidio Press, 2004.

Weinberg, Gerhard. *A World at Arms: A Global History of World War II.* Cambridge, UK: Cambridge University Press, 1994.

Wheeler, Richard. *A Special Valour: The U.S. Marines and the Pacific War.* New York: Harper Collins, 1983.

Whyte, William. *A Time of War: Remembering Guadalcanal, a Battle Without Maps.* New York: Fordham University Press, 2000.

Wilson, Stewart. *Aircraft of World War II.* Sydney: Australian Aviation, 1999.

Wright, Derrick. *A Hell of a Way to Die: Tarawa Atoll, 20–23 November 1943.* London: Windrow & Greene, 1996.

Wukovits, John. *One Square Mile of Hell: The Battle for Tarawa.* New York: New American Library, 2006.

Yahara, Hiromichi. *The Battle for Okinawa: A Japanese Officer's Eyewitness Account of the Last Great Campaign of World War II.* New York: John Wiley and Sons, 1995.

Articles

Alexander, Joseph H. "Bloody Tarawa." *Naval History* 7 (Nov–Dec 1993).

——. "Tarawa: The Ultimate Opposed Landing." *Marine Corps Gazette* 77 (Nov 1993).

"Army: Discipline Wanted," *Time*, 13 October 1942.

Bartsch, William. "Operation Dovetail: Bungled Guadalcanal Rehearsal, July 1942." *The Journal of Military History* (April 2002).

Bateman, Robert. "Cause for Relief." *Armed Forces Journal* (June 2008). Accessed at *http://www.armedforcesjournal.com/2008/06/3468975* 18 October 2012.

Chambers, John Whiteclay. "S. L. A. Marshall's *Men Against Fire*: New Evidence Regarding Fire Ratios." *Parameters* 33 (Autumn 2003).

Glisson, Bill. "Reflections of a 27th Division Artilleryman." *The Orion Gallivanter*, December 1994.

Heinl, Robert D. "D-Day, Roi-Namur." *Military Affairs* 12, no. 3 (Autumn 1948).

Hill, Vice Admiral Harry W. "Marshall Island Operation—Eniwetok." *Military Review* 12, no. 3 (Winter 1948).

"Japanese Defense Notes." *Intelligence Bulletin* 2, no. 4 (December 1943).

"Japanese Explanation of S. W. Pacific Reverses." *Intelligence Bulletin* 1, no. 8 (April 1943).

Leigh, Mark. "Fighting in the Atolls." *Military Illustrated* (Jan 2003).

Love, Edmund G. "Smith vs. Smith." *Infantry Journal* 63 (Nov 1948).

Miller, John, Jr. "Crisis on Guadalcanal," *Military Affairs* 11, no. 4 (Winter 1947).

———. "The Casablanca Conference and Pacific Strategy." *Military Affairs* 13, no. 4 (Winter 1949).

Mitchler, Robert. "Heroes—Drafted or Volunteer—Are Made, Not Born." *Leatherneck*, 30 January 2009.

Morton, Louis. "Command in the Pacific, 1941–1945." *Military Review* 41, no. 12 (Dec 1961).

———. "Pacific Command: A Study in Interservice Relations." *The Harmon Memorial Lectures in Military History Number Three*. United States Air Force Academy, Colorado, 1961.

———. "Review: The Island War." *Military Affairs* 11, no. 2 (Summer 1947).

"Notes on the Japanese—from their Documents." *Intelligence Bulletin* 2, no. 2 (October 1943).

Pace, Eric. "Gen Ralph C. Smith, Honored for War Bravery Dies at 104." *New York Times*, 26 January 1998.

Railey, Hilton. "Morale of the United States Army: An Appraisal for the *New York Times*." Report, Washington, DC, 29 September 1941.

Russell, William H. "Genesis of FMF Doctrine." *Marine Corps Gazette*, Nov. 1955.

Shoptaugh, Terry. "These Farmboys Can Fight." *The 164th Infantry Newsletter*, Oct. 2007.

"Some Defense Techniques Used by the Japanese." *Intelligence Bulletin* 2, no. 3 (Nov 1943).

Strobridge, Thomas, and Bernard Nalty. "From the South Pacific to the Brenner Pass: General Alexander M. Patch." *Military Review*, June 1981.

Tyson, Donald. "All Might Not Go as Expected." *Proceedings*, Nov 1999.

"West Point Breaks Graduation Record." *The New York Times*, 2 Nov 1918.

▬ INDEX ▬